ELITES, LANGUAGE, AND THE POLITICS OF IDENTITY

ELITES, LANGUAGE, AND THE POLITICS OF IDENTITY

The Norwegian Case in Comparative Perspective

GREGG BUCKEN-KNAPP

State University of New York Press

HØGSKULEN
I VOLDA

Cover photo: David Hogsholt, Tine Milk Cartons.

Published by
State University of New York Press, Albany

Printed in the United States of America

For information, address State University of New York Press,
90 State Street, Suite 700, Albany, NY 12207

Production by Kelli Williams
Marketing by Anne M. Valentine

Library of Congress Cataloging-in-Publication Data

Bucken-Knapp, Gregg.
    Elites, language, and the politics of identity : the Norwegian case in comparative perspective / Gregg Bucken-Knapp.
        p. cm. — (SUNY series in national identities)
        ISBN 0-7914-5655-2 (alk. paper) — ISBN 0-7914-5656-0 (pbk. : alk. paper)
        1. Norwegian language (Nynorsk)—History—19th century.   2. Norwegian language—Social aspects—19th century.   3. Norwegian language—Social aspects—20th century.   4. Sami language.   5. Nationalism—Norway— History.   I. Title.   II. Series.

PD2915.B83 2003
306.44'09481—dc21   2002042641

10 9 8 7 6 5 4 3 2 1

For my parents,
and for Lisa

Contents

Tables

Acknowledgements

This book began as a paper in one of Harvey Feigenbaum's graduate political science seminars on European politics at the George Washington University in the fall of 1994. He didn't profess to have any familiarity with Norwegian language policy, but he was willing to trust that I had a puzzle that merited further investigation. Over the next few years, as this project moved from paper, to proposal, to fieldwork, and eventually became a completed dissertation, his guidance was invaluable. Few graduate students could ask for an advisor that was more committed to the process of shaping a raw research question into a polished, finished product. I am enormously grateful for the skillful way he managed to push me in the right direction while always acting as a source of encouragement for this and other endeavors.

I have also benefited from Jeff Henig's and Jack Wright's willingness to step outside the fields of American politics and public policy to serve as committee members for a project on a distant and peripheral European state. Their careful reading, and constructive criticism, of earlier drafts has been of great value in helping me to target this book to a significantly wider audience. While I have clearly learned more from them than they have from me, I should also say that their Norwegian pronunciation improved considerably over the course of this research.

My stay in Norway during 1996–1997 was partially funded by a U.S. Fulbright Grant. In Oslo, I was fortunate enough to be a visiting scholar at the Department of Scandinavian Studies at the University of Oslo. Both Dagfinn Worren and Lars S. Vikør were, repeatedly, of great assistance during this year of fieldwork, and never hesitated in helping me to locate information, to make contacts, and more generally, to feel at home in Oslo. My time in their department is a period that I recall with only the best of memories.

Sheri Berman, Maurice East, Lee Sigelman, Michael Sodaro, Charles Herber, and Susan Wiley have also read parts of, or in some cases, the entire manuscript, and I greatly appreciate both the time and energy they put into helping this project along and moving it from dissertation to completed book manuscript. Stephen Walton has, like Morris Zapp in the David Lodge novels, come along to offer wit, wisdom and razor-sharp insight that went well beyond the scope of the task at hand. His expertise in Norwegian language policy kept me on my toes and constantly learning, and our conversations about academic life have been a welcome addition to the past few years.

I'd also like to thank my former graduate school colleagues at the George Washington University. Alistair Howard, Kelly Kollman, Elizabeth Matto, Justin McKenna, Jennifer Saunders, Rachel Caufield, Terry Casey, Zsuzsa Csergo, Gulnaz Sharafutdinova, John Riley, Jackie McLaren and others made relieving the pressures of graduate school a bit more enjoyable than was probably wise. I'm lucky to have gone through that experience with them. At various points, Mary and Erik Baumann, Simon Andersen and Anna Harboe, Anne Grönlund, Helga Gudlaugsdottir and Gudmundur Asmundsson (and their family), Kyrre Knutsen, Knut Ellingsen, and Dorota Porada all provided a roof over my head and, more often than not, served as much-needed conversation partners in the far-flung pubs of Europe. Their kindness and friendship means the world to me. People distant to this process also deserve recognition, as they (unknowingly) made the writing flow just a bit more smoothly. Thanks are owed to Lloyd Cole, Declan McManus, Patrick Fitzgerald, David Gedge, and Terry Hall. You've done some good work over the years.

I doubt this project would have ever been completed, let alone started, had it not been for my family's support. Having gone to college in the United States, I am fortunate enough to have been raised in a family that could provide the expensive educational opportunities that I wanted. I only hope that my parents see this book as some small repayment on the financial investment that they made in my future. As they say, "Without you, I'm nothing . . ."

Finally, thanks, thanks, and more thanks to Lisa Broadwell. Her patience, understanding, humor, and presence were the greatest of rewards upon returning to Washington, D.C., in 1997 to begin the writing process. She's been the coolest of muses ever since.

Chapter 1

Language, Politics, and Modern Norway

INTRODUCTION

In the summer of 1996, leaders of all the major Norwegian political parties, covering a political spectrum from left socialist to extreme neoliberal, appeared briefly together for the universal ritual of the photo opportunity. Grinning broadly, armed with shovels, the leaders were posed awkwardly around a young tree. The tree was being planted in honor of Ivar Aasen, the Norwegian scholar who had died a hundred years earlier and had devoted his life to the development of Nynorsk, the minority written Norwegian language. When questioned by the press, each party leader managed to find a way to tie the legacy of Aasen and Nynorsk to the ideals of her or his party. To outsiders, this joint appearance to celebrate cultural heritage might evoke no attention, or at best, the usual references made to the cultural symbols of smaller European nations as being nothing more than folksy and quaint. Further, outsiders may find it remarkable that this small nation has witnessed three versions of written Norwegian compete for official recognition over the past 100 years: Bokmål, the dominant standard, derived from Danish and widely used in urban areas; Nynorsk, the minority standard constructed out of rural western dialects; and Samnorsk (Common Norwegian), a proposed fusion of the previous two into a standard that reflected the language usage patterns of everyday Norwegians. However, as the subsequent case study chapters will show, this photo opportunity would not have been possible only a few decades earlier. For much of modern Norway's existence, language has served as a tool that elites of varying ideological stripes have used in order to wage political

1

battle. From the 1880s up to the 1960s, struggles over language went hand in hand with struggles over Norwegian national identity, economic ideology, and electoral politics.

This book explains what factors led to the initial politicization of language in Norwegian society, why it remained a salient political issue throughout much of the twentieth century, and why elite desire to focus on the language question declined in the 1960s. Despite this extensive focus on the particulars of the Norwegian case, my chief aim is not to cast light on events that are solely of interest to specialists in Scandinavian political history. Rather, I argue that an investigation into Norwegian language politics has merit because it adds to a much larger debate about the relationship between group identity and elite political objectives.

I show how political elites create group identity based on linguistic characteristics. This, in and of itself, is nothing new to either political science or contemporary sociolinguistics. Two of the key works on nationalism, Anderson's *Imagined Communities*, and Hobsbawm's *Nations and Nationalism*, provide what are generally considered to be some of the strongest accounts as to how language is employed in the construction of national identities.

Where my own investigation differs is in demonstrating that language has potential for elite use well after state construction. Specifically, my own investigation of Norwegian language politics suggests a link between language and identity that has not frequently been explored. The Norwegian case demonstrates that while language was initially politicized to aid in the creation of the new Norwegian state, elites found language to be politically valuable in the following decades as well. Moreover, these subsequent constructions and manipulations of *Norwegian* linguistic identity, taking place well after the consolidation of the Norwegian state, did not involve relations between different ethnic groups.[1] Linguistic differences among Norwegians are correlated with class and regional differences. Social democratic political elites promoted the construction of linguistic identities that merged linguistic characteristics from different social classes. The intent of these newly constructed identities was to assist in forging and maintaining broader cross-class alliances between the urban working class and rural inhabitants.

Prior to the case studies, it is useful to begin by focusing on the varying role that language has been assigned both within political philosophy and in contemporary political science. In doing so, this review draws attention to a division among scholars regarding language's ability to be employed as a tool in changing society and in obtaining political objectives. Marx's argument that, on the one hand, language is mostly a reflection of a given set of social relations, will be presented. Yet many twentieth-century thinkers who were influenced by Marx arrived at a sharply different conclusion. That is, it has also been argued by some that language can be employed not only to reinforce social relations, but can also fundamentally alter those relations. As the case study chapters will demonstrate, the history of the Norwegian language conflict speaks powerfully to these opposing views on language, lending credence to a view of language as a policy instrument that has ramifications far beyond the cultural arena.

LANGUAGE AND POLITICAL THOUGHT

One importance of language is that it inherently contains insights on the social relations of a given society. In this regard, Ludwig Wittgenstein's *Philosophical Investigations* stands out, rejecting the Platonic view of language as a tool whose function was to mirror an objective reality. Wittgenstein argued that the Platonic view of language, in which language gained meaning by naming objects in the real world and expressed an objective universality, was sharply flawed. His alternative is posited through the construction of "language games." In these games, the use of words as object names did not just label them within reality, but also implied a set of commands issued by the speaker and to be obeyed by the listener. Wittgenstein's example of this is the master builder and the apprentice: The builder states only the name of an object that he needs, and the apprentice passes him the appropriate object when requested.[2] Naming the object lends symbolic representation to it as a physical object, and also carries the message that certain relations exist between two individuals sharing this simple "language": namely, the speaker is commanding the listener to engage in a certain activity, and that the authority for him to do so is understood by both. Thus, the lesson is clear: language, even in its most basic form, goes beyond communication and represents a set of social relations that can assign both speaker and listener to certain roles, each with varying degrees of power.

However, if language is not charged with the task of defining universalities, but is rather the subjective expression and description of a given society, one can inquire as to whether language also has additional functions. That is, once produced, are languages limited only to communication and to mirroring (however loosely) existing social relations? Specifically, can languages be used to alter the society in which they were produced? In this regard, a brief discussion of Marx and twentieth-century Marxist thinkers will be instructive.

Marx and Engels were more explicit than Wittgenstein about the connection between language and the organization of society. In *The German Ideology*, they argue that man first makes history by engaging in four circumstances or moments on a near simultaneous basis. Stating that "life involves before everything else, eating and drinking, clothing, and many other things," the production of the means to satisfy the basic needs becomes the first activity. Following the fulfillment of these basic needs, new needs immediately arise that must also be fulfilled through production. Third, as a practical function of fulfilling these needs, humanity propagates its own kind, and engages in reproduction. Finally, Marx and Engels state that the "production of life, both of one's own in labour and of fresh life in procreation" is also mirrored in a social relationship, which is considered the cooperation of individuals under any given set of conditions.[3] A result of these four moments, particularly that of social relationships, is the production of consciousness within individuals. For Marx and Engels, consciousness is a *product* of the necessity that individuals have social relations.[4] Language enters into this formulation by being the "practical expression" of that consciousness:

> Language is as old as consciousness, language is practical consciousness, as it exists for other men, and for that reason is really beginning to exist for me personally as well; for language like consciousness, only arises from the need, the necessity, of intercourse with other men.[5]

Thus, Marx and Engels, in sketching their materialist view of history, place language in the same framework: language is a product of material and social relations. One must question whether the vulgar reductionism which implies that language (as an element of the superstructure) cannot be transformed without first transforming the material relations of society (base), or that language, once produced, does not have the ability to alter the material relations of society. However, there are significant elements of this line of thinking in Marx's work. For while Marx indirectly considered language in the *Grundrisse*, one cannot conclude that he offered any support for the idea that "language as superstructure" could exercise influence on the current mode of production. Specifically, Marx discussed labor as a "category" that had taken on different meanings under different modes of production. To locate language in Marx's discussion, it is important to recognize that a "category" can be interpreted as an abstraction that is synonymous with language. In precapitalist times, the category of labor had quite limited and specific meanings that were linked to certain concrete activities. However, under capitalism, Marx argued that labor as a category had lost these specific connotations and now existed as only an abstraction, and that it "has ceased to be organically linked with individuals in any form."[6] Marx goes on to observe that:

> This example of labour shows strikingly how even the most abstract categories, despite their validity—precisely because of their abstractness—for all epochs, are nevertheless, in the specific character of this abstraction, themselves likewise a product of historic relations, and possess their full validity only for and within these relations. . . . The categories which express (bourgeois society's) relations, the comprehension of its structure, thereby also allows insights into the structure and the relations of all production of all the vanquished social formations out of whose ruins and elements it built itself up . . ."[7]

In this passage, Marx reaffirms the argument made in *The German Ideology* that "categories" are products of historic relations, but he also is commenting on how these categories can have influence of their own. Marx suggests that the category of labor (as conceived of under capitalism), while only fully valid to describe elements of capitalism, is nonetheless employed by bourgeois economics to describe labor in precapitalist times. According to Marx, the influence that categories/language have is in shaping our present-day understanding of a very different set of historical circumstances. One should note very carefully that Marx is not arguing that (present) superstructure has an influence on (past) base, but rather on our understanding of past bases.

Yet, as a strategy, the use of noneconomic forces in society to *alter* the material base is not fully enunciated until Antonio Gramsci takes the term "hegemony" on loan from the Bolsheviks and the Third International and employs it as the cornerstone of a cultural and political "united front" against capitalist forces. Antonio Gramsci is of course widely noted for his theoretical contribution of identifying the "ideological predominance of the dominant classes in civil society over the subordinate" as the hegemony of the ruling class, yet one can argue that an equal contribution was made when he offered his tactical suggestions for combating the totality of ruling class domination.[8] Gramsci argued that for the proletariat to fight the bourgeois state successfully, it is necessary to engage in a counterhegemonic effort that consists of a three-prong war of position for control of the state and civil society. It is the second and third elements of this war of position that are of interest in this context and are in fact interrelated.

As opposed to a direct attack (i.e., the use of violent force) on the bourgeois state, Gramsci argued that the key to working-class success lay in the creation of a specifically working-class culture. This working-class culture would be in opposition to bourgeois cultural norms, which, of course, only served to perpetuate bourgeois domination. While Gramsci never directly addressed the role of language conflict in the construction of his counterhegemonic strategy, chapter 3 will show how language conflict can serve in the war of position: The Norwegian Labor Party (DNA), after decades of a traditional Marxist focus on purely "economic" questions and the need to promote potentially violent revolutionary struggle, eventually came around to recognizing the significance of combating the bourgeois control of culture in general and language in particular.

Linked to this is the third component of Gramsci's war of position, which proved to make the tactics of coalition-building around language possible. Gramsci suggests that there need to be certain shifts in consciousness before the working-class can be successful in its attempt to fight bourgeois control of the state and civil society. One of the transformations that an individual must undergo is to leave behind the identification with only his or her own respective economic class and instead come to see him or herself as a member of *all* subordinated classes, who can "come together to form a counterideology that frees them from the subordinated position."[9] However, Gramsci appears to have held contradictory stances as to whether or not a successful counterhegemonic war of position should be waged that involved language as a unifying force. On the one hand, he argued that as many of Italy's dialects were low prestige, it would be necessary for working-class Italians to take advantage of the "normative grammar" offered by standardized and hegemonic Italian if they were fully to take advantage of the modern and unified Italy.[10]

Yet, in personal writings to his sister, Gramsci expressed a far different view on the abandonment of nonstandard linguistic patterns for the new, modern Italian. In dealing with the question of what language his nephew ought to be educated in, Gramsci strongly came out for the use of Sardinian, as opposed to Italian, and justified this view by labeling Sardinian as an entirely separate language.[11] Regardless of the tension between these views, Gramsci's development of a united front that would employ a strategy of political and cultural counterhegemony moves us a great deal away from both Wittgenstein and Marx.

What may be thought of in Gramscian terms as a counterhegemonic project utilizing language can also be expressed through Pierre Bourdieu's focus on cultural capital in general and in some of his specific remarks on the nature of language. The broad outlines of Bourdieu's analysis have centered around an extension of Marx's work on capital and the insight that capital as a form of domination cannot be conceived in strictly economic terms. Rather, it is supplemented by at least three additional types: social, cultural, and symbolic. Of particular interest to us here is cultural capital, which can be viewed as the cultural traits that are necessary for children from nonbourgeois backgrounds to attain if they are to achieve a shift in membership from an underprivileged to a privileged group. Alternately, as "natural" members of the advantaged group, bourgeois youth by definition are already rich in the necessary cultural capital that will be of use in perpetuating their dominance over the nonprivileged classes.[12] For Bourdieu, cultural capital, along with the other forms, are thought of in highly strategic and utilitarian terms. He states that the "social world can be conceived of" by:

> discovering the powers or forms of capital which are or can become efficient, like aces in a game of cards, in this particular universe, that is, in the struggle (or competition) for the appropriation of scarce goods of which this universe is the site. It follows that the structure

of this space is given by the distribution of the various forms of capital, that is, by the distribution of the properties which are active within the universe under study—those properties capable of conferring strength, power and consequently profit on their holder.[13]

While Bourdieu's own shorthand for bourgeois cultural capital is "style, taste and wit," it should be obvious from the earlier discussion in this chapter that language is also an important element of cultural capital. Bourdieu notes in his discussion of the educational system that "the culture of the elite is so closely linked to the culture of the school" that the two are virtually indistinguishable. Yet the style, taste, and wit of the upper class are not the only cultural traits reinforced or transmitted in an educational setting. Certainly, the language and grammar of the dominant group is also given privileged status. In bilingual nations where language use is closely correlated to class differences, this form of cultural capital takes on the greatest of significance. According to Bourdieu, where the language of the dominant group is the official state language and therefore the official language of schooling, one of the key requisites for moving away from a disadvantaged societal position is to adopt that aspect of elite culture that has been codified as the sole means of official communication. This is necessary not only because one understands that "language" serves as a signifier of membership in the "proper" group, but also because of the very concrete reason that becoming socialized in the elite culture via the educational system is not possible in any other tongue than in the language of the dominant elites. To learn the cultural values of the dominant class, one must also learn the medium through which they are transmitted and in learning that linguistic medium, one is also learning an additional cultural value.

In addition to a general discussion of noneconomic forms of domination, Bourdieu has also made the discussion of language and domination a specific focus of his work on capitalist society. In writing on "linguistic capital," Bourdieu follows the same line of thought employed when discussing all other forms of capital: namely that it is by default yet another trait that inevitably involves power relations. Bourdieu notes that, ". . . *linguistic relations are always relations of symbolic power* through which relations of force between the speakers and their respective groups are actualized in a transfigured form."[14] Elsewhere, Bourdieu points to the coercive nature of a dominant language by noting that:

> When one language dominates the market, it becomes the norm against which the prices of the other modes of expression, and with them the values of the various competencies are defined . . . it has a social efficacy in as much as it functions as the norm, through which is exerted the domination of those groups which have both the means of imposing it as legitimate and the monopoly of the means of appropriating it.[15]

While Bourdieu's discussion poses cultural and linguistic capital as tools that certain groups maintain in order to perpetuate their domination and that other groups must obtain in order hopefully to leave behind their disadvantaged societal status, one must wonder if Bourdieu has neglected an alternate strategy, particularly for those that are disadvantaged in terms of linguistic capital. Is the only successful path to increased linguistic capital a strategy in which the dominated group takes on the tongue of the dominant class? Collins' discussion of Bourdieu's work on language concludes by observing that recent work in sociolinguistics has taken Bourdieu to task for not recognizing that linguistically oppressed groups can devise strategies that allow for the flowering of nonelite language in certain public spheres.[16] Specifically, he points to recent studies on the Catalan region of Spain, in which the state-sanctioned domination of Catalan has been resisted in the "everyday" sphere of family, work and other face-to-face interactions. However, even these studies fall short of suggesting a truly viable counterstrategy to that of assimilation, for they ultimately must acknowledge that the bulk of the gains are made in nonofficial settings.

As I will show in chapter 3, not only did the Norwegian Labor Party's treatment of the language question ultimately develop into a counterhegemonic project, but it also suggests an alternative to Bourdieu. Ultimately, one may argue that Bourdieu sets forth a type of determinism, in which those that have the necessary linguistic skills are thankful, and those who don't, hope to acquire them. Yet the Norwegian case demonstrates how the intervention of political elites pursuing other, nonlinguistic ends, can have a spill-over effect onto what constitutes valuable linguistic capital. In forging the linguistic coalition between workers and farmers in the 1930s, and in elevating Common Norwegian to a position of official prestige through subsequent policy, Norwegian Labor Party elites altered the linguistic playing field. Those groups, workers and small farmers, that Bourdieu would consider disadvantaged in terms of linguistic capital, did not have to fully adopt the dominant class' language in official settings. Legislation and orthographic reforms would instead carve out significant sanctioned space in the public arena for the use of this "lower-class" speech alongside the speech belonging to privileged groups. Further, and in even greater contradiction to Bourdieu, in order for the advantaged groups to maintain continued access to the educational and other credentials deemed necessary for success, members of the dominant group would be forced to accept two key linguistic changes. First, through orthographic reforms, Riksmål would be significantly altered to closely resemble the language used by everyday Norwegians. Secondly, through legislation such as the alternative norm essay law (sidemålstilen), even members of advantaged groups who considered Riksmål to be their "mother tongue" would be required to show competence in Nynorsk. For Norwegians, language was to become less of a barrier in accessing other forms of prestigious societal capital.

LANGUAGE IN CONTEMPORARY POLITICAL SCIENCE

Though it is often dismissed as a significant political variable, language and the struggles surrounding language planning should be of interest to political scientists for a number of reasons.[17] As David Laitin points out, the sanctioning by the state of one language as the official standard has implications for the social mobility of all linguistic cultures within the nation.[18] In the most basic sense, the language which is the official currency of the corridors of power becomes the requisite one for all members of society. Related to that, Ernest Gellner observes that for there to be mobility among various groups within society, a state ". . . cannot erect deep barriers of rank, of caste or estate . . ." between members of society.[19] Societies that have a multilingual population, yet only make provisions for one language to be codified as the official standard, erect both formal and informal barriers to those whose primary language is another. The sanctioning of a specific language by a state is then an example of the elite exercise of power to shape the rules of political access. Thus, the ability or the requirement to use one linguistic standard over another can have real implications for individuals and groups seeking to compete with other forces in society on an equal footing. Each of these observations suggests that there is a politics of language and that studying this aspect of politics involves examining ". . . the relation between the distribution of language skills on the one hand, and political power and high status or prestige on the other hand in a society with more than one variety of language."[20] For social scientists then, one key reason to engage in the study of language planning conflicts is that it is yet another arena where competition among elites and counterelites takes place and where various societal groups battle for increased rights and access to political power.

Despite this apparent importance of language as an issue that promotes or prevents groups from accessing political power, political science has not granted language a larger role in questions over societal conflict. In political science, the role of language generally appears in conjunction with investigations into national identity. In the literature on nationalism, language figures prominently among those who seek to explain the rise of states and nations.[21] David Laitin, for example, has devoted several works to explaining the choices of language planners in postcolonial African states;[22] Jonathan Pool has focused attention on the manner in which emerging states can efficiently adopt an official language policy suitable for a bilingual state;[23] and William Safran has focused on "superordinate languages as state-building instruments" in both European and non-European settings.[24]

After state formation, and over the course of a state's history, language has generally received less attention from political science, with the exception of those states where language cleavage is thought to be an underlying source of conflict. In this area, Belgium, Switzerland, Canada, and Spain often stand out.[25] Each of these cases has a shared characteristic: these states possess specific geographic zones where distinctly different languages are dominant, and where distinctly different ethnic groups are also dominant. Further, each of these states has not imposed "language rationalization" upon its citizenry; that is, the state has not mandated the exclusive use of one national language. Finally, while the state may not have rationalized the use of language, the state has been a key player in the attempt to create language policy. Each of these examples is emblematic of state efforts to mediate some balance acceptable to all of the chief linguistic subcultures. Ultimately, that language is a salient or significant conflict in these states is generally not questioned.

The Norwegian Case

An interesting contrast to these cases is the example of multilingual Norway. The Norwegian language has two official written standards. The hegemonic language variant, Bokmål, is used mainly by high status groups, particularly the petit bourgeois in urban centers of eastern Norway. The alternative, Nynorsk, is a collection of rural dialects and used primarily in western Norway, but also favored by many of the country's intellectuals and activists on the political left. Until 1929, Bokmål was officially known as Riksmål, and Nynorsk was known as Landsmål. (In this case, however, for the sake of simplicity and also to avoid confusing the reader, I use the term Nynorsk throughout this book, even when discussing Landsmål in the pre-1929 period.) Written Norwegian also has had a third standard, Common Norwegian, which primarily existed as the policy aim of a gradual fusion between Nynorsk and Bokmål. This third written variant remained mostly an aspiration on the language planning horizon throughout the twentieth century and was eventually discarded as a policy option by the Norwegian Labor Party in the 1960s.

Since the establishment of parliamentary sovereignty in 1884, the conflict between adherents of the two languages has played itself out frequently in the Norwegian policy arena. Legislation regarding the two languages initiated with a parliamentary resolution granting equal status to the two standards and has continued over the past 110 years to include laws on the use of the language in government institutions, education, textbooks, and broadcasting institutions. The impact of this legislation has ranged from what some may dismiss as the symbolic, such as the requirement that certain stamps and currency be labeled with both official renderings of "Norway" (Norge/Noreg), to legislation that has had substantial impact on the behavior of both individuals and institutions in Norwegian society. This includes the requirement that all Norwegian citizens pass exams certifying their competency in both standards upon graduation from secondary school, the requirement that all civil servants conduct official business in the language of the individuals they are interacting with, and the guidelines that have increased the amount of Nynorsk in state broadcasting institutions to roughly twenty percent of broadcast time.

In observing the conflict that has evolved between adherents of these two standards, it is important to note the key manner in which Norway differs from other multilingual European states. Language conflict between the two official Norwegian standards is not an expression of ethnic differences.[26] Unlike the use of the Sámi languages, using one version of Norwegian over another does not mark an individual as being an ethnic outsider. An additional difference between Norway and its other European counterparts is that language has not become exclusively compartmentalized by region. While Nynorsk experiences its strongest base in the west of Norway, it is required that the general population have sufficient Nynorsk training for communication in the minority standard. It is also worth noting that language cleavage has never been the key cleavage in Norwegian society. A number of scholars have shown that while language is a powerful group symbol in Norway, it has ranked behind both regional cleavages and the left-right divide. Finally, the Norwegian party system has never seen the rise of parties that primarily reflected language issues at the expense of other political questions. Without these parties, Norway is lacking a factor critical in other bilingual/multilingual European nations where language policy has received substantial attention from political elites.

Thus, the case of modern Norway presents an interesting puzzle, and one with significance to political science.[27] Norway is similar to Belgium in that both states have a long history of language legislation that has had real impact on the behavior of society.[28] However, Norway's language conflict differs Belgium's and other European nations in terms of the lack of multiple ethnicities, exclusive geolinguistic zones, and single-issue language parties. Thus, the case of Norway leads one to ask why Norwegian elites have chosen language policies in the manner that they have over the past century. More generally, in terms of the interplay between language and policy, the puzzle is phrased as follows: What forces lead political elites toward the adoption of certain types of language policies; and what forces make them more or less inclined to devote space on the political agenda to language issues?

LANGUAGE POLICY AND LINGUISTIC
IDENTITY AS POLITICAL TOOLS

The objective of this research is to explain the broad variation in Norwegian language policy from the point of parliamentary sovereignty until the late 1960s. While a number of specific policies have been enacted since the late 1960s, this period marks the most recent shift in orientation by Norwegian political elites to the language question.

The specific thesis I formulate is that the impetus for linguistic policymaking in Norway has generally come from the top-down, from political leaders who advocate linguistic policies in an effort to advance nonlinguistic political objectives, rather than from the bottom-up through pressure from political activists and organized interests. More specifically, I argue that Norwegian political elites primarily viewed language as an instrument for the construction, manipulation, and maintenance of national and subnational identities.

This thesis draws largely on major works dealing with nationalism, such as that of Anderson, Hobsbawm, and Breuilly, who have stressed that national and ethnic identities are largely a political creation.[29]

Perhaps most apparent in the case of Anderson, language plays a critical role in the emergence of broad-based nationalist movements and the construction of sovereign states. For Anderson, language assumed a key role in conjunction with the rise of print capitalism and higher literacy rates among the masses. He argues that the intelligentsia in many European states were able to garner popular support for nationalist movements by directing appeals toward the increasingly literate masses via print media written in the popular language.

However, it was not just the practical component of communicating in a language comprehensible to the masses that was of importance to the creation of national identity. Rather, the intelligentsia also glorified the common vernacular by making it a defining characteristic of the new nation. By using the common vernacular and making it a focal point of the nationalist movement, Anderson argues that language became both the medium and central component of the nationalist message.[30]

Similarly, Hobsbawm's focus on the link between language and the establishment of national identity in the nineteenth century emphasizes how nationalist political activists drew on the emergence of linguistic and cultural revival movements in order to generate mass support for the national idea.[31] In both cases, language and nationalism are portrayed in rather instrumental terms, with their proponents employing these symbols and ideas as a way to gain access to increased resources and political power.

The findings in the case study chapters offer powerful evidence in support of Anderson's "instrumentalist" view that language is employed by political elites to construct nations. However, there is an additional implication of the story that will unfold in the following chapters. The Norwegian case demonstrates that the political value of language need not be limited to the elite construction of a national community. Language also plays a key role in the elite construction of subnational groupings—in this case, a united cultural front between the dialect-based working class, and the more Nynorsk-oriented farmers. In constructing a united front or counterhegemonic project and in altering the nature of valuable linguistic capital, this study will show that not only are languages employed to imagine national communities, but that they have importance in other types of "imaginings": Namely, those that center around the strategic need to unify subordinated classes in an effort to gain state power.

This view of the "use" of culture has come under attack by a number of scholars, most prominent among them, Anthony Smith. Smith attacks the "instrumentalist" view of national and cultural symbols, in which the focus is on how "ethnicity and nationalism (come to be used) in the power struggles of leaders and parties." For Smith, these types of investigations are flawed for two reasons:

> Instrumentalism, on the other hand, fails to explain why ethnic conflicts are so often intense and unpredictable, and why the 'masses' should so readily respond to the call of ethnic origin and culture. It also fails to address the problem of why some ethnics are so durable and persistent, and why so many people lay down their lives for their nations.[32]

As this case study proceeds, it will become clear that I address this criticism by focusing on the contexts that made cultural symbols salient. At the same time, it is important to specify that I do not claim that the complete details of every language policy are the successful result of elite manipulation. Rather, one of the recent major works in American public policy may be of use here. Kingdon's analysis of agenda-setting in American politics suggests that policy can be conceived of as having two chief components. There is the overall agenda that will be adopted in regard to a political issue, such as whether a given party opts to support one of any number of linguistic standards or whether it wishes to distance itself from the linguistic fray.[33] Kingdon maintains that this broad orientation is largely autonomous of societal pressure and that the position chosen at this level is more likely the result of "visible participants" such as elected elites, high-level bureaucrats and institutions such as political parties. In the case of elected officials, Kingdon observes that they are not "shrinking violets" and that the incentives for participating in the visible activity of agenda setting is of course related to their ambitions for office. However, policy is not simply the choice of an agenda, it is also the choice among alternatives that can be used to implement a given agenda. Here, Kingdon affords room to various types of societal pressure and suggests that the specific alternatives of a given policy may reflect the whims and desires of pressure groups, bureaucracies and academics, labeling these groups as "hidden participants."[34]

There is little doubt that as alternatives within Norwegian language policies have been revised and the finer elements debated, that experts and other interested parties have had their say. However, what has not been sufficiently clarified by other studies is whether Norwegian language policy as a whole has reflected the will of society or that of political elites. Uncovering the extent to which language policy has been an arena that elites have been able to shape for their own ends and independently of other forces in society is the chief aim of this work.

One alternative hypothesis for the formation of language policy in Norway will also be investigated. An interest group led strategy, that is, the extent to which policies are a response to the surges and declines in the activism of linguistic organizations independent of larger political movements and issues, will also be explored.

At this point, I will briefly turn to the literature that informs the research hypothesis and the alternative. Following that, a historical overview of language conflict in Norway will be offered so as to demonstrate the varied and substantial policy outcomes that must be accounted for by the research hypothesis. Finally, I will spell out the methodological guidelines that were used to obtain and evaluate data gathered in the course of this research.

LITERATURE REVIEW AND HYPOTHESES

The Political Exploitation of Language

Riker observed that to the political challenger, the art of politics is to find some alternative to the current winner. This "art" is both possible and necessary as a result of the potential disequilibrium that results from authoritative decisions made through a majority rule mechanism. Through the use of Arrow's Paradox we know that while decisions may be arrived at in a majority-rule society, they will under some conditions be unsatisfactory to the majority of participants, given that any alternative chosen is not the preferred outcome of a majority of the participants.[35] In issues that are considered trivial, this outcome would not produce a high degree of dissatisfaction, yet it is more likely in trivial issues that there will be unanimity as to the preferred alternative. According to Riker, most political choices involve issues that are "morally scarce," that is their results benefit some segment of society while punishing others. Therefore, given that a majority of participants in a society will generally be dissatisfied with the outcome of most nontrivial political decisions, "losers" seek to beat the current winning coalition through creating a new winner. In creating this new winner through the formation of a new coalition, the existing equilibrium is then displaced.[36]

Certainly, it is possible to characterize the broad outline of Riker's argument in a purely opportunistic manner, where elites adopt any issue that may be available to either gain access to or maintain political power. However, the reality of his claim is subtler. Riker states that:

> The outcome of efforts at manipulation is also conditioned by the external circumstances in which the manipulation occurs, the underlying values, the constitutional structure, and the state of technology and the economy. Numerous efforts are made at manipulation. Not all succeed. The choice of which ones do succeed is partially determined by these external circumstances.[37]

Elsewhere, Riker suggests that outcomes are "of course, partially based on tastes because some person's tastes are embodied in outcomes." However, for Riker the critical question appears to be not the existence of these values or tastes, but rather "the ways (in which) the tastes and values are brought forward for consideration, eliminated, and finally selected . . ." Riker sees this process as heavily influenced by political institutions, and in particular, how political party elites shaped the selection of an issue.[38]

Shifting the focus to language, contemporary sociolinguistists and the occasional political scientist have problematized the claim that language policy outcomes are secondary to other goals held by political elites. Cooper disagrees strongly with the prominent view of language planning espoused by Einar Haugen that language planning occurs "wherever there are language problems." Instead, he asserts that:

> Language planning is typically carried out for the attainment of nonlinguistic ends such as consumer protection, scientific exchange, national integration, political control, economic development, the creation of new elites or the maintenance of old ones, the pacification or cooption of minority groups, and mass mobilization of national or political movements. In any war, one uses all the ammunition at hand.[39]

Yet, despite Cooper's claim that "language planning is typically motivated by efforts to secure or maintain interests, material or nonmaterial or both," he places the argument in a broader framework and concedes ground to other forces. Among his concluding series of generalizations is this: "Language planning cannot be understood apart from its social context or apart from the history which produced that context."[40] In that sense, one might infer that Cooper also sees a place for values, tastes, and ideology in the language planning process.

Weinstein does not merely concede ground to other social forces; he considers them ultimately decisive. He notes that, "The masses have the last word, however, even though they are always subject to considerable manipulation by elites."[41] For Weinstein, the question of whether a language policy succeeds is ultimately a question of whether there is resistance to it at the mass level. As I will show, the Norwegian case presents numerous examples where protests against policies were orchestrated at the mass level, yet the policies were implemented and remain on the books. Thus, at the very least, Weinstein's claim needs to be tempered by the reality of the Norwegian case.

Laitin claims that rulers of African states may be less interested in the building of nations than in the construction of states when engaging in the use of language policy. Implicit in this distinction is that the rulers of a given state use the symbols of a nation and certain ethnic groups, but do not do so primarily for the end of advancing the status of those symbols. Rather, the goal of the rulers is to employ the symbol of language for the ends of "maintaining order in society and extracting resources from society." Thus, to Laitin, language is also seen as ammunition, and in this case, the battle is "for the institutionalized domination over society by a ruling cadre, otherwise known as state building."[42]

In sum, the previous discussion forms the basis of the research hypothesis, which can now be stated more generally:

Hypothesis #1   Official support for a given language policy in bilingual/multilingual states varies with the extent to which political leaders believe language policy can be manipulated for their own political gain.

The Alternative Hypothesis: Pressure Group Activity

There is a considerable amount of literature dealing with Norwegian language policy. The largest portion of this literature has been produced by Norwegian sociolinguists and lexicographers. While producing a vast amount of material on the conflict, the general tone of this literature is descriptive in nature and does not explicitly deal with how the variations in Norwegian language policy came about. Ernst Håkon Jahr, for example, has contributed a large number of essays on all the periods of the conflict and the multitude of actors and institutions involved, yet he does not attempt to assess the relative impact of any particular set of events or circumstances.[43] Almenningen and Torp and Vikør are similar in that they present broad histories of the development of the Norwegian languages and the recent conflict, yet they do not view it as their task to offer explanations for the events they are describing.[44] Within this largely descriptive literature, however, is one chief theme that serves as the basis for my alternative research hypothesis.

Linguistic interest groups: A repeated theme of the literature surrounding the Norwegian language conflict, if in fact not the dominant theme, is that language pressure groups have played a key role in shaping language policy outcomes. Recent scholars of the Norwegian language conflict, such as Dalhaug, have devoted significant attention to *Fedraheimen*, a newspaper that in the decades prior to the establishment of parliamentary sovereignty agitated for increased use of Nynorsk in such arenas as education.[45] Also focusing on the period prior to the Norwegian parliament's attainment of sovereignty, Brunstad makes note of the establishment of the first two pro-Nynorsk linguistic organizations, *Det Norske Samlaget* and the regional *Vestmannalaget,* both founded approximately twenty years before the 1884 legislation. Both organizations served the purpose of publishing books in the Nynorsk standard, and it is assumed that the dissemination of printed Nynorsk is a contributing factor to its growth in usage.[46]

The bulk of the attention on the role of interest groups in the Norwegian language conflict, however, has centered around Noregs Mållag and Riksmålsforbundet. Lars S. Vikør, one of the top scholars researching the language question, provides one of the few English-language works on the Norwegian language conflict, explaining the history of the conflict in terms of *The New Norse Language Movement.*[47] Jahr points to the role of the East Norwegian movement of dialects as a contributing factor in the agitation supporting the orthographic reforms of 1917, and also the manner in which this dialect movement increased sensitivity for dialects that were not based on the rural western coastal area.[48]

The role of Riksmål activists is also given attention in the accounts of the conflict. Jahr notes that the response to the 1917 orthographic reform was a 200,000 signature petition drive on the part of Bokmål organizations and a nationwide series of protest meetings to urge the repeal of the reforms.[49] Both Lien and Almenningen, in describing the events of the post-World War II years, state that the combined action of over eighty Bokmål organizations in school district language referenda was a factor in the decrease in the usage of Nynorsk among school children.[50] Finally, the classic work in the field is Haugen's *Language Conflict and Language Planning.* Haugen offers not only the most comprehensive history of the language question in the twentieth century, but in doing so, sketches the relationship between the various language pressure groups and changing government stances on what constitutes official Norwegian.[51]

Yet, the idea that policy outcomes are driven by competition among pressure groups, in an effort to persuade policymakers towards a desired outcome, is by no means unique to the Norwegian language question. Beginning from the observation that political science is "the study of how political preferences are formed and aggregated into policy outputs by governments," Baumgartner and Jones suggest that two "grand initiatives" have emerged within the discipline in an effort to understand how government does in fact aggregate preferences and develop policy.

One of these key approaches is social choice theory, partially discussed earlier in conjunction with Riker. Baumgartner and Jones identify the other main approach as group theory and the subsequent pluralist off-shoot. Policymaking, for the group theorists, features "interest associations (that) interacted as vectors in Euclidean space, and public policy was the net result of this struggle." In this formulation, the state and the political elites that occupy institutions, are "there" to be captured by the pressure groups that have the necessary resources to dominate.[52]

Pluralist scholars offered a view of policymaking that relied less on the idea of a neutral state that was "there for the taking" and offered a more nuanced vision in which policymakers "brokered coalitions" with pressure groups in certain policy areas. Key to both group theory and pluralism is that pressure groups, to a greater or lesser extent, play a highly influential role in shaping policy outcomes.

Thus, one of the major justifications for choosing pressure group influence as the key alternative to the idea of elite manipulation is the prominent role that pressure groups have received in the political science and public policy literature as a whole. Coupled with the high degree of emphasis on the role of pressure groups in the literature on Norwegian language policy, this choice of an alternative hypothesis seems all the more "natural" and is formulated as follows:

Hypothesis #2   Official support for a given language policy in bi-/multilingual states is primarily the result of mobilization activities taken by language-oriented interest groups.

USAGE OF THE TERM *ELITE*

The major theme of this book is that Norwegian political elites have repeatedly used language policy as a tool to help achieve other political and ideological ends. While much of this chapter sets out the general argument explaining why the exploitation of language policy should be a matter of importance for political science, as well as why the case of Norway is particularly appropriate, this section addresses the term *elite* as is used in this study.

My strong reliance on the term *elite* should not be taken as an indication that I would characterize Norwegian political culture as elitist. The term *elitist*, as it was frequently used in the debates of American political scientists and sociologists during the 1950s and 1960s, arose from "sharp challenge(s) to the validity of widely pre-vailing assumptions about popular government,"[53] and was associ-ated with a belief that policy decisions in a given political community were largely determined by a set of overt or covert ruling elites.[54] In the elitist understanding of democracy, which stands in contrast to the pluralist contention that "competition among various power centers is the essence of the political process,"[55] the mass citizenry is thought to play a sharply limited role in the policy-making pro-cess. For proponents of the elitist view, the masses were thought to possess a characteristic set of "inadequacies" that excluded them from the policy-making process. Namely, the masses were consid-ered to be "passive, inert followers who have little knowledge of public affairs and even less interest."[56] Aside from Dye and Ziegler's classic (and much-needed) introductory American government text, *The Irony of Democracy*, such questions over elitist versus pluralist understandings of democratic government are not at the core of the American political science discourse, and it is not my intention to reopen the debate here.

But, if it is not my intention to characterize Norway as elitist, then why do I opt for the term elite? Dahl himself avoided the use of the term *elite*, because "no matter how much an author may try to sterilize the term by definition,"[57] it carries connotations that others are quite willing to read into it. Despite the risk, I will nonetheless put my faith in both definition and clarification.

My use of the term *elite* is primarily guided by both Ezra Suleiman and Robert Putnam's work within the field of comparative politics. For both of these scholars, the term *elite* does not involve a normative judgment being made regarding a lack of societal en-gagement on the part of the masses. Rather, I use the term *elite* in largely the manner that they have: a definitional term intended to describe the group of individuals in democratic society who hold, and periodically compete over, the reigns of government, which carries along with it the ability to make and enforce policy. For Suleiman, this group of "governing elites" exerts the key influence on "political or economic decisions," and unlike "military, religious, intellectual (or) academic" elites, has both power and influence that "transcends a particular sector" or domain.[58] Putnam describes this group by first specifying political elites as "very loosely . . . those in any society (who) rank toward the top of the (presumably closely intercorrelated) dimensions of interest, involvement and influence in politics" and then narrowing his focus to the subgroup of "professional politicians."[59] Putnam's interest in elites as "professional politicians" is of course a key area of investigation in his decades-long research project that led up to the publication of one of the contemporary classics of the comparative politics field, *Making Democracy Work*.[60] Thus, using definitional shorthand to refer to Norwegian politicians as elites is just that: a mere definition that is an accepted practice in comparative politics, and not a pronouncement on the character of Norwegian democracy.

METHODOLOGY

In explaining the methodological guidelines that I employ in this study, a useful starting point is to ask a simple question: Is it possible somehow to disentangle the history of the Norwegian language struggle in order to determine whether or not issue exploitation is the most viable explanation? While a substantial amount of research has been cited in the preceding pages of this chapter that points to the plausibility of issue exploitation as the motivating force behind Norwegian language policy, criticisms have been raised in the language politics community of an approach that emphasizes self-interested behavior at the expense of other factors.

In focusing on the motivations of language activists, Pool does acknowledge that if one looks far enough that one can "usually find ulterior goals if we look or ask," but he also claims that it is possible to locate evidence that language activists "genuinely care" about the policy they are pursuing. For Pool, the entire effort of attempting to clarify the weight that these factors carry seems to be futile and he prefers to treat language and politics as interdependent equals.[61] For language activists and language policymakers, simply because competing explanations can all be conceived of as occurring simultaneously does not imply that we should shy away from determining their relative merit. It is to this task that I now shift my attention.

Variation in Norwegian language policy: Language policy of Norwegian elites, the dependent variable in this project, can take on one of the following six categorical values:

- Pro-Nynorsk language policy
- Pro-Bokmål language policy
- Pro-Common Norwegian language policy
- Opposition to all forms of language planning
- No official party stance on language policy
- Support for language policy that aids all linguistic cultures simultaneously[62]

Elite preferences towards language policy is constructed by considering both a political party's official platform stance on the Norwegian language question and the language policies that it has promoted in the Norwegian parliament. There is, of course, not always a perfect fit between the two; yet on the whole, none of the parties involved in this analysis adopted language policies at platform discussions that supported one linguistic standard while offering parliamentary support to the opposing standard in the subsequent session of the Norwegian parliament. Official party language policy stances are analyzed in terms of the following laws and parliamentary actions:

- 1885 parliamentary declaration giving Nynorsk and Bokmål/ Riksmål equal status
- 1907 law requiring a second essay written in Nynorsk for graduating secondary school students
- 1938 parliamentary orthographic reform
- 1952 establishment of The Norwegian Language Commission (Norsk språknemnd)
- 1972 establishment of The Norwegian Language Council (Norsk språkråd)

These cases have been chosen for a number of reasons. First, the period 1885 to 1968 represents the time span in which successive Norwegian governments adopted and altered their policies with regards to the language question. From 1968 to the present, the official language policy has remained largely static. Additionally, these policies are representative of the major policies that have had real and substantial impact on the behavior of Norwegians. While the policies will be described in greater detail in the following chapters, it can be noted here that the 1885 parliamentary declaration provided the precedent for all subsequent Norwegian language policies. The 1907 law required that a certain degree of proficiency in both Norwegian standards be attained by students; the 1938 orthographic reform dictated the accepted official usage of both Norwegian standards; and both the 1952 and 1968 parliamentary appointed councils established the guidelines for permanent bodies that would administer "nonpolitical" solutions to the language conflict. Further, these are the policies that have received some of the most extensive treatment by scholars of the Norwegian language conflict and which have been explained through the alternative hypotheses under investigation. Finally, these policies have been chosen because their various outcomes have often benefited different linguistic constituencies and, as such, it is possible to test whether this variation in the dependent variable can be accounted for by the mobilization activities of the relevant constituencies.

It is necessary to point out that not all of the preceding policies are representative of the claim that new issues can be introduced onto the political agenda, or that existing issues are redefined, in order to alter the current dimension of political conflict. I argue that the 1885 parliamentary declaration, the 1938 orthographic reform, and the establishment of the Norwegian Language Council fall into that camp. These three policies, as I will show, represented an attempt by political elites to fundamentally restructure some aspect of political competition via the use of language. In the case of the first policy, elites who supported its introduction sought to make the construction of a uniquely Norwegian national identity of primary importance. In doing so, they also employed language as a way to infer that their political opponents were rooted in the old Danish colonial order.

In the second case, elites supporting the reform were formalizing the cultural basis of a cross-class coalition that had provided the Social Democrats with broad electoral support. And in the case of the establishment of the Norwegian Language Council, Labor Party elites, increasingly supportive of urbanization and economic growth, sought to cast off an association with language that was contradictory to the new image and goals of the party.

The remaining policies do not represent fundamental attempts at manipulating the political agenda. Rather, they are examples of political elites seeking to preserve the advantages they had gained through adopting a given stance on the language question. As I will show, preserving these stances implied managing the language issue such that interest groups and parliamentary rivals, while having some degree of input, could not ever succeed at fundamentally altering the course of language policy that elites had chosen.

Linguistic interest groups: In analyzing whether interest groups can account for the elites' choice of language policy, I consider the following:

- Mobilization activities undertaken by language interest groups prior to the adoption of party platforms and parliamentary policies
- Policies desired by the relevant language pressure group as stated in convention proceedings or election manifestos distributed to political parties
- Statements from language pressure groups made subsequent to the adoption of party platforms and parliamentary policies

It is necessary here to pause and further consider the question of interest group pressure to specify what is expected to have occurred when a claim of an interest group-led strategy is made. In a general fashion, how do we know when interest groups have succeeded or failed in their attempt to shape the political agenda? As I consider the evolution of time from when an interest group adopts a stance on the language question, to the point when a policy is adopted by political elites, are there certain cues that we might expect to see from both activists and elites that assist us in ascertaining who actually "controlled" the agenda? So that we have the ability consistently to compare the events of different policy struggles to one common group of reference points, the following set of guidelines will be used throughout the course of this investigation, with the added assumption that the relationship between pressure groups and political elites is one that takes place in a democratic society:

1. The interest group must have a goal that they wish to be enacted by a given group of political elites, and the goal needs to have been articulated by the group in as clear a manner as possible. Further, the goal must be one which can feasibly be translated into public policy form.

The assumptions behind this first of our guidelines are relatively clear. If there is no goal sought by the interest group, any question of seeking to influence political elites can be immediately ruled out. The question of how clearly the goal is stated is also critical, as if political elites are left to infer the goals of an interest group from a vague set of principles, there is the distinct possibility that political elites will not be able to perceive correctly what it is that the interest group wishes them to do. The question of feasibility bears mention in that the goal of an interest group must be something that is capable of being rendered in public policy form. If the goal is not feasible, and elites obviously fail to implement it, we cannot realistically assess a pressure relationship between the activists and elites.

2. The political elites must initially have a stance toward the goal that is: explicitly contradictory to the position of the relevant interest group; have no stance toward the goal among their own stated list of goals; or not be prioritizing the goal highly enough to satisfy the relevant interest group.

   This portion of our guidelines is also straightforward. Interest groups must have information about the stances of political elites for the issues that are dear to them. With no information about whether elites completely oppose or express indifference to a given issue, or about whether they simply do not view an issue as meriting a high place on the agenda, interest groups cannot realistically be expected to devise a strategy in which they target that portion of the political elites' stance that they disagree with.

3. If the interest group decides that the relevant political elites hold a stance toward the goal that is not in keeping with the preferences of the interest group, then a strategy of persuasive actions and the threat of sanctions must be adopted by the interest group.

   The concept of pressure implies that some measure of actions will be taken by the interest group to bring about the desired change on the part of political elites. One can envision this as occurring in one of two fashions that are closely interrelated. On the one hand, interest groups may first engage in activities that are informative in nature. Through mass rallies, meetings with officials, and use of media, interest groups may try to persuade elites that their initial stance is ill-conceived and should be re-thought.[63] However, there is little guarantee that the mere presentation of information to the relevant elites will bring about the desired shift on a given policy. Thus, interest groups augment their presentation of information with threats of sanction. Interest groups may decide that if the political elites do not alter their stance within a fixed period of time, they will cease their efforts at persuading this group of elites and coalesce around other elites that they believe are more likely to champion their cause; or the interest group may enter into the political arena itself and challenge the elites who were not sufficiently in favor of the group's policy goal.

4. If political elites change their stance, this change must be directly attributable to the actions of the interest group.

This final observation rests on the point that may be most critical to our investigation of the Norwegian language struggle and can be summed up in a simple rule of social science investigation: correlation does not imply causation. That an interest group has a preferred stance on a policy matter and that the relevant elites adopt a similar stance at some later time in no way demonstrates that an interest group explanation has been substantiated. Other variables must be controlled for in terms of their possible influence. Only once we have ruled out these possible alternative explanations can we suggest with some measure of certainty that the alignment between the desires of an interest group and the actual outcome is due to interest group activities.

The possibility of an interest group-led strategy appears to constitute the major alternative to the research hypothesis. While I note again the possible complementary nature of the research hypothesis to the alternative, the alternative appears to be an ad hoc attempt at accounting for specific occurrences in the Norwegian language conflict. The disconfirmation of the alternative hypothesis as a general explanatory framework will allow for the research hypothesis to be accepted.

However, my argument that elite manipulation of language serves as the best explanation for shifts in Norwegian language policy does not simply rest on ruling out the major alternative hypothesis of interest group influence. From a methodological standpoint, an explanation that suggests a key explanatory role for "elite manipulation" and "elite interest" may present certain difficulties. As King, Keohane and Verba note, causal explanations that assign explanatory power to concepts such as "national interest, utility or motivation" can often be suspect, as scholars will frequently fall back on tautological explanations in an effort to demonstrate the alleged validity of these explanations. In observing the major shortcomings of tautological explanations involving these concepts, they note that:

> . . . the evidence that the act maximized utility or fulfilled intentions or achieved the national interest is the fact that the actor or the nation engaged in it. It is incumbent upon the researcher formulating the theory to specify clearly and precisely what observable implications of the theory would indicate its veracity and distinguish it from logical alternatives.[64]

Thus, in the case of Norway, the question becomes how to best determine whether actions taken by political elites for or against a given linguistic standard, if not the result of pressure group activity, were in fact the result of an elite desire to manipulate language for other political ends.

In evaluating the actions taken by Norwegian political elites towards the language question, I expect that at the minimum, the first of the following two points will be met:

1. A plausible linkage between the language question and other elite political goals must be observable.

   The assumption behind this point is quite straightforward. As my argument rests on the claim that shifts in Norwegian language policy were the result of elites that did not have language-related concerns as their primary motivation, it becomes necessary to locate the political goals that could potentially serve as the impetus for elite action on the language question. It must be stressed though that it is not enough to simply locate other political goals that interested Norwegian elites while language policy was being altered, and to then declare these goals as a determining factor in language policy shifts. Rather, for there to be a genuine linkage between the two, it needs to be shown that manipulating language policy could have some specific benefit for political elites in terms of achieving one of these other goals. Thus, I repeatedly look to the broader political environment that Norwegian political elites operated in and ask the question, "To what extent would language policy serve as an effective tool in helping political elites achieve some other end?"

2.   Where possible, it needs to be shown that elites are aware of the plausible linkage between language policy and other political goals, and that elites seek to capitalize on this perceived linkage.

Ideally, it would be desirable to have the "smoking gun," perhaps in the form of an official memo or an acknowledgement in the memoirs of an elite, that a given language policy primarily reflected the desire to maximize political advantages elsewhere. Of course, such definitive statements of causality are few and far between in social science research. Thus, in some instances, the case for elite manipulation needs to be made by first ruling out interest group pressure and then showing a plausible linkage between language and other questions at a time when language policy was being made or altered. Quite obviously though, evidence of the "smoking gun" would be preferable. As I will show in the following chapters, such evidence can arise in two chief manners. First, through writings, speeches and other activities, the relevant elites explicitly acknowledge that language served a valuable function as a political tool. Alternately, while not directly acknowledging the desire to exploit a linkage between language and some other political end, elites engage in some observable activity that demonstrates an awareness of a link between language and other political goals.

My data comes from a variety of primary and secondary sources. The bulk of the primary sources were located in the Norwegian Parliamentary Archives, the Norwegian National Archives, the archival material of the various language pressure groups, and the official parliamentary record. Many of the speeches made by elites outside of the Norwegian Parliament are from the large number of anthologies produced by Norwegian language conflict historians for use in research. As the overwhelming number of years under investigation in this study do not allow for elite interviews, the use of "histories" forms the other major data component. Accounts of policy and platform struggles were gleaned from a large number of historical works, both published and unpublished. I have taken pains to attune myself to the fact that all historical accounts argue one perspective over another. Therefore, I have made great use of historical material that academics from various sides of the Norwegian language conflict of the question have produced.

The following three chapters detail the case of Norwegian language policy, not only showing the weakness of a pressure group argument, but casting light onto the conditions that allow political elites to see language as a necessary weapon in their battle to gain and hold onto elected office. Chapter 2 will focus on the first decades of the modern Norwegian state and how the emerging Liberal party was able to employ language as a symbol of Norwegian nationalism against an urban elite with strong ties to the old Danish order. Chapter 3 will show that language has relevance to political elites that are not just concerned with questions of nation-building. In particular, it will emphasize how the Norwegian Labor Party has gone through three distinct stances on language policy during the twentieth century, and how each has been linked to larger political concerns. Both of these chapters will offer substantial evidence that a pressure group explanation cannot account for Norwegian language policy.

Chapter 4 considers another case of Norwegian language policy: the treatment of the Norwegian Sámi. The first half of this chapter focuses on how language policy towards an ethnic minority formed part of a larger set of policies designed to promote the establishment of a Norwegian national identity. The latter half of this chapter shows how limited promotion of the Sámi language became a possibility in the changed political climate following World War II.

As will be seen in chapter 5, the Norwegian case also has value in a comparative perspective. In Belgium, ethnic groups that faced shifting economic fortunes employed language and other cultural symbols in an effort to gain increased economic and political power. As the traditional lines of cleavage in Belgian society were organized around religious and ideological differences, Belgian elites repeatedly resisted efforts to define conflict in ethnolinguistic terms. However, once it became clear to Belgian elites that they could no longer avoid seriously dealing with ethnic-based demands, they redesigned Belgian institutions such that their power could be maintained in a quasi-federal state that emphasized the significance of ethnic division.

The concluding chapter will draw attention to some of the general conditions under which political elites may find language politically useful, and will suggest additional variables that ought to be given greater attention in future studies of language policy.

Chapter 2

National Identity, Party Identity, and the Role of Nynorsk in the New Norwegian State

INTRODUCTION

Before turning to an evaluation of the pressure group hypothesis, an initial comment is in order about the place of the language conflict in Norwegian society. Those not familiar with the history of modern Norway frequently have difficulty understanding how language policy could have played such an important role in Norwegian society over the past 100 years.[1] Even Norwegian scholars of the language conflict have acknowledged that "(t)o many foreigners, Norway stands as a puzzling example, being linguistically so divided and pluralistic."[2] Yet the importance of language as a political issue on the nineteenth- and twentieth-century Norwegian political agenda has been well-documented.

Primarily, political scientists and sociologists who focus on Norway locate language, along with religion and teetotalism, as one of the three important expressions of a peripheral counterculture movement that has been active with varying degrees of strength against the urban center of Oslo throughout the past century.[3] According to Rokkan et al., the territorial center, representing secularized values and the widespread usage of Bokmål, can be characterized by three factors: military-administrative centers (location of legislative assemblies, courts, ministries, etc.); economic centers (location of major industrial corporations, banks, stock exchanges, etc.); and cultural centers (location of academies, universities, dioceses, etc.).[4] Rokkan et al. point out that a center:

> controls the bulk of transactions among holders of resources across a territory; it is closer to any alternative site to the resource-rich

33

areas within the territory; and it is able to dominate the communication flow through a standard language and set of institutions for regular consultation and representation.[5]

In contrast, peripheral regions, which in the Norwegian case are marked by broad usage of Nynorsk, along with the popularity of teetotalism and support for the Lutheran Church, are defined as those areas that control:

> at best only its own resources, is isolated from all the other regions except the central one and contributes little to the total flow of communication within the territory, particularly if its language and its ethnic identity set it apart from other regions controlled by the center.[6]

According to Rokkan et al., the importance of these peripheral regions and their trademark cultural values is that the distinct culture of the peripheral regions has made them ideal candidates that are available for mobilization by political elites.[7] The history of modern Norway is rich with examples of political conflicts between the center and periphery, including questions over the establishment of a national identity in the late nineteenth and early twentieth century, pitting the traditional rural areas against the Danish-influenced capital; the rural-urban divisions that served as a potential obstacle to Labor Party ascendance in the 1930s; the decision by the post-war Labor Party to promote economic centralization and urbanization at the expense of traditional rural ways of life; and most recently, the strong center-periphery overtones that have marked the two Norwegian EU referenda.

As both this and the following chapter will demonstrate, language has repeatedly appeared on the Norwegian political agenda in the past 100 years. However, the political use of such a regionally based issue, particularly in a society where center-periphery relations are salient, has meant that Norwegian elites have had to be aware of both the opportunities and problems that stem from the promotion of any given language policy. The chief problem has been that advantages accruing from the choice of a specific language policy in one region or with one group have rarely translated into the same advantages on a nationwide basis or with all classes in Norwegian society. Thus, I will argue that Norwegian political elites, as they have looked to make use of language as a tool, have had to be primarily concerned with this dual realization, and that they have been far less concerned with the activities or desires of the language pressure groups.

THE INTEREST GROUP HYPOTHESIS

The goal of this chapter is to explore whether the Nynorsk language pressure groups were able to dictate the language policy of the Liberals. In doing so, this chapter will form the first of two that explores the viability of the interest group hypothesis:

> *Hypothesis #2*   Official support for a given language policy in bilingual/multilingual states is primarily the result of mobilization activities taken by language-oriented interest groups.

Such extensive treatment of the interest group hypothesis is necessitated by the fact that both academic and popular accounts of the Norwegian language conflict inevitably devote great attention to the role of the two chief language interest groups, Noregs Mållag (the chief pro-Nynorsk interest group) and Riksmålsforbundet (the chief pro-Riksmål/Bokmål interest group), their less organized precursors, and smaller language organizations that came and went during the twentieth century.

While a number of other language policies were adopted in the following years, the focus in this chapter will be on two of the earliest, which are widely seen by Norwegian scholars as forming the official basis for the advance of Nynorsk. The 1885 parliamentary declaration of equivalency between the Nynorsk and Riksmål standards provided the parliamentary precedent for all subsequent Norwegian language policies, and the 1907 "alternative norm essay law" required that a certain degree of proficiency in both Norwegian standards be attained by students. Additionally, this policy is widely seen as the first that advanced beyond a policy of "passive equivalency" to one of "active equivalency," whereby Norwegians were required to make changes in their linguistic behavior to afford Nynorsk a greater societal space.

The Liberals were the leading liberal party in the emerging Norwegian state, from 1884 to 1931. In this period, proponents of

Nynorsk saw their first policy victories championed by the Liberals in the newly sovereign Norwegian parliament. First and most critically, following a propaganda campaign by Nynorsk organizations, the Liberals passed a parliamentary resolution giving Nynorsk and Dano-Norwegian formal equivalency in the eyes of the state. This resolution, the language equality law (jamstillingsvedtaket) is the basis for all subsequent language policy dealing with the status of the two standards. In addition to the language equality law, a 1907 school law mandating that all candidates for graduation from secondary school be able to write one essay in that language which was not their chief form of instruction, was adopted shortly after the national Nynorsk organization requested such.

Taken jointly, the adoption of these two policies presents an initial picture suggesting that language policy in Norway was driven by the whims of the organized Nynorsk advocates. A closer review of the struggles surrounding these policies will suggest something quite to the contrary. Namely, this chapter will demonstrate that Nynorsk adherents had, at best, a close relationship with those elements of the Liberals that were already aligned with the Nynorsk movement, and they were not able to expand their "pressure activities" beyond this group. As a parliamentary party, the Liberals did implement language policies that were to the benefit of Nynorsk; however, they were not the result of interest group pressure. Rather, the orientation of these policies can be traced to other questions that were high on the Liberals' political agenda: specifically, the construction of a Norwegian national identity in the wake of both parliamentary sovereignty in 1884 and the dissolution of the union with Sweden in 1905, and the need for the Liberals to differentiate itself in the eyes of the electorate from its chief rival, Høyre (the Conservatives). Insofar as Liberal elites chose to pursue these goals, language policies that aided in this quest mattered, but any proposals that might have been at odds with the Liberals' larger political agenda were either dismissed or strongly watered-down.

ACTIVITIES LEADING UP TO THE LANGUAGE EQUALITY LAW

Parliamentary sovereignty was introduced in Norway in 1884. Two years earlier, a radical liberal majority (later to become the Liberals) was elected to the Norwegian parliament. This new majority would have the necessary number of seats eventually to impeach the conservative government for misuse of its royal veto. Like all others under the union with Sweden, this conservative government had been appointed by the Swedish king and was formally responsible to the Swedish crown and not to the Norwegian people. Law professors at the national university observed that there was no valid case to be made against the government. However, the Liberals' strong position in the new Norwegian parliament allowed it to pack the court of judges with enough members to outvote the professional judges that were expected to support the stance of the law professors, and the government was sentenced to "deprivation of office." This bloodless parliamentary coup signaled the beginning of Norwegian governments that would be dependent on political support in the Norwegian parliament in order to rule, and not the royal backing of the court in Stockholm.[8]

It was commonly thought at the time that there was a "natural alliance" between advocates of Nynorsk and the emerging Liberals. As is the case with almost all other examples of linguistic nationalism in the late nineteenth century, these advocates of Nynorsk were strongly represented by school teachers and academics, those groups that stood the most to gain from seeing their language become one of the accepted variants for official business and cultural reproduction.[9]

The nature of their seemingly natural alliance with the Liberals is the result of two similar forces. On the one hand, many prominent members of the Liberals, hailing from the core usage areas of Nynorsk, used spoken dialects that formed the basis of the new language and as such, were seen as standard bearers for bringing Nynorsk to the corridors of power in the formerly Danish Christiana. But it was not just the language of rural and peripheral Norway that Nynorsk advocates saw the Liberals bringing to the Norwegian capital. For the Liberals' victory in 1884 also represented a strengthening of the role of countercultural, peripheral values in a time when traditional economies and ways of life were increasingly under threat by the growth of industrialization in Norway.[10] As a party, the Liberals did not specifically seek to block the broad transformations that Norway's traditional economies were undergoing. However, in coming to power, the Liberals not only displaced the urban-based elite that had its roots in the Danish bureaucracy, but the Liberals brought with them a sense that the values of people in the districts were not to be disregarded and that their values and ways of life could now serve as a counterweight to the earlier hegemony of urban-based aristocratic values.

Upon coming to power, the Liberals were greeted by a strongly enthusiastic Nynorsk print media. In a well-known quote, the biweekly Nynorsk paper, *Fedraheimen*, announced on June 28, 1884, that, "We now have four fully committed Nynorsk advocates in the government, and the prime minister himself is the fifth. . . . Now the language issue can become one of the first matters to be dealt with in the nation. The time has come, Norwegian men and women, let us work now, quickly and without tire, so that we may hold victory in our hands!"[11] Along with Det Norske Samlaget, a Nynorsk publishing house, *Fedraheimen* served as the main organizational basis for the Nynorsk movement until the establishment of Noregs Mållag in 1906.

But such enthusiastic and hopeful rhetoric was not about to be met with a similar degree of response from the Liberals' central committee. When the draft party platform was issued for the 1885 Norwegian parliamentary elections, Nynorsk advocates, who had expected so much from a government that seemingly had Nynorsk friendly ministers at its very core, were quite disappointed to find that a seven-point platform had been issued and no mention of Nynorsk had been made therein. Additionally though, a five-point program of future policy areas had been issued and Nynorsk was found among these, albeit only in passing, as part of the fifth point that focused on subjects that should be introduced at the junior/high school level. Haugland notes that the disappointment on the part of the Nynorsk advocates was understandable, as the Liberals' central committee contained at least four prominent supporters of the language, including prime minister Sverdrup.[12]

While Arne Garborg, the key figure in *Fedraheimen*, mocked the Liberals for equating the importance of Nynorsk with that of straw-weaving as a subject of school instruction, he also suggested one reason why the Liberals may have been wise not to give immediate and explicit support to Nynorsk: electoral politics. Garborg suggested that a detailed party platform focusing on a number of issues might have been more of an advantage at the polls to the newly united Conservatives than it would have been to the Liberals.[13] It is interesting to note that only four days after Garborg's critique of the Liberals, *Dagbladet* made public a memorandum written by Sverdrup that painted a picture of a party that would come out of the election with a heavily proactive Nynorsk policy. Specifically, Sverdrup, writing in the capacity of a "private person," suggested to the minister of the Department of Church Affairs that arrangements should be made to ensure that a sufficient number of texts were available in Nynorsk across the array of school subjects. Additionally, he proposed that local school districts take up the decision as to which of the two official languages would be the primary one used for instruction in their district.[14]

However, *Fedraheimen's* official response came in the form of an editorial that focused only on Garborg's criticism of the Liberals' central committee. The editorial encouraged all local party organizations to pass resolutions that would demand increased support from the Liberals for Nynorsk.[15] To supplement this call, and aided by *Det Norske Samlaget, Fedraheimen* issued 12,000 flyers that employed both national and pedagogic arguments in an attempt to gain official status for Nynorsk. To adherents of Benedict Anderson's analysis of nationalism, this joint effort had meaning far beyond an acceptance that both organizations were genuinely interested in promoting Nynorsk for altruistic reasons. As a newspaper and a publishing house, both were part of the rise of print capitalism that necessitated a literate market. Both were active in marketing products that were written in a minority language for the population as a whole. Thus, it should come as no surprise that those whose business was Nynorsk were behind the effort at agitation and that we do not find a groundswell of activity from the farmers and other residents of the periphery on whose tongue Nynorsk was based.

That only publishers and others who had a vested material interest in the promotion of Nynorsk led the effort to influence the Liberals is interesting, but a more important question remains. How was this first attempt at organized pressure by Nynorsk advocates met by the Liberals? The answer appears to differ depending on whether one looks at party organizations and candidates at the local level, the party convention prior to the election, or the parliamentary party in power after the election. The differences in response by each of these components, albeit subtle, are distinct enough to suggest that the Liberals, as a party, were not at the service of Nynorsk advocates. Rather, what motivated the Liberals as a whole were concerns about political competition and ideological profiling.

At the local party level, the pressure of this 12,000 flyer campaign appears to have had mixed results. Roughly twenty-five local Liberal organizations responded with resolutions of support, but a full third of those were concentrated in the most heavily Nynorsk "amt" or county of Romsdal, on the western Norwegian coast. Additionally, to the extent that other counties were strongly represented, they appear to have been counties that were also part of, or close to the core area of, Nynorsk use. Kristians and Akershus, respectively the county for the capital and the next-closest county, only had one local resolution of support each from Liberal organizations.[16] These numbers suggest that the pressure activities being undertaken by Nynorsk advocates were meeting geographically predetermined responses. In those areas where Nynorsk already had a significant base, namely the rural Western counties, support for their efforts was great and in those areas where there was not broad usage of Nynorsk, generally in the eastern "urban" areas, support in the forms of resolutions was rather limited. Far from applying pressure on the Liberals as a national party, the issuance of 12,000 flyers calling for support appears to have better succeeded at mapping out current levels of support for Nynorsk as a political issue.

Similarly, an attempt in the following decade to build a national organization of Nynorsk youth (also closely affiliated with the Liberals) was also hampered in terms of effectiveness by the borders of language use. Once again, in counties or districts where Nynorsk was not widely used, the youth organizations were not able to make broad inroads and the attempt at building youth organizations as language pressure organizations often had to be supplemented with other issues of "national restoration" that were more in keeping with the local culture.[17] Both of these early efforts at organizing and pressure on the part of Nynorsk activists appear to point to the regional limits that their success was to have.

However, the strategy of the Nynorsk activists was designed not just to attain resolutions of support from around the nation, but to convince the Liberals as a whole to re-think its placement of Nynorsk in their political platform. Prior to considering the party's response as a whole, it is interesting to consider the way in which Liberal members of the Norwegian parliament responded to the resolutions. Given the regional-based strength of the calls for official status for Nynorsk, the path chosen by the Liberals in the Norwegian parliament is predictable. In January, 1885, 41 Liberal representatives, out of 145 Liberal party members in the Norwegian parliament, put forth a suggestion that the Norwegian parliament would declare formal equivalency between Nynorsk and the then Dano-Norwegian. Of these 41 representatives, only 4 came from urban areas, while the remaining 37 came from predominantly rural counties. It also appears that as one moves further from the core Nynorsk usage areas, the number of Liberal representatives sponsoring the suggestion became far less.[18]

It is at this point that one would strongly have to question a piece of conventional wisdom in the story of Norwegian language policy. According to Haugland, the resolution put forth by the forty-one representatives was designed to show Nynorsk advocates that the Liberals were willing to promote their cause. However, Haugland's own evidence suggests quite a different story. The overwhelming geographic skew towards rural areas among those who sponsored the resolution suggests that, prior to the election, the Liberals may have been less willing publicly to commit to the issue as a whole, and that only those Liberal representatives and candidates that hailed from pro-Nynorsk counties were willing to do so. That the Nynorsk issue may have carried negative implications for the electoral fortunes of urban Liberal candidates is strengthened when our focus shifts to the final platform discussions at the Liberal convention of 1885.

How did the Liberals as a whole respond to the increased attention being focused on Nynorsk through the flyer campaign, the string of local party resolutions, and the proposal set forth by forty-one of its own representatives? Just as Garborg criticized the Liberals for drawing up an initial platform that was possibly "too clever" in both including Nynorsk and at the same time relegating it to an issue that would be prioritized at a later date, the party seems to have once again opted for a preelection evasion. Instead of issuing a platform that ranked individual goals or issue areas that the Liberals would work on in the coming Norwegian parliamentary period, the party opted simply to state that it had faith that prime minister Sverdrup would properly develop both the content and direction of its future policy stances.[19]

It is useful to sum up the events that occurred prior to the Norwegian parliamentary election and the debate over the language equality law. First, one sees that the hopeful rhetoric of the Nynorsk activists was met with a lukewarm degree of support by the Liberals as a whole, though support from Norwegian parliamentary members in Nynorsk districts was far more forthcoming, as it was from local Liberal organizations found in the core area of Nynorsk usage.

Additionally, despite the introduction of a resolution by the Nynorsk wing of the party and a leaked memo from the prime minister, both of which having indicated strong support for Nynorsk, the party officially chose to skirt the issue. It did this first through putting it on the back burner of policy questions and secondly through avoiding any detailed platform at the final convention. The lack of complete support for the Nynorsk issue in the Liberal party prior to the election can be traced to the fact that it was an issue with strong geographical ties: people simply did not use the language in all areas of the country. Additionally, the strong regional nature of the language went hand in hand with a certain set of counterelite, rural values, that were more difficult to rally around in the eastern and populated areas of the nation. In both cases, for Liberal candidates to have actively campaigned on a plank of party support for Nynorsk created the potential that their prospects would be hurt at the polls. Thus, the events leading up to the election already hint at the limits of support that would be found in the party for the demands of the Nynorsk activists. Regardless of what Nynorsk activists wanted, only those candidates who felt "safe" enough in their districts to attach themselves to the language question did so, and the party as a whole avoided committing to the issue, a stance that was to continue up through 1906. It is what occurs in the Norwegian parliament after the 1885 election that shows how the party was able to satisfy a key demand of the language activists as part of their efforts both to construct a national identity and to paint the opposition into a very unflattering ideological corner.

A "TRULY" NORWEGIAN LANGUAGE

If the previous section has emphasized how the Liberals had to dance very carefully around the language issue in the period prior to the 1885 Norwegian parliamentary election, it is still necessary to explain why the Liberals considered the language question to be an attractive candidate for political exploitation. While the party as a whole refused to officially commit itself to Nynorsk prior to the election, the parliamentary party did embrace official status for Nynorsk only a few months later. In this section, I argue that, by necessity, the Liberals had an ambiguous relationship with Nynorsk. On the one hand, as we saw in the previous section, a certain degree of distance needed to be kept from the language question given regional variations in language choice. I show that regional differences among the electorate were often supplemented by differing views within the party over what type of status and rights Nynorsk should be given. Finally, I show how a resolution with vague enough wording could be made in support of Nynorsk, such that the Liberals would emerge from the parliamentary debates as not only the clear friend of Nynorsk, but also as a party that stood in sharp contrast to the Conservatives.

After the dissolution of the union with Denmark in 1814, the Norwegian language situation was similar to that of many other European nations. There was an upper-class spoken language—Danish, as pronounced by the inhabitants of Oslo—employed chiefly by the aristocracy, civil servants, and businessmen in the nation's capital. Its corresponding written standard was official Danish. For the remaining 80 percent of the population (farmers and rural inhabitants), local dialects were generally spoken, and these were accorded relatively low social status by the ruling elite of Oslo. However, after the union with Denmark had ceased, the official written language became, in political senses, a foreign language.[20] Whereas in nations such as France or Sweden, the official written language had been the result of the dialect of the capital, this was not the case in Norway, or rather, was the case in an indirect manner. The language of the capital was the language provided by its "partner" in the union. Thus, as feelings of independence and nationalism grew among the relatively small educated strata of the new Norwegian state, along with it rose the question of how to assert these feelings of nationhood in a way that would visibly differ the counter-elites from the Danish-based ruling class. Among those that would form the leadership of the Liberal party, such efforts found fruit in a philological debate going on over the nature of the Norwegian language.

Over the course of the nineteenth century, two schools of thought had emerged on the question of the Norwegian language. On the one hand, school teacher and language reformer Knud Knudsen argued that the way to construct a national language was gradually, using the Oslo spoken dialect and written Danish as the departure points.[21] While practical in that there were models for this in other European nations, and that it already had an existing written standard as a basis for development, such a strategy was not without political implications. For implicit in this road to a national language was the belief that the Norwegian nation was new and had its origins in 1814. The contending point of view was provided by Ivar Aasen, who argued that the dialects being spoken by the 80 percent of the rural/peripheral population were in fact based upon gammalnorsk (Old Norwegian) and could be both described and cataloged without making any reference to official Danish. Aasen maintained that the union with Denmark had provided a false sense that the dialects were variations of spoken Danish, while he hoped to contribute to a national consciousness through arguing that the dialects constituted a particularly Germanic and Nordic form of language.

Aasen's method for the construction of "New Norwegian" was to travel the rural areas of the nation in the mid-nineteenth century and collect dialects. The result was to be the construction of a national written form that was based on all Old Norwegian-derived dialects, so that Nynorsk could be a reflection of Norway as a nation, not just of Norway as one regional dialect.[22]

In his discussion of the link between languages and emerging nineteenth-century European nationalism, Anderson notes that the leaders of these nationalist movements were those persons whose education and occupations put them in the position of the "handling of languages," and that as a result of work being conducted on and about national languages, larger political goals of explicit nationalism could be advanced.[23] While both Knudsen and Aasen can be thought of in this manner, it was Aasen's view that had the immediate impact on an emerging political counter-elite who would benefit greatly from the use of linguistic nationalism. In the long run, Nynorsk would become threatening to the unity of the Liberals. Still, the initial emphasis on a language that derived from a view of Norway as an entity with a history preceding that of Danish rule provided the Liberals with a powerful national symbol and proof of national identity independent from that of their former rulers. Knudsen's concept of establishing a Norwegian language could not provide this, for, as his solution was a gradual shift based on the Danish language, the implication was ultimately a starting point of a Danish national identity.[24]

Awareness of the usefulness that Nynorsk would have in the construction of Norwegian nationalism can be found decades before the first round of organized pressure activities against the Liberals. Sverdrup is cited in an 1868 letter as having told prominent Liberal elite Aasmund Vinje, "If we are to believe there is a future for this nation, we must expect help from the language movement and the whole of the Norwegian national movement if we are to oppose the bureaucracy and the political and literary slavery that we face."[25] One decade later, Sverdrup would state, "It is my desire to work for the enlightenment of the people and the language issue. I can go so far as to say that it is my duty to not spare any effort to achieve these goals, insofar as I wish for self-rule for my people."[26]

As we have seen earlier in this chapter, Liberal members of the Norwegian parliament handled the Nynorsk issue quite differently from one another, depending on their geographical location. However, in addition to focusing on the electoral reasons that contributed to such differential treatment, there is the question of whether Liberal representatives had one unified view of the language question on the floor of the Norwegian parliament. That is, regardless of the linguistic make-up of the constituencies, did Liberal elites as a parliamentary party subscribe to the agenda that was put forward by Nynorsk advocates? Did the parliamentary Liberal party wish to see Nynorsk triumph as Norway's sole written linguistic standard? The evidence, which is taken primarily from the events surrounding the debates on the language question in the spring of 1885, suggest that there was far from a unanimous degree of support for the Nynorsk agenda. Yet, despite this uneven support for a Nynorsk agenda, we know that the Liberals, with one exception, wound up pushing through the language equality law. What explains this eventual support? The answer to this comes from understanding that while the party may have had different groupings around the language questions, there were larger ideological questions in the party that allowed even the least zealous supporters of Nynorsk to get on board for the language equality law.

In particular, Bull and others make the argument that the Liberals can be considered to have had only one view on the language question and that this view derived from the need to utilize language as part of the nationalist agenda. While the argument I am making does require a "larger issue" such as nationalism for language to be tied to, I maintain that, in order to understand how language was manipulated, one needs to recognize that the Liberals did not have one unified view of the language question. The most critical of the early language policy outcomes did not just come about because of the link to nationalism, but because the party, with different wings on the language question, could only be united on a view of language that drew heavily on liberal ideology.[27]

Specifically, like many of its European contemporaries in the late nineteenth century, the Liberals' rise to power was largely based on a critique of the way aristocratic society limited access to power to those that had either been born into the proper circles, or those that had the wealth to join those circles. The alternate view of access to power, as put forth by liberal counterelites, was one that would increase access by allowing the growing educated and merchant classes the ability to compete with one another for the reins of the state. In this sense, as the liberal ideology came to influence questions of governing and questions of the economy, we can also see the Norwegian case as one where it came to influence cultural policy. Casting official support for Nynorsk in terms of formal equivalency allowed it the chance to compete with Dano-Norwegian and was consistent with the emerging liberal ideology. As such, "formal equivalency" implied that the state was guaranteeing the citizenry the right to choose from among two linguistic choices; however, it was not dictating what that choice should be, or to what extent the linguistic behavior of Norwegians should be altered.

As noted earlier, the evidence of this differing view within the Liberal party on the degree of official support to be given to Nynorsk can be discerned in the Norwegian parliamentary debates of spring 1885. A small body of literature has arisen in Norwegian sociolinguistics that attempts to interpret the intent behind these debates, less from the perspective of assessing the support that the Liberal party had for Nynorsk, but more from a starting point concerned with whether the term *det norske Folkesprog* (the Norwegian people's language), used in the resolution, implied Nynorsk or the more Danish-inspired Knudsen variant.[28]

Despite the difference in emphasis, one can use these same debates to show the existence of support for state promotion of Nynorsk that was, at best, quite passive. In particular, one need look no further than Church and Education Affairs Minister Elias Blix, who stated during the 1885 debate that he wished to place the two written forms side by side on an official basis, just so that each of them could have the ability to freely develop their strength.[29]

Additionally, one can look to the floor comments from the Conservatives for evidence that there was, at the very least, uncertainty on how the Liberals were treating the language issue. As prime minister Sverdrup's stance on the language question came to be seen more and more in line with that of the Nynorsk advocates, one Conservative representative warned that Sverdrup's words revealed that what the Liberals were really trying to do was to bring about the introduction of Nynorsk as Norway's sole national language.[30]

But ultimately, the clearest evidence that the Liberals were experiencing a divide on the language question from the very start came in the form of the regional party organs and their coverage of the language equality law. In an analysis of Liberal press coverage of the resolution, Haugland notes that there is broad discrepancy of how the various regional Liberal organs put a spin on the issue. In the Nynorsk friendly constituencies, he finds that the Liberal press unabashedly emphasized the pro-Nynorsk aspect of the Liberals' parliamentary activities. Yet, in the noncore areas, the Liberal press needed to cast a different light on the issue and, for that, it fell back on the party's commitment to a liberal ideology, which demanded that it allow for all languages to compete on an equal footing.[31] This was also the case in the national urban press, where *Dagbladet* attempted to downplay the pro-Nynorsk efforts of Sverdrup by stating that, "Mr. Sverdrup, just like all of the other friends of the language movement, wants to afford the same freedom for growth to both languages."[32]

Quite simply then, the combination of a party that was spread over different linguistic-geographic core areas, along with representatives that had differing views over the extent to which formal rights should be granted to Nynorsk, meant that not only would the Liberals not be at the beck and call of the Nynorsk movement, but its policy approach to the issue would be strongly conditioned by the need to contain the issue from becoming one that could split the party along linguistic lines. To do so, passive state promotion of Nynorsk, formalized through the granting of formal equivalency for the two languages, was chosen as the politically safe route. But most importantly, in raising the status of Nynorsk to official status, the Liberals took a language that very few spoke, and that featured less than 100 written overall works, and elevated it to both a symbol of the newly independent Norwegian nation and the party that had successfully challenged the old aristocratic order.

BEYOND NATIONALISM

Finally, it should be remembered that while Liberal ideology explains why it was possible for political elites from different areas and with different views on language to join in a common effort on the language policy front, it does not account for why the Liberals thought it necessary to make the language issue politically salient. Much of that answer, of course, lies in the preceding discussion on nationalism, particularly in the need of rising counter-elites to find a mythical past with which to associate and justify their rise to power. However, while less important, there is a more concrete party politics explanation. Admittedly, while the role of competition among political parties is not entirely divorced from the part that nationalist ideology played, there is little doubt that party competition would frequently be a chief issue when language policies came to a vote in the Norwegian parliament.

The need to use the language issue in competition among the two main parties, the Liberals and the Conservatives, stems from the realization that they while many of the players were the same from the decade immediately preceding parliamentary sovereignty, the parties were themselves quite new and had not developed any sense of tradition, policy legacies, or organizational identity that could become shortcuts in the minds of the voters. Thus, it appears logical that the available political landscape was surveyed for issues that could define one's own party in the best light, while of course casting one's opponent in a suitably negative fashion. For the Liberals, this attempt is made all the more challenging given that the Conservatives appeared to adapt rather quickly to the new political reality of sovereignty and did not base its appeal around the need to maintain the old order.[33] Schattschneider has observed that one of the least favorable situations for a group locked in cleavage with another is that "irrelevant competitors" may appear and compete for the attention of the mass public, thus rendering the current political division less salient.[34] The Liberals by no means comprised an "irrelevant competitor," but the language issue was not the central one under the old lines of cleavage, and as such, constituted a new attempt to gain the attention and loyalty of the voting public. And while it would be an exaggeration to say that the Conservatives shared the same inclination toward liberal democracy that the Liberals did, the fact remained that the easiest ideological reference point—the Conservatives as the domestic representatives of the old colonial order—was no longer entirely valid. In accepting the new rules of the game, the Conservatives had in fact changed the symbolic nature of the game. Yet in reaching to language, the Liberals would be able to restore and build upon those differences between the two parties.

We witness this use of language policy to define the Liberals' political opposition occurring in two ways. First, the Liberal-friendly press, such as *Dagbladet*, painted the outcome of the language equality law in such a way as to dredge up the recent historical past, painting the Conservatives guilty by association. During the week of the debates on the language equality law, *Dagbladet* stated that, "The issue is such that the Conservatives, with an instinct for self-preservation, do not happily view the farmer's language as coming from the most cultivated of behavior. The Danish language is the language of the bureaucracy. Just as the bureaucracy's power has been weakened, so has its language, which in having been brought here from Denmark, has lost its purity."[35] The use of language to associate the Conservatives with the old colonial order was a clever device. Whereas the Liberals suffered internal divisions on the issue, the Conservatives were unanimous in their continuous and principled opposition to any official inroads for Nynorsk. The principled nature of this opposition is critical, in that insofar as it was constant, the Liberals knew that attacks based on language would not be met by shifts in the Conservatives' language policy. Therefore, the Conservatives' unwavering stance on the language question provided an enduring symbol for showing differences between the two parties on a whole host of issues: democracy, the rights of rural peoples, and their sense of patriotic loyalty to the new Norwegian state.[36]

An example of how the Liberals were able to use language as a defining issue between the two parties comes in the year immediately following the language equality law. The county of Holmestrand had requested that it be exempt from paying fees for one of the western railway lines, and the majority report from the railway committee in the Norwegian parliament concurred, but did so in Nynorsk. The two minority members of the committee, both Conservatives, dissented and claimed that it was unwise to allow the use of Nynorsk in amendments to legislation. The Liberals countered with reference to the language equality law, and when the issue was put to a floor vote, the

Conservatives lost along straight party lines.[37] The point is quite simple: whereas the Liberals may have had internal divisions on what rights Nynorsk should officially have, when it came to the question of ideology, there was a unanimous understanding that language could be used to draw new battle lines where current substantive differences did not always exist and where the question of parliamentary sovereignty no longer existed.

In terms of the four conditions noted in the previous chapter, I maintain that only two of the four were actually met. Condition one, that of a specific goal on the part of an interest group, was met in that pro-Nynorsk forces made clear their desire to see Nynorsk attain official status.

The second condition, that of an elite stance different from that preferred by the interest group, was met when the Liberals took two separate stances on the adoption of official status for Nynorsk prior to the 1885 election. Neither of these was in keeping with the desires of pro-Nynorsk forces. First, the party made no mention of the language in its initial draft platform and, in the later official election platform, the Liberals skirted mention of *any* specific political issues.

I argue that the third condition, that an interest group adopts a strategy of persuasive actions along with the threat of sanctions for noncompliance, was not met. While pro-Nynorsk forces did issue flyers and call for resolutions of support, these attempts at persuasion carried no real credible threat of sanctions against Liberal elites that chose not to comply. Pro-Nynorsk forces simply stated their preferences, and asked that Liberal elites adopt a similar stance. Those in the rural and western areas, who were already friendly to the new language, had no problem in offering up their support. Eastern and urban Liberal elites were quite a different matter. Given that the organizational and numerical resources for the pro-Nynorsk movement was negligible in the eastern and urban areas, Liberal elites in those regions were under no obligation to support the call. Nynorsk advocates simply did not have the ability to damage the electoral fortunes of those elites outside of the core usage areas.

Thus, I also argue that the fourth condition, that the change in elite stance on the relevant issue be directly attributed to interest group efforts, was not met. As pro-Nynorsk forces could not compel members of the Liberal parliamentary group to adopt their desired stance, one must look elsewhere to understand why Liberal elites chose to throw their support behind a resolution giving official status to Nynorsk. The reasons for this support, I have argued, can be found in the link between language and national identity, the manner in which liberal ideology looked favorably upon competition among ideas and the need for the new elites to differentiate themselves from the old order.

THE ALTERNATIVE NORM ESSAY LAW IN NYNORSK

In April and May, 1906, the Norwegian parliament voted to introduce an alternative norm essay for all candidates pursuing the artium degree. This new requirement, in practice, meant that while students could still answer both main essay questions in Dano-Norwegian, they would now be required to answer a third, less demanding question in Nynorsk. The most authoritative study surrounding the introduction of this alternative norm essay concludes by stating that Nynorsk language activists saw the key points of their political program realized, even if it was in a different form than originally thought.[38] And while such a conclusion is largely born out by the historical record, the other main conclusion of the study, that the policy outcome is the direct result of pressure activities on the part of Nynorsk activists who had recently formed Noregs Mållag, is not. Nor is Haugland alone in making this type of assessment. Almenningen's exhaustively documented study of the first seven years of Noregs Mållag's organizational life also supports the impression that the 1907 alternative norm essay law can be ascribed to the pressure activities of Noregs Mållag.[39]

I do not wish to take issue with the factual evidence gathered by these two studies, as they are the definitive accounts of the era and in that sense are quite valuable contributions. Rather, it is the way in which the evidence has been assembled and the conclusions that are implicitly or explicitly drawn as a result, that I question. The story of the adoption of the alternative norm essay law in 1907 is not a story of the successful application of pressure politics. It is a story of political elites, within and across parties, who endeavored to manage the language issue in such a way so that electoral fortunes could be boosted and so that party identities could be maintained or transformed in the face of larger societal changes.

Historical Background

As Trond Nordby has noted, 1905 in Norway was an "ideological year zero." The end of the union with Sweden left many political elites wondering if the old lines of party division that had hardened in the 1880s could remain viable. It was largely understood that a key difference between the two major parties was that the Liberals represented a radical constitutionalism and favored the dissolution of the Swedish union, whereas the Conservatives, while accepting parliamentary sovereignty, preferred the maintenance of close links with the Swedish court.[40] Economically, the nation was undergoing a rapid degree of industrialization and politically, the horizon already showed the first signs of the organized working class, with a small group of socialist elites having emerged in the Norwegian parliament. All of this spelled significant difficulty for the Liberal identity, as its "image" had largely been centered on the farmer's rural values and economy, as well as the need to oppose the cultural linkage of the urban elite with foreign circles.

　　Compounding this situation, and not just for the Liberals, but for all political parties, was a recent change in the institutional rules. In 1905, an electoral commission appointed by the Norwegian parliament undertook a reform of the way in which members of parliament were chosen. Prior to 1905, members were chosen indirectly through nominating conventions. However, the reform of 1905 brought both smaller and single member districts to Norway. The election commission saw this as an attempt to better divide the number of seats among the political parties such that their current strength among the Norwegian electorate could be better reflected.[41] Thus, Norwegian politicians, regardless of party, were now put in direct competition with one another and had to face directly the voters of individual districts.

　　The implications that this change in electoral rules has for strategy among the parties in terms of the language question, particularly the Liberals, should be clear. As Weaver and Rockman note, the facilitating electoral rules of a system can have a significant impact on the policy-making capabilities of political elites.[42] However, one can argue that these types of institutional rules also have an impact on the issues that potential members of parliament choose to emphasize during the election. In a single-member district system, political elites, with the primary goal of being elected, need largely to concern themselves with the policy preferences of the constituency in their electoral district.

Specifically, the changes in the electoral rules of the young Norwegian state placed individual candidates in a more difficult situation vis-à-vis district interests than the parties had previously experienced. Prior to the shift to the single-member district system, the demands set forth by organized interests were more easily balanced by the parties, in that parties could frequently make sure that a wide range of district interests were placated by granting them each a candidate considered to be their own. The new system provided no such easy balancing act, given that only one candidate was to represent the interests of the entire district. Those that sought to be the candidate now had to contend with multiple interests, each demanding that he give commitment and high prominence to their issue.[43]

The smaller district size also played an important role. Intense group interests at the local level were suddenly magnified in importance vis-à-vis the candidates, as they now were able to contend in a smaller arena. These interests, that under a proportional representation list system, might have been placated by receiving the final slot on a party slate, now had the potential to dictate policy stance to a candidate, even when the desired stance was out of keeping with that of the candidate's national party. This potential for influence on candidate stance came about, because as Mjeldhiem notes, interest groups were now looking at small district size and seeing that they had a viable new threat: either the candidate adopted the required stance on their issue, or they would withhold support and run a person of their own choosing as an alternative within the district.[44]

Thus, the changes in the electoral rules resulted in an increased sense of power and activity among interest groups at the local level. Both political elites and the Norwegian media were aware and concerned that the new election law had produced an unintended by-product: the linkage of a candidate's electoral fortunes to the successful fulfillment of localized and particularized interests' political demands.[45]

As we will see though, this potential increase of interest group influence at the *local* level did not result in changes at the *national* level of policymaking for the language question. The reason is that interest groups suffered due to uneven regional strengths and were unable to "pressure" any candidates other than those running in sympathetic districts.

To recap though, it seems probable that we can expect to see certain types of behavior exhibited at both the party and candidate level in terms of salient campaign issues. At the party level, the continuous salience of cleavages in Norwegian politics would lead us to expect that those parties with strengths in western, rural (Nynorsk) areas would choose to emphasize the issues that play best in those regions, while the opposite would be expected from urban/Bokmål parties.[46] At the level of individual candidates, we can expect party differences to have significantly less importance than in a system of proportional representation. That is, within districts, candidates from different parties will have a markedly closer position on certain issues than they may share with candidates of their own party from a different district, where the prevailing public opinion is different.

Finally, the last key change in the post-1905 environment came with the founding of Noregs Mållag. It is the timing of their founding convention, along with the demands they put to the major political parties, that has produced the mistaken impression that their activities are responsible for the 1907 alternative norm essay law. That a national Nynorsk organization did not come into existence prior to the early twentieth century should be understandable for a number of reasons. The regional Nynorsk organizations that did exist often had sharply contrasting views on how far Nynorsk should go in becoming the official language of Norway. For the western regional language organizations, such as Vestlandets Mållag, the stance taken was that Nynorsk should be the only Norwegian language, while those groupings in the east tended towards a more conciliatory line for those who did not have a Nynorsk-based dialect as their spoken tongue. Additionally, the regional Nynorsk organizations were poorly financed and it was often argued that they did not have the necessary resources to be a lasting national organization, though a national youth Nynorsk organization was founded in 1896.[47] Finally, the emphasis on democracy and decentralization that was core to the linguistic politics of the Nynorsk movement also seems to have been an initial roadblock to its national organization. And though all of these were technically overcome in 1906, the history of Noregs Mållag has often revealed profound dissent, quite frequently geographically based, as to what political course the organization should take.

The Conventions of 1906

Largely as a result of the change in electoral laws, and the strengthened sense of nationalism that the dissolution of the union brought
about, a nationwide call to Nynorsk activists was issued in the beginning of 1906. It is interesting to observe from the very beginning that
the organizational choices made by Nynorsk activists suggested
that they did not have the ability to put pressure on the Liberals and
that they were in fact dependent on the party to see their demands
translated into public policy. Unlike the teetotalist movement, Nynorsk
was in no way a national movement. As such, it did not have the
human resources necessary to conduct sustained agitation campaigns
in non-Nynorsk areas. Nor did most Nynorsk activists see the need to
organize a separate party in the western core areas, as Liberal candidates had already long espoused a Nynorsk-friendly stance. Thus, going
into their founding convention, Nynorsk activists were strongly opposed to the formation of a single-issue political party, for they understood that their cause was already championed by the Liberals in
regions where the language had strength. In those regions where Dano-
Norwegian was dominant, no chance of winning could be expected.
Thus, the pressure that Nynorsk activists hoped to exert was specifically
on the Liberals.

The record of founding convention attendees suggests that not
only was Noregs Mållag going to be strongly dependent on the Liberals, but also that there was a symbiosis between the two organizations.[48] Convention records reveal that over half of the Liberal
parliamentary group was part of the founding convention. And while
the intent at the founding convention was that pressure would be
applied by Noregs Mållag on the Liberals' platform and parliamentary committees, the substantial overlap that existed between the elite
membership of both suggests that pro-Nynorsk sentiment was already
well-entrenched in the party before the founding of Noregs Mållag.
Given this, one has to question whether the participation of Liberal
MPs at the Noregs Mållag convention might have had an additional
significance that others have not addressed. This convention provided
a public setting for western Liberal MPs to engage in one of the three
key types of activity that is expected of any candidate for representative office: position-taking. As Mayhew has observed, the benefit that

comes to candidates (or office-holders) from this type of activity is, ". . . not that he make pleasing things happen, but that he making pleasing political judgments. The position itself is the political commodity."[49] The convention provided Liberal candidates with an early opportunity to be in the public spotlight as the key supporters behind the alternative norm essay law; one that in their Noregs Mållag hat, they would strongly push, but one that as members of the Liberals, they would lack an effectively binding stance.

At the convention itself, the newly-formed Noregs Mållag issued a political platform that consisted of two demands. The first addressed the alternative norm essay and stated that one of the required essays for the artium degree would need to be in Nynorsk. The second point demanded that all candidates for the civil service be required to take a test in Nynorsk. Following this, there is no record of any discussion about the tactics that were to be used to pressure the Liberals or the other parties for the attainment of these goals. Rather, participants turned to internal organizational matters, and sufficed themselves with merely sending on the political platforms to the conventions of the Liberals and Conservatives that were to begin the following day.[50]

The Liberals went into the 1906 convention with a suggested language plank, hammered out prior to the Noregs Mållag meeting, that centered around "working towards the Norwegianization of the language, including the goal that Nynorsk be the equivalent of the generally accepted written language (Dano-Norwegian)."[51] However, according to the Nynorsk/Liberal paper *Den 17de Mai*, a "large majority" of convention delegates passed a far more pro-Nynorsk language plank.[52] This new plank, the fifth of nine items, called for "the continued work for the rebirth of the Norwegian language, which will include among other things, that one of the required essays for the artium degree would need to be in Nynorsk."[53]

As noted earlier, the question of the alternative norm essay took place against the backdrop of changes in the party system. Whereas up until the dissolution of the union, the Liberals and Conservatives had been poles apart, the new era found the central committee of the Conservatives establishing a committee that would look into the possibility of cooperation with some of the more moderate members of the Liberals. The Conservatives informed the Liberals of this move and asked that it do the same, a request that was immediately rejected by the Liberals.[54]

Herein lies the most plausible cause for the adoption of Noregs Mållag's proposed language plank by the Liberal convention. In the face of a possible realignment of political elites within and across parties, the radical nationalist faction at the convention was able to dominate on a number of platform issues. This was done in an attempt to prevent cooperation between the two parties and the resulting platform went so far as to state that the party was choosing to reaffirm its "faith in its traditions."

One Liberal elite noted in his memoirs that, as it was well-known that the Conservatives were by and large an exclusively Dano-Norwegian party, the Liberals chose to distance themselves decisively from the Conservative platform on a few key issues, chief among those the language issue and on teetotalism."[55] Thus, in a defensive attempt to maintain party identity, the most radical faction appears to have cast about for suitable alternatives that would differentiate the party from the Conservatives. In that sense, Noregs Mållag was quite lucky. Not only did it already have preexisting support from half of the party's MPs, but it could also benefit from being a key symbol in what was to be a complex war of ideological position.

The complexity of this period of party conventions is made all the more daunting when one recalls that the government, a coalition of moderate members of the Liberals and the Conservatives, also issued their own election platform under the name Samlingspartiet (the United party).[56] Just as the radical faction within the Liberals was attempting to maintain the traditional "farmer-nationalist" identity, the United party had its eye on detaching the more moderate grouping of voters that had ascribed to the Liberals' political liberalism, but not its cultural radicalism.[57] And again, just as the Liberals had found language to be a convenient way at convention time to differentiate itself from the Conservatives and the growing desire by some in both parties to formalize the middle of the road coalition, the United party was able to use the language question to signal how it differed from the other political groupings in this unstable period. While it may be tempting to label the resulting language plank as a mere compromise between Liberal and Conservative members of the coalition, the reality shows there was no small degree of strategic thinking involved. The language plank stated that the United party would work for the continued equivalency of both languages in public life and would use education to ensure that youth had sufficient knowledge in each standard. As such, it specifically reaffirmed the liberal component of the Liberals' language strategy, but it was sufficiently vague on what educational measures would be taken to bring about increased knowledge and it did not endorse the Noregs Mållag/radical Liberal call for the alternative norm essay. The Conservative central committee seemed to be cognizant of the way in which this vague plank would be of use to candidates on the stump: ". . . individual planks pave the way for differences of opinion regarding ways and means . . ."[58]

While the Conservatives chose to endorse the United party's election platform and in fact ran all of its candidates under that name, it left its party program intact, which in terms of language meant that the party was still formally committed to the stance that Riksmål was the basis for the future linguistic development of Norway. Like many party programs and platforms worldwide, one might be tempted to think of this as no sooner written than forgotten. However, its explicitly anti-Nynorsk stance, when combined with the vague Nynorsk support in the election platform and the newly instituted single member districts, meant that Conservative candidates in western Norway were in a bind if we consider their primary goal to be the attainment of office. Despite the fact that the Conservatives were in general at a disadvantage in the Nynorsk core areas, the stances taken in both the party program and in its election platform left western Conservatives too vulnerable under the new electoral rules. As such, one more party faction emerged into the mix and, by definition, used language to distinguish itself from other elements in its party. In several electoral districts across western Norway, local Conservative organizations adopted platforms that varied from vague support for pro-Nynorsk work to explicitly binding themselves to the activities of the Nynorsk movement.[59] In doing so, these local Conservative organizations were going well beyond the ambiguous support found in the United party's platform and were throwing their support behind the call for the alternative norm essay. In the next section, we will see how candidates from different parties and in different regions handled the alternative norm essay issue and the various language planks while on the stump.

The Election Campaign and Afterwards

As expected, the key factor in determining whether candidates exhibited a stance that was favorable to Nynorsk and the adoption of the alternative norm essay was whether or not they were in a core Nynorsk usage area. Liberal candidates in the west, who had always formed the largest and most active base for parliamentary support of Nynorsk, continued to stress their pro-Nynorsk credentials. To the outsider, these efforts at times may have appeared near comic. Some western Liberal candidates showed up at meetings with voters and stressed that despite the fact they could not write in Nynorsk themselves, they would champion it at every available opportunity. However, the story was entirely different for Liberal candidates in either eastern or urban areas. On the whole, these candidates either downplayed the significance of the proposed legislation or ignored it outright. Carl Berner, chair of the Liberal central committee, dismissed the concrete nature of the Liberal language plank and claimed it was something that the party merely regarded as something that they would work on in the future. Local Liberal papers in Bokmål areas supported the efforts of their candidates to sidestep the issue and were generally silent on the language plank.

The mixture of geographic and electoral considerations also appears to explain the stump behavior of Conservative candidates. In the eastern part of the nation, a full twenty percent of the candidates formally distanced themselves from the language plank, largely on the basis that the question of increasing student knowledge of Nynorsk had too much of an "obligatory" tone to it and thus could be interpreted as being in line with Noregs Mållag's demand. Western Conservative candidates had of course pledged themselves to a language plank that was roughly the equivalent of that adopted by the Liberals in many cases.[60]

The election produced something of a mixed result. In terms of seats, the Liberals were the clear election winner; however, a large number of these MPs then pledged themselves to the governing coalition. The end result, in general terms, was that moderate Liberals and Conservatives stayed in power as a coalition. It is interesting to note that as the issue moved through the Norwegian parliament, at no point did either Noregs Mållag or the Liberal election plank receive consideration as a serious final proposal. Rather, in the bill that was introduced by Liberal members who had been at the founding Noregs Mållag convention, and in the recommendation issued by the government, there was a clear retreat from what had been approved by a large majority of Liberal convention delegates. In each of these, the demand that one of the two essays be answered in Nynorsk was now downgraded to a call that students had the right to answer the essays in the language of their choosing and that when they opted to answer both in one language that they would then be required to write a shorter, easier third essay in the language they had not chosen for their main essays.[61]

The story from here on is one of compromise between various parliamentary groupings and is only relevant insofar as the record shows no evidence of even attempted pressure on the part of Noregs Mållag to influence the parliamentary proceedings. Rather, to the extent that there were attempts at pressure on the Norwegian parliament's treatment of this issue, it came from the Riksmål/Dano-Norwegian side, which organized a series of mass meetings in Bergen and Christiana (Oslo) during the proceedings that culminated in the formation of Riksmålsforbundet, the national pro-Riksmål organization. A key thrust of their efforts was the forwarding of petitions and resolutions to the Norwegian parliament urging that there be no legislation requiring the Nynorsk alternative norm essay as part of the artium degree. This pressure was ignored by the Norwegian parliament and when the final piece of legislation was eventually hammered out, which modified the Liberal sponsored bill by allowing a dictation test in Nynorsk for the first five years of the law's life, geography once again appeared to play a major role. All of the western Conservative representatives were part of the group that supported the alternative norm essay proposal.[62] Similarly, on the Liberals' side, 61 percent of those who voted against the implementation of the alternative norm essay represented larger urban districts where Nynorsk was not used. If "urban-Liberal" or "western-Conservative" did not prevent or cause the alternative norm essay from being adopted, then we need only to recall the bigger point. Given electoral rules and a political culture in their districts that differed from their parties' national appeal, they looked to language as a convenient way to send voters the message that they were not out of touch with the whims of the district.

Finally, how did the newly organized Nynorsk movement view the outcome of its first foray into pressure politics? The clearest way in which the dissatisfaction manifested itself comes from an account provided of the 1908 Liberal convention. Here, unlike the positive spin that *Den 17de Mai* had tried to put on the essay outcome a year earlier, a number of radical Liberal delegates who were also Noregs

Mållag members spoke out and attacked the party for betraying the stance it had taken in 1906. Members not only accused the Liberal parliamentary group of not having been "entirely loyal" to the language plank, but also stated that they were not pleased with the way a "peculiar" interpretation of the Liberal program had been applied.[63]

All in all, then, the 1906–1907 alternative norm essay controversy reveals that despite claims made by some, Noregs Mållag did not attain what they originally set out for, nor did they significantly labor to see the implementation of the alternative norm essay at any other point than the platform stage. In terms of resources, they appeared to have relied exclusively on political elites that had a larger loyalty to a party, and not solely to the regional constraints of just one issue. In relying on these elites, they were in fact dependent on whether and how elites would choose to employ the alternative norm essay issue. The alternative norm essay was of value to political elites, but it was useful in a modified form that suited their dual needs. On the one hand, it was of use in differentiating elites in one political faction from those of another faction. On the other hand, the alternative norm essay was a key instrument in the 1906 election for sending cues to the home electoral district indicating whether or not one was aligned with local political culture.

The case of the alternative norm essay can also be summarized in terms of the four conditions for pressure group influence. I argue that when looking at the conflict surrounding the adoption of the alternative norm essay, only the first two of four conditions was in fact met. Condition one, that of a specific goal on the part of an interest group, was met when the newly formed Noregs Mållag issued a platform calling for, among other things, the adoption of a alternative norm essay in Nynorsk.

The second condition, that of an elite stance on an issue different from that preferred by the interest group, is more ambiguous in this case. Initially, the Liberals merely had a language plank that spoke vaguely about the need to offer continued support for Nynorsk, which can be interpreted as not directly supporting or opposing the specific policy preferences of Noregs Mållag. Yet, the Liberals then adopted an election platform that called for the introduction of a Nynorsk alternative norm essay. Ultimately, following the election, the Liberals in parliament opted for a new stance on the alternative norm essay in which Nynorsk would now most likely be a student's choice on a much shorter and less demanding third essay. As noted previously, Noregs Mållag expressed dissatisfaction with this final stance well after the new law had been adopted. Thus, it is interesting to note that the Liberals' second stance on the issue was actually much closer to the policy desired by Noregs Mållag than was their final stance on the alternative norm essay.

The third condition, that an interest group adopts a strategy of persuasive actions along with the threat of sanctions for noncompliance, was also not met. Noregs Mållag's chief attempt at persuading elites to adopt the alternative norm essay came when the organization's founding convention issued a call to political parties that they place support for the alternative norm essay on their election platforms. While the Liberals initially responded by adopting the required stance, it became clear that the party as a whole did not see itself committed to the goals of Noregs Mållag. As in the case of the language equality law, Noregs Mållag, lacking sufficient organizational resources, could not threaten those parliamentary candidates outside of core usage areas who chose not to support the goal of an alternative norm essay. Additionally, once the proposed measure was being debated in the Norwegian parliament, Noregs Mållag did not play a role in attempting to dissuade the Liberals from the watered down proposal that ultimately proved to be less than satisfactory.

Thus, I argue that the fourth condition, that the change in elite stance on the relevant issue be directly attributed to interest group efforts, cannot possibly have been met. I largely argue this on the basis of the difference between the final appearance of the alternative norm essay law and the preferred stance of Noregs Mållag. To the extent that the Liberals shifted their stance on this issue, they shifted it away from the position desired by Noregs Mållag.

Additionally, I have provided evidence that lacking any real pressure from Noregs Mållag, Liberal elites took a stand on the alternative norm essay that was largely motivated by two factors: the dual need to appear in sync with the political culture of the local district and the desire to differentiate the party from its conservative opponents.

CONCLUSION

The focus of this chapter has been on the relationship between Nynorsk activists and the use of the language question by Liberal elites. Far from the conventional wisdom found in the historical literature on Norwegian language policy, we have discovered that the Liberals' use of language policy has been strongly contingent upon their desire to link language to a larger political agenda. Pressure group influence has quite frequently been asserted as the causal factor behind the Liberals' decision to go ahead with both the language equality law and the alternative norm essay in Nynorsk. The evidence presented here fails to confirm that hypothesis on a number of fronts. In both cases, a primary obstacle to efforts by language activists was the over-riding geographic nature of the language cleavage. Nynorsk activists did not have the resources to operate effectively outside their core area and in the western counties, their attempts at pressure were by and large targeted at political elites who already supported their agenda. Further, Nynorsk activists developed no strategy of threats or persuasive actions to bring about the desired change in elites and were content with merely communicating their political preferences prior to each of the elections. Unlike their Dano-Norwegian/Riksmål counterparts, Nynorsk activists appear to have been by and large absent from efforts to influence proceedings in the Norwegian parliament on these two policies and instead relied on the Liberal MPs that were already committed to the issue.

Ultimately, one must look elsewhere to discover why language became politicized in the late nineteenth and early twentieth century. The Liberals acted on the language issue, not because they were pressured to do so, but rather because if handled carefully, it could be of great assistance in presenting the party as the most democratic and Norwegian in the post-colonial order. Choosing a language strategy that not only emphasized their common links to the "Norwegian-ness" of the peasantry, but that also painted the Liberals' political opposition as the elitist leftovers of the old Danish order, put the Liberals clearly on the side of the 80 percent of the population that did not have urban Norway as a home. For the Liberals, language was the clearest symbolic statement of building the Norwegian nation. Yet, as a national party, the Liberals had to maintain a very careful eye on the role of language in the party. The regional nature of the question had the potential to damage the rural/liberal urban counterelite coalition if it assumed too much prominence in the party or if a stance too clearly in support of the strong Nynorsk demands was chosen. In balancing the symbolic usefulness of Nynorsk with these concerns, the party opted for a purposeful vagueness on the language question, which was consistent with its liberal ideology and allowed for candidates to embrace or avoid the issue depending upon their own electoral needs. The 1906 election law reform extended this, allowing candidates to have some autonomy on the language issue, and support or opposition to Nynorsk became a useful electoral strategy all across the nation.

In the next chapter, I will focus on how the Norwegian Labor Party (DNA) used Samnorsk (Common Norwegian) both to build a socialist cultural politics and to design a language strategy meant to appeal to the broadest possible segment of the electorate. As I continue to focus on the interest group hypothesis, substantial attention will be devoted to how DNA resisted the pressure group efforts from both the radical leadership of Noregs Mållag and the conservative Riksmål movement. In doing so, the next chapter will show how a party with a very different political world view and with a very different set of language politics was in fact quite similar to the earlier Liberal elites on one important count. Namely, I will argue that DNA also recognized that language conflict had the ability to be harnessed and transformed into a tool that served the needs of a political movement.

Chapter 3

Language and Social Democracy in Twentieth-Century Norway

INTRODUCTION

This chapter continues the focus on how Norwegian political elites were or were not able to withstand "pressure" activities from the various language interest groups. In doing so, however, this investigation of DNA's stance on language politics reveals some of the clearest evidence showing that political elites do in fact view language as worthy of political manipulation. The evidence also shows *why* they view language in this fashion. The evidence supporting these claims is drawn from a historical survey focusing on some of the key moments and debates in the formation of twentieth century Norwegian language policy.

This chapter shows how one party, DNA , has gone through three major stances on language politics in the twentieth century. Throughout the first three decades of the twentieth century, DNA's official line on the language question followed strict Marxist lines: language conflict undermined the importance of class conflict, and as such, the party did not lend support to any of the official standards. From the 1930s until the early 1960s, DNA propagated a stance of bringing the two written forms together into one joint form, Common Norwegian, and made "the people's language" a highly visible part of its socialist cultural politics. From the mid-1960s to the present, DNA has substantially backed away from its support for the Common Norwegian project and has instead sought to maintain the official status that the two standards possess. As we consider the adoption of

65

each of these stances, it should become clear that the primary force in each case has been a view on the part of DNA elites that language politics is subsidiary to other party goals and that language matters when it can be framed in such a way as to advance or symbolize the larger objectives of the party.

The interest group hypothesis will once again be shown to lack support. Primarily, despite the fact that Nynorsk adherents benefited from the policies of Common Norwegian, the official leadership of Noregs Mållag remained in opposition to this DNA stance through-out much of its policy life. Additionally, Riksmålsforbundet was in constant and clear opposition to this set of policies. Secondly, I will explain how independent interest group support for the policies of Common Norwegian only came about in the waning days of the policy, once it was under broad attack from a number of conservative forces. Finally, I will consider DNA's retreat from the policies of Common Norwegian in the mid-1960s. As the definitive shift away from almost thirty years of support for Common Norwegian, it is surprising that this period has not merited further investigation by Norwegian sociolinguists. Still, as we will see, such reticence on the part of researchers is to be understood. More so than any earlier period in the history of the Norwegian language conflict, this one raises questions of multiple causality, particularly in terms of how a growing grass-roots movement in opposition to government language policies came to combine with a DNA government that had new policy priorities and was increasingly less certain about its fortunes with the electorate.

DNA AND THE LANGUAGE QUESTION
PRIOR TO THE 1930s

While the period after the Bolshevik revolution saw many Second In-ternational parties split, with communist wings pledging loyalty to Moscow and reformist wings opting for the parliamentary route to democratic socialism, the Norwegian Labor Party was an exception. DNA had gone through much of the 1910s as a reformist party, but in 1918, this social democratic party pledged itself to a radical pro-Moscow line and joined the Comintern. This rather extreme shift is explained by some as a result of the first-past-the post electoral system that Norway used for the first decades of the twentieth century. Despite receiving large numbers of popular votes in Norwegian parliamentary elections, the party suffered under the single-member district rules, and DNA radicals were able to argue persuasively that the ballot-box route to socialism was a sham.[1] Of equal importance was Norway's place as a newly industrializing nation in the world economy. Proponents of this economic view, according to Katzenstein, stress that the relatively late industrialization of the new nation, centered on the exploitation of natural resources and finance having been provided by foreign capital, created easy rallying points for a powerless working class.[2]

This radicalized social democratic party officially took no stance on the language question, allowing its parliamentary party group full autonomy on the matter. But behind this neutrality on language, one can find evidence that language as a political problem was viewed by the ruling faction in one of two ways. In the period 1903–1920, language was seen by DNA as just one more issue that was designed to detract from the real point at hand, namely class struggle, while after that the official stance of neutrality also included a growing debate within the party about the role of language. One review of the DNA party organ, Social-Demokraten, for the period 1903–1920, repeatedly showed that language was viewed as an issue that could split the party if it were to come up for debate, "Who would defend, or tolerate, that such a dividing question as (language) would be allowed to gain a foothold in our party?"[3] Official editorials in the paper also encouraged readers to, "continue our work for the material well-being of all, and not be divided by today's passing battles."[4]

The official neutrality towards the language question and the apparent disdain for its place as a serious political question is of course not just a function of crass Marxist reductionism. Rather, if one bears in mind the way in which chapter 2 has shown how the two leading nonsocialist parties were able intimately to tie the concept of language to the national question, one can easily understand the reluctance of DNA to become involved in an issue that was heavily tinged with bourgeois associations. After all, a central tenet of the Communist International was that the concept of the nation masked the unequal power relations between the two classes.

However, while DNA did not drop its stance of neutrality on the language question until the 1930s, this official distance from language politics did not imply that there was no discussion of it within the party. Particularly from 1920 onward, one can note the emergence of Halvdan Koht, a historian who would later become Norwegian foreign minister prior to the German invasion, as the central and decisive figure in championing a line that urged DNA to trade its neutrality on language for active support of Common Norwegian.

Koht's roots in the language movement were that of a bridge-builder, having been in the leadership of Østlandsk Reisning (an organization championing the eastern Norwegian dialects) and Noregs Mållag at a time when the latter was still exclusively dominated by radical pro-Nynorsk westerners. To Koht though, the major organizational arena for his language work came when he joined DNA in 1911. According to Koht, DNA needed to take a stance on the language issue because, ". . . a socialist party could not just have an economic or a social program, but it also needed a cultural program. DNA could not turn away from one of the most important questions of our time."[5] Koht's first breakthrough to the party elite on the language question came on the heels of the 1917 orthographic reform, in which he defended the Common Norwegian nature of the orthographic reforms. The central committee of DNA charged Koht with issuing a report for the party on the relationship between the labor and language movements.[6] Issued in 1921, *Arbeidarreising og målspørsmål* (The Labor Movement and The Language Question) offers an early insight into why Koht thought party elites needed to abandon their neutrality on language conflict.

The heart of the pamphlet is geared towards explaining why the small farmers ought to be made part of DNA's push towards socialism.[7] Koht acknowledges the basic conflict between the rural and urban classes and he notes in particular that, despite the propensity of the rural class towards "conservatism" and defense of a nonindustrial economy, it was the rural class that fought for the introduction of democracy in Norway through opposition to the old Danish and Swedish elites. Claiming that the working class should never forget its debt to the farmers, Koht suggests that the reality is that both classes are of course united by a common enemy in the capitalist class. Additionally, he notes that both the farmers and the working class have suffered linguistically at the hands of the urban upper classes. Yet, he states, it is only with the Common Norwegian reforms of 1917 that the working class has seen the emergence of the right to raise their children with a spoken language that they can truly claim as their own. Koht goes on to urge the working class to intensify its linguistic demands and call for a literary language that allows it full freedom of linguistic choice.

But why does Koht see this as important? What is the need to convince the working class that it has a common cultural struggle to be waged alongside the small farmers? The answer, according to Koht, is that involvement in the language struggle on the part of the workers will increase the likelihood that the farmers will be better disposed towards joining the class struggle:

> If you can join forces with the farmers on this issue, then it will be of help in winning the farmers over in the social struggle. When the farmers see that the workers value their spiritual heritage, then it will be easier for them to see how socialism can also appeal to them. Nobody can expect that the farmer would become a socialist without seeing some advantage in it, and in the language question we have a demand where the workers could and should help the farmers, for their own sake.[8]

There is, however, an additional practical reason for why the DNA leadership was becoming interested in the language question. Jahr notes that while periodic overtures had been made to the Nynorsk movement by various party organs, public figures in the Nynorsk movement were often highly placed in various interest organizations that the DNA base considered to be politically antagonistic.[9] The concern, according to Jahr, was that many of the places where the working class looked to in terms of organized cultural opposition, Nynorsk appeared as an overriding symbol. Thus, one cannot ignore the possibility that when the DNA leadership tried to convince supporters that the language struggle was also a struggle of the working class, that it was in fact trying to prevent language from contributing to a permanent divide between farmers and workers. Yet, despite its temporary appearance as a central issue in the first few years of the 1920s, DNA took no steps beyond that of issuing the pamphlet and maintained its neutral stance.[10]

Where did Noregs Mållag stand in the midst of this first phase of DNA's language politics? The official history of the organization looks back on the 1910s and notes that it was by and large a period where the leadership was increasingly disenchanted with the Liberals' lack of willingness to deliver policy on some key demands. A sense was developing in the organization that it would have to rely increasingly on itself to push pro-Nynorsk policies.[11] As always, the organization was divided between two wings, one largely made up by radical Nynorsk purists from the western portion of Norway and those that were in support of gaining advances for Nynorsk through the support of Common Norwegian. And while the organization's 1921 political platform, distributed as always to all parties in advance of the Norwegian parliamentary election, once again reaffirmed its desire to see Nynorsk as the only national language in the land, a more realistic accounting of the organization's internal division is that both Nynorsk radicals and Common Norwegian supporters such as Koht sat on the central committee.

However, pressure activities towards DNA in this first phase appear to have been relatively nonexistent. Rather, the notable difference was that Noregs Mållag was now fully out from under the wing of its association with the Liberals. Realizing that the once dominant liberal party was now in decline after the 1921 elections, Noregs Mållag took notice of other parties and joined publicly with DNA at a forum on the working class and the language question. The 1921 elections had produced a dramatic defeat for the Liberals, with a popular vote decline from 28.3 percent to 20.1 percent.[12] And while the elections had also produced a very similar decline for DNA, from 31.6 percent to 21.3 percent, the single member electoral district rules had been scrapped for the 1921 election, when proportional representation was introduced. As a result, despite this decline in the popular vote, DNA saw its share of seats jump from eighteen to twenty-nine, while the Liberals saw their number of Norwegian parliamentary representatives plummet from fifty-four to thirty-nine.

Some enthusiasm existed in Noregs Mållag when Bondepartiet, (the Farmers' Party), was founded in 1920 out of frustration with the Liberals' focus on rural culture at the expense of attention towards the profits of larger farmers. However, the hope was short-lived that the Farmers' Party would champion the radical Nynorsk line. In 1920, the party approved a language plank that fully supported the continued implementation of Common Norwegian, leading a key Noregs Mållag figure to note with disappointment that the language activists should not be expecting any help or support from the new party.[13]

It is important to note that the Liberals' decline was not simply perceived as a short-term setback that might be reversed at the next election cycle. The election results of 1921 were simply a continuation of the electoral misfortunes that the party began suffering in 1918, when it lost a full one-third of its seats. While those who focus on the language question ascribe this to the fierce debate over the way the Liberal government attempted to implement the 1917 orthographic reform, general historians of Norway note that a larger factor was anger in the electorate over the Liberals' inability to deal with wartime profiteering and large-scale inflation.[14] Additionally, industry employment figures for the first three decades of the twentieth century confirm that the Liberals' natural electoral base was slipping sharply. From the turn of the century, when a full one-fifth of all Norwegians over the age of fifteen were employed in agriculture, the percent declined by 1920 to 16.8 percent. At the same time, the emerging working class remained hovering at approximately 12 percent.[15] Thus, Noregs Mållag had good reason to begin looking for a new institutional venue that it could pressure for further Nynorsk legislation.

THE SHIFT TO COMMON NORWEGIAN

As noted in the introduction, DNA, prior to the 1930s, viewed language conflict as an issue that detracted from the more critical importance of advancing the class struggle. Yet, from the mid-1930s onward, DNA not only found a place for language politics in its platform, but championed the necessity of complementing the class struggle with the struggle for people's cultural traditions, and it chose to symbolize this struggle largely through the party's embrace of Common Norwegian.[16] This dramatic shift in stances can be understood when one considers the importance of two related occurrences: the full-scale electoral defeat that the party suffered at the polls in 1930 and the particular decline amongst DNA's rural portion of the Norwegian electorate. For DNA, which was on the verge of becoming the hegemonic political institution for decades to come, the timing and content of language policy was determined above all else by the drive for electoral power.

My explanation begins distant from language politics and is grounded in the events surrounding the 1930 Norwegian parliamentary election. Electoral defeat for DNA in the 1930 election came in the form of losing a full 20 percent of its seats in the Norwegian parliament, dropping from fifty-nine to forty-seven seats. The leading study of DNA during this period provides a detailed account of how DNA elites responded to this loss, where they chose to assign the blame, and what they ultimately considered to be the only viable course of action at the 1933 convention.[17]

The real culprit behind DNA's 1930 setback could be found in how the bourgeois parties were able to portray DNA as a dangerously radical party that was not fully committed to the "rules of the game" under parliamentary democracy. The DNA platform itself was a result of debate in the late 1920s over whether the party ought to mirror the changes in its voting base, which saw increases amongst farmers and other rural Norwegians. Hard-liners in the party were concerned that the increasing number of nontraditional voters for the party could dilute its socialist politics and as such pushed strongly for a "sharpening" of the party platform, such that party loyalty to the old class line would be the key emphasis. The alternative vision of party strategy and ideology was that the party ought to be fully committed to a parliamentary strategy and ought to base its appeal to the masses on national lines, through championing such slogans as "the party's national task," and respecting "the views of all the people." This "national" line was rejected by the party central committee, if only narrowly, and the party went to the polls in 1930 led by a wing that advocated extra-parliamentary action as the sole path that could lead to the attainment of socialism.[18]

That the bourgeois parties and press had a field day with this electoral strategy is, of course, an understatement. Dahl notes that the bourgeois press attacked DNA on what we might label "the three R's": revolution, religion, and Russia. DNA was repeatedly portrayed by its opposition as supporting extra-parliamentary activity, that it was antireligious, and that it hoped to build a Bolshevik state in Norway. The first and third points were easily substantiated by pointing to DNA's own platform, while even the second was shown without great difficulty by pointing out that an architect of the revolutionary line, Edvard Bull, had authored brochures for DNA in the early 1920s that contained bitter attacks on Christianity as the enemy of the working class.

DNA's postmortem of the election defeat demonstrates that party elites clearly blamed the bourgeois attacks on their platform and less directly the nature of the platform itself. Explicit links were made by party elites to other social democrat losses around Europe where bourgeois opponents had successfully linked them to more revolutionary stances. The truth, however, was that DNA did in fact have these stances and they were not simply tactical attributions on the part of the opposition. DNA had in fact briefly formed a government after the 1927 elections and attempted to put into practice its plans for the socialization of society along traditional Marxist lines, with the rather quick and inevitable result of capital flight and a bourgeois vote of no confidence.[19] Martin Tranmæl, perhaps the key figure in the Norwegian socialist movement and an ardent supporter of the revolutionary line, conceded immediately after the election that perhaps the party platform had scared "a few" supporters away, but cautioned against a full-scale shift to a more reformist posture. Just two weeks later, reversing his opposition to a more inclusive line, Tranmæl expressed his support for a DNA stance that would take full account of the "will of the majority of the people."[20]

However, the need to rethink a failed political platform was made all the more necessary by the economic depression sweeping Europe. The period after the 1930 election disaster for DNA saw economic crisis hit Norway through a GNP fall of 8 percent in 1931, a loss of over seven million workdays due to labor conflict, and the Norway's Bank departure from the gold standard, with no other currency being chosen against which to peg the krone.[21] Additionally, others have noted that the economic crisis was augmented by a rising political specter: the growth of a domestic fascist threat in the guise of Quisling's Nasjonal Samling party.[22] Thus, on many fronts, it appears that a failed revolutionary line was no longer viable for DNA, either in terms of trying to appeal to its unusual mix of a rural and urban constituency or in terms of responding to the pressing economic and political crises.

The 1933 DNA convention reflected both of these realities along with the earlier discontent that party elites had expressed about the 1930 election setback. The new platform moved clearly in the direction of reformism and spoke of the necessity to avoid violence in pursuing the class struggle. It also spoke of the need to come up with practical solutions to the ongoing economic crisis. Additionally, in an implicit response to those in the bourgeois camp that tried to play the Bolshevik card, the platform stated that Norwegian socialism would be built on the basis of domestic considerations and realities. But most importantly, the departure from the revolutionary line was replaced with the explicit effort to win a parliamentary majority through the construction of an electoral coalition that would combine the working class with the small farmer.[23]

While there is no direct evidence of the influence of outside events, one does have to consider that advocates of state power through electoral coalitions benefited strongly from the social democratic successes in Denmark and the social democratic failures in Germany. With a tradition of throwing ideological rigidity to the wind, the Danish Social Democrats were the first of the Scandinavian parties to forge the worker-farmer coalition. They successfully managed to unite workers and farmers in 1929, at the very time when the Norwegian socialists were on the verge of defeat.[24] As Germany plunged deeper into economic and political crises, the failure of the German social democrats to broaden their appeal beyond that of a working class party was available as further ammunition for those reformists that wished to show the importance of coalition-building in responding to economic and political threats.[25]

Perhaps above all else, the 1933 DNA convention demonstrated that the party had now come to terms with an inevitable challenge faced by all Marxist parties that choose the parliamentary route as an element in their strategy. That is, DNA had successfully grappled with what Esping-Andersen has referred to as "the need to subordinate class purity to the logic of majority politics."[26] The new politics of coalition building that the party opted for in 1933 stressed the need for DNA to broaden its appeal far beyond the traditional working class to capture an electoral majority. This subordination of the class line ultimately took the form of the party's decision that voters should rally behind the slogan, "A Majority and State Power for The Labor Party!" Interestingly enough, although the party had now fully abandoned the disastrous 1930 platform, DNA elites were quite candid in the explicitly tactical and "means to an end" nature of their new stance that stressed bringing the small farmer into the party's voting ranks. One key figure noted at the convention that, "Our position about (bourgeois) democracy has not changed . . . but we cannot forget that this fictitious term "democracy" plays a much larger role for those that we must have on our side."[27]

Where does language politics fit into this story? The answer is that Koht's rather impassioned effort throughout the 1920s to see the party jettison its linguistic neutrality and come down on the side of Common Norwegian appears to have fit perfectly with both the electoral and ideological goals of DNA in the mid 1930s. This variety of language politics was not useful to the "old" DNA, as it stood in sharp contradiction to the traditional Marxist line in emphasizing the value of cultural politics. Additionally, though, it emphasized the culture of the small farmer, a class that DNA elites still felt a strong degree of ambivalence to as part of their socialist project. But, to the "new" DNA, which had seen over half of its 1930 parliamentary seat losses come in rural areas, the emphasis was on the need to win elections and power by bringing small farmers over to the side of DNA. Language politics as promoted by Koht could serve as a valuable symbol, both in uniting the two classes on a concrete issue and in demonstrating to rural Norwegians that DNA would treat their concerns with respect.[28] A policy of Common Norwegian, or promoting the "people's language," was not only consistent with DNA ideology, but it could even serve as a tool to advance the party's doctrine.

The shift away from neutrality on the language question for DNA came when the party decided in 1933 to publicize both a resolution and a speech by Koht. The resolution and the speech had occurred at the 1930 convention, but had not received broad attention by the party. While not able to convince the party to abandon neutrality on the issue in 1930, Koht had succeeded in spearheading a call for the party to establish a working committee that would draft an official stance on language and other cultural questions. At the same time, Koht delivered a speech to the convention in which he laid out the basis for why DNA ought to give up a policy of linguistic neutrality, and also back the Common Norwegian line.

In 1933, the party printed up both the committee resolution along with Koht's well-argued plea for a socialist cultural politics centered around "the people's language" and sent them out to all local party organizations for discussion.[29] The committee draft of a language and cultural policy stressed that one future goal of a language policy in DNA would be to promote a sense of solidarity among the working class such that it would fight for a view of the nation that was "real," as opposed to a nationalism promoted by opponents in the class struggle. More importantly, the stance that DNA members were to debate as their future linguistic line read as follows:

> Therefore, (DNA) will always fight for the real spoken language of the people when it comes to the language question. In the press and in schools, (DNA) will push for the living people's language, such

that it occupies a greater and greater portion of the official languages in this country, so that they can eventually wind up as one.[30]

Koht's speech went straight to the heart of the matter and emphasized
that the party had significant cause, both tactically and in principle,
to take a stance on the language question. In terms of tactics, he
noted that the language issue was increasingly difficult to avoid in
Norwegian politics and that it had the potential for preventing linguistic opponents from becoming allies in other circumstances, which
is seemingly an allusion to the cross-class coalition that would be
sanctioned by the party three years after Koht's speech. In terms of
principle, Koht's adept linkage between language and class struggle
seemed tailor-made for the manner in which DNA would officially
promote it during the 1933 election: Koht continued to argue, much
as he had done in the 1920s, that Bokmål, as a language of the upper
class, helped to preserve a class culture in Norway. Koht acknowledged that Bokmål had gone through many shifts since the turn of
the century, yet none of this could "disguise" the fact that it was still
a language of the upper-class. Ultimately, his attack on the language
of privileged Norwegians ended with the call to understand that those
who are not part of the upper class and did not use Bokmål are part
of the linguistic underclass. This, according to Koht, revealed that "in
this country, language struggle is a natural part of the class struggle."[31]

At this point, the reasons for the transformation should be plainly
clear. The Norwegian Labor Party, responding to a large loss of seats
in the 1930 election and to the economic crisis that strongly affected
both workers and farmers, abandoned its revolutionary stance and
committed itself to bringing small farmers into its electoral coalition
so as to achieve an electoral majority. Continued neutrality on the
language question could potentially harm this coalition, given the
strong Nynorsk base among farmers. Even in its draft form, the highly
promoted departure from neutrality on the language issue squares
very nicely with Downs' observation of how parties organize both
their ideology and their policies to maximize their vote share at election time.[32] Downs states that parties can only implicitly "woo" a
limited number of social groups, given that an appeal to some will
inevitably alienate others. DNA's support for Common Norwegian
was a rational and clever response to this dilemma. Supporting Bokmål
was clearly not possible, as along a spectrum of ideology and lan-

guage, such a choice would have necessitated that DNA move away from its ideological position as the representative of the working class and adopt a linguistic position that was aligned with a far more conservative ideology. To have adopted a strictly pro-Nynorsk platform, as Noregs Mållag called upon all parties to do at each election, would not have been rational, given that DNA's voter base was split roughly down the middle between rural and working class voters and would have required DNA to move away from its original class constituency. Additionally, the reality that Nynorsk speakers only comprised one-fifth of the population made such a stance ill-advised. No linguistic movement existed that championed the rights of the working class at the expense of those who used Nynorsk or Bokmål, thus such a choice could not be made. Thus, the sole viable solution was to alienate neither of its desired constituencies and to find a language policy that promoted both the working class and the small farmer as natural allies. As a policy choice, this had of course been available since Moltke Moe's writings at the turn of the century. Politically, though, it was not necessary for DNA until the 1930s.

DNA's revisionist platform of 1933, which stressed the need to face the economic crisis with practical solutions and which sought to gain power for the socialists through an alliance of farmers and workers, was an unqualified success. The party achieved just over 40 percent of the popular vote and saw its number of Norwegian parliamentary seats increase from forty-seven to sixty-nine.

DNA formally tied itself to the Common Norwegian line in 1936, with unanimous support for a language post put forward by Koht calling for a "broader place for the people's language." Tranmæl, who had moved from revolutionary to revisionist on the broader ideological front, also did so in terms of language politics, stating that the party was now fully committed to "linguistic liberation" as well. For the party as a whole, the new stance appeared in the 1936 DNA election pamphlet, stating that the party would "continue its work to create a unified language in this country based on the people's language." With that goal as an end, the election brochure also pointed out that the current DNA government was undertaking plans for yet another orthographic reform.[33] It is to this reform that I now turn, for it demonstrates the practical and far-reaching consequences of adopting a language policy plank. Far from being symbolic in nature, promoting Common Norwegian in Norwegian society would dramatically reshape language usage in all spheres of society. Perhaps more importantly, though, for the advancement of an argument that centers on elite autonomy from the whims of language pressure groups, the 1938 orthographic reform reveals that DNA was able to implement the concrete components of a language policy to which the two major language organizations were vehemently opposed.

PUTTING THE PEOPLE'S LANGUAGE INTO PRACTICE

The work for the 1938 orthographic reform had actually been initiated in 1934, thus suggesting that the truly critical turning point in the party's language shift was the promotion of Koht's line during the 1933 election campaign. The Norwegian parliament mandated the establishment of a Department of Education and Church Affairs committee that was charged with two chief goals. First, on the basis of the "Norwegian people's language," it was to decrease the distance between the orthographies of the two written languages. Secondly, the committee was expected to address the issue of "optional forms" that existed in both languages, and to limit their usage.[34] As we will see, the route that the committee took in fulfilling this second goal was very much in keeping with casting language as a tool in the class struggle.

From the perspective of Noregs Mållag, the question of additional orthographic reforms sharpened the already existing cleavage between the two camps in the organization. Western Nynorsk purists (the conservatives, as they are known in the existing literature) were opposed to any such orthographic changes, while a less powerful faction advocated the furthering of Common Norwegian through additional reforms (the radicals).[35] For the purposes of evaluating whether or not Noregs Mållag had influence over DNA's Common Norwegian line, this might be expected to present certain difficulties. Most notably, one has to consider whether or not the question of interest group influence might need to be recast so as to take account of factional influence on DNA. However, as Vikør notes, the radical faction of Noregs Mållag were "often, but not always, the same people" who were already working on the reforms from within the DNA.[36] But, as will be shown in the following, the conservative faction was the dominant group in Noregs Mållag, and was not able to prevent this implementation of Common Norwegian from going forward. As

Vaagland noted, in the mid 1930s, Noregs Mållag was so deeply divided on the question that it simply avoided taking any official stance on the coming orthographic reform, despite the heated debate that occurred at both annual meetings and in the pro-Nynorsk press.[37] More than anything else, this lack of resolve to take the issue on speaks to Noregs Mållag's inability as an organization to have been a driving force behind the design of the 1938 reform.

As one might expect by this point, no such division existed within Riksmålsforbundet, the chief opponent to Noregs Mållag. Much as they had done in the past, Riksmålsforbundet held to a line in the 1930s that stressed, "All attempts to bring 'Riksmål' and 'Nynorsk' together on an artificial basis must be dismissed. The two forms of language must have the freedom to develop, and in the practical sphere they should have the chance to demonstrate their ability as the people's natural means of expression."[38]

Issued in 1936, one has to be surprised at how candidly the committee report explained that it did not use any scientific principles or statistics in reaching its conclusions. Rather, as Haugen notes, each of the members appears to have gone with a type of linguistic gut instinct as to both what forms were truly representative in Norway and what modifications needed to be made.[39] Scholars of the Norwegian language conflict have generally considered it the case that the committee had great difficulty in achieving both of its assigned goals simultaneously and chose to prioritize bringing the two language standards closer together over the reduction of dual forms.[40] But, in doing so, and again, without much basis in philological matters, the committee focused more heavily on the need to reform Riksmål, citing its Danish roots. Nynorsk, on the other hand, was seen as having a natural connection to the people's language that the planners were trying to build, thus it required far fewer changes. The thrust of the proposed reforms was that the so-called optional forms that came out of the 1917 orthographic reform would now be replaced by two separate categories: obligatory and optional forms. The obligatory forms struck most hard at Riksmål, removing much of the standard spelling in the language and replacing it with forms that had been used in Nynorsk. A good portion of these new obligatory forms had been optional under the 1917 reform and were therefore largely unknown to the Norwegian public at large. Limited obligatory changes were suggested for Nynorsk, but the committee's key desire for reworking the Nynorsk variant was to add in those urban working class dialects that had been absent from Aasen's original model of Nynorsk. The optional styles also affected Riksmål far more than they did Nynorsk. The committee simply employed optional forms in Riksmål as a further way of giving Nynorsk usages an equivalent status to traditional Riksmål spelling patterns that had not been struck down.[41]

The practical implications, at least in the educational sphere, were staggering. If approved by the department, all school texts would need to be drastically overhauled and reissued to reflect the legally mandated forms of Norwegian, teachers would be required to teach the many obligatory and side forms as all being worthy of a similar degree of respect, and strong pressure would exist for other segments of society, including the media, to follow suit.

The main language pressure groups were opposed to the orthographic reform, both in its initial form, and even after the committee attempted to take into account the divergent criticisms. Despite the fact that Nynorsk would be the chief beneficiary in terms of usage from this reform, it initially was the source of the bulk of the criticisms. Keilhau notes that of the 231 communiqués that the Norwegian parliament received on the proposed reform, 191 were in opposition to it, with 176 of those coming from Nynorsk advocates.[42] While the bulk of these were the result of activity organized by Noregs Mållag's chapter in western Norway, others have observed that even within the organization, a clear majority of Noregs Mållag members were opposed to the proposal. Opposition was voiced on a number of issues, including the concern that western variants of Nynorsk would be most hard hit in the Nynorsk portion of the reform, that it already had a viable norm (1901), and that Riksmål users would not implement their required changes. However, the most important criticism by Noregs Mållag of the DNA proposal was the complaint that Common Norwegian in and of itself was the wrong tactic. Nynorsk simply could not achieve its status as the sole national language if it were forced to enter into a watered-down compromise with Riksmål.[43] A small minority in the organization supported the proposal, though these forces were led by Koht and an ally that had served on the committee. In one brochure, Riksmålsforbundet condemned the proposed reforms on the basis that the government committee "did not have a clear view of the significance of language in the nation's administrative and cultural center. It is proposing forms that go against the entire system of pronunciation that is used in the southeastern portion of the nation and in the cities."[44]

While the committee attempted to take into account some of the specific criticisms from both camps (i.e., backtracking on altering certain conjugational patterns), the overall thrust of forging a new orthography with Common Norwegian at its core remained, and the proposal was approved by the Norwegian parliament, with DNA and the Conservatives voting along party lines. Each language interest group followed up the adoption of the new Common Norwegian orthography by observing there had been victories on some minor points, but dissatisfaction remained. Riksmålsforbundet explicitly advised against the use of the new standard, while conservatives in the Nynorsk camp did the same.[45]

The vocal opposition by the main language pressure groups, both before and after the adoption of the 1938 orthography, demonstrates how the preferences of language pressure groups could not have been the driving force in its adoption. As they did at all other points in Norwegian history, the two standards remained mutually intelligible, allowing one to discount the reforms as a response to communication difficulties between the two language groups. Further, one has to discount a claim that the revisions were necessitated for economic reasons, that is, that having two standards in such a small country was a financial drain on the education and administration sectors. In the long run, that may have been the case, but the standard approved by the new orthography dictated the introduction of a third written variety of Norwegian and therefore brought about even further expense for the state. Ultimately, when asking why the Norwegian Labor Party opted for radical implementation of a Common Norwegian line in the late 1930s, the answer has to be political. On a cultural front, the committee proposal solidified and embodied the alliance that DNA had forged between workers and farmers. Through linguistic planning, the government fully intended to reduce the linguistic privilege that the Norwegian upper-class maintained in imposing their written language on the nation as "proper" and "official." What would be substituted in its place was not a preexisting alternative, but rather a linguistic creation, one that patched together the spoken dialects of workers and farmers and would be given full state backing as the true "people's language."

The identity of the Norwegian language, and in a certain sense the Norwegian people, was in the process of being transformed by this orthographic proposal. Previous reforms had a widely understood notion that language was altered to serve the needs of creating a nation and to help Norwegians differentiate themselves from their colonial rulers. This time, however, those who used Riksmål would not be thought of as tied to the former Danish rulers, but rather as being representatives of the Norwegian ruling class. This association was certainly strengthened by the Conservatives' steadfast support for many of the goals advocated by Riksmålsforbundet and by their strict ideological opposition to any efforts at planning undertaken by DNA. Those that adhered strongly to a pure Nynorsk were no longer proponents of a progressive Norwegian nationalism, but were portrayed as being out of step with the realities of industrial society. And while Common Norwegian was a distant dream for the DNA government, the use of farmer or working class dialects was no longer to be interpreted as a sign of being uneducated. Rather, DNA had every intention that the use of these dialects would be a powerful symbol of cooperation between different sectors of the underclass in their battle to achieve socialism.[46]

DNA AND COMMON NORWEGIAN IN THE FIRST DECADES OF THE POST-WAR ERA

As we are primarily concerned with the interplay between pressure groups and political elites in a democratic society, the Nazi treatment of the Norwegian language falls outside of the boundaries of this chapter. However, the wartime years did feature substantial Nazi involvement in Norwegian language planning, which was entirely consistent with elite manipulation of a cultural symbol for political purposes. Particularly, it is noteworthy that within a year after the Nazi invasion, the pro-Nazi government put forth their own proposal for an orthographic reform, drawing on the more conservative variants of both Norwegian standards.[47]

For our purposes though, the account of the political use of the Norwegian language resumes with the end of World War II and the restoration of a democratic government. At the ballot box, DNA was stronger than ever, taking its first majority of Norwegian parliamentary seats in 1945, while its share of the popular vote continued to hover in the low 40-percent range. This lock on state power would continue until the early 1960s. The general political platform of DNA in the immediate post-war years was committed to the restructuring, rebuilding, and modernization of Norwegian society along the lines of a planned social democratic state. All during this time span, DNA would officially remain committed to the politics of Common Norwegian. Only when their lock on power was threatened by a rightward shift in the electorate would DNA elites begin to rethink their language policies.[48] Yet, policy shifts are of course preceded by discussion amongst elites about the merits of staying the course or opting for a fresh start. In the case of DNA and language politics, the continued implementation of Common Norwegian was accompanied by internal party discussion in which certain key members began to push for a reevaluation of the Common Norwegian line. Such discussions did not bring about any results until the early 1960s, and will be explored later in this chapter.

With this background in mind, this section focuses on DNA's ability to continue concrete implementation of Common Norwegian policies despite ongoing opposition from the two traditional language organizations. What is particularly noteworthy in this regard is that, on the Riksmål side, opposition to Common Norwegian greatly intensified to its most visible level. Yet, despite this growth in Riksmål pressure activities, and despite continued opposition to Common Norwegian from Noregs Mållag officials, DNA was able to hold the line in the two major language policies of the first fifteen post-war years: the establishment of the Norsk språknemnd (Norwegian Language Committee) and the approval of the committee's proposal for textbook revision in 1959. Figures for language usage on a national level, by region, along with figures showing the regional makeup of the 1957 vote for Bokmål/Riksmål users are provided in tables 3.1 and 3.2.[49] In reading these tables, it should be noted that Østlandet is the eastern portion of the nation in which Bokmål/Riksmål has its strongest base. Vestlandet and Sørlandet are respectively the western and southern portions of the nation, where Nynorsk has its strongest level of support. Briefly, these tables continue to show that Nynorsk was very much a minority language and that its use was confined primarily to the West, but also the South of the nation. As I will show in a subsequent portion of this chapter, table 3.2, in only focusing on how Bokmål/Riksmål speakers split their vote by region, does not take into account one of the critical pieces of information in this investigation: the level of interest

Table 3.1
Norwegian language usage across region, 1957. Percent. (N=1506)

Language	Østlandet	Sørlandet	Vestlandet	Trøndelag	Nord-Norge
Riksmål	.78	.55	.47	.80	.51
Bokmål	.15	.13	.20	.17	.43
Common					
Norwegian	.00	.01	.01	.00	.00
Landsmål	.02	.11	.12	.01	.01
Nynorsk	.02	.18	.20	.01	.05
Mixture	.00	.02	.00	.00	.00
As taught	.00	.00	.00	.00	.00
Regular	.02	.00	.00	.00	.00
Both main	.01	.00	.00	.01	.00
Total:	100.00	100.00	100.00	100.00	100.00

Source: Norwegian National Election Survey, 1957

Table 3.2
Party choice in the 1957 Norwegian parliamentary election. Bokmål/Riksmål users only. Percent. (N=774)

Party	Østlandet	Sørlandet	Vestlandet	Trøndelag	Nord-Norge
Communist	.02	.00	.01	.02	.00
DNA/Labor	.59	.44	.50	.72	.57
Liberal	.05	.33	.11	.02	.03
Christian					
Peoples	.07	.05	.16	.09	.11
Farmers' Party	.06	.15	.06	.04	.05
Conservative	.18	.03	.17	.11	.18
Bourg. List	.03	.00	.00	.00	.06
Bourg.	.00	.00	.00	.00	.00
Total	100.00	100.00	100.00	100.00	100.00

Source: Norwegian National Election Survey, 1957

in language policy. Once this additional variable is added to the mix, we will get a much stronger picture of how language mattered for DNA among the electorate.

A major theme of all accounts of post-World War II Norwegian language politics is the growth of pressure activities by the Riksmål forces. Their increased visibility came partly through the establishment of a journal, *Ordet* (The Word), in 1950, which provided accounts of the growing grass roots movements of parents against the politics of Common Norwegian, attacks on specific government directives involving Common Norwegian, and general propaganda that Riksmål forces might use in fighting the Labor Party's Common Norwegian line.[50] This was followed two years later by the weekly newspaper *Frisprog* (Free Language) that served a similar function, and was "officially" the organ for Foreldreaksjonen mot Samnorsk (The Parents' Action Against Common Norwegian). In terms of the small scale actions being taken by parents in the urban areas, one is struck that the opposition was far different from that of the 1930s, when it appeared to be confined to a small number of purists on both sides. Rather, that each issue of these papers was inevitably filled with accounts of various forms of protest against Common Norwegian suggests that mobilization at the mass level against Common Norwegian was now catching on. However, much of their ire was directed against government plans for the establishment of a permanent language planning committee. Proposals for a permanent committee had emerged from the government in the late 1940s, largely in an effort to establish a textbook norm that would adhere to the 1938 reform. However, a key participant in the proceedings suggested an interesting additional reason for why the language committee was being proposed in the years following 1945. Alf Hellevik observed that academics on all sides of the language question had been influenced by the wartime years and that the crisis of the war had produced a sense of cooperation that was hoped would now carry over to the language conflict.[51] Among language activists, who had expressed interest in a permanent language committee throughout the late 1940s, there was a vast difference on the function the committee should have. These differences among the government and the main language organizations of course reflected their different goals in language policy. Riksmål advocates, who were in general opposed to the idea that language planning should become a matter for public policy, strongly denounced the idea that the committee would institutionalize the government's commitment to Common Norwegian and instead suggested that the committee be formed along the lines of an independent academy that would be free of any government oversight.[52]

For Noregs Mållag, the conservative faction continued to constitute the majority throughout much of the 1950s and as such, was a bitter opponent to the idea of a permanent language committee formed along Common Norwegian lines.[53] More important for the chief Nynorsk pressure group, however, was the fact that the organization never fully recovered to the level of activity that had been seen prior to the war. The available resources were smaller, membership was far less motivated or willing to commit itself to another push, and accounts of the organization in this period implicitly suggest that the greatest amount of activity was spent not on trying to influence the state's language policy, but rather on fighting internal battles between the two camps. Still, Noregs Mållag's conservative camp prevailed again and asked the Norwegian parliament to postpone the establishment of any permanent language committee.[54] Even in the face of more intense opposition, DNA's parliamentary party saw only two defections, both representatives of urban areas, and in a vote mostly along party lines, united with the Liberals, the Farmers' Party and the Christian People's Party to defeat the Conservatives ninety-five to forty-one and establish the permanent language committee.

The first major undertaking of the newly formed Norwegian Language Committee was of course to establish a textbook norm. The goal was to produce a workable norm that drew on forms in both languages, such that new textbooks would be produced for the entire nation. The key draft of this new norm was issued by the Norwegian Language Committee in 1957, producing the expected opposition from the Riksmål side. Riksmål groups pooled their resources and issued a joint pamphlet, with each organization denouncing the proposed norm in various colorful fashions. André Bjerke had the honors for Riksmålsforbundet and did so by leveling his closing criticisms less at the reform itself, but at the Common Norwegian orientation of the Norwegian Language Committee:

> The language committee's founding paragraph expresses a pure contradiction when it demands that one should "on the basis of scientific investigation, bring the two written languages closer together on the basis of the Norwegian people's language." When researchers are told ahead of time by the authorities what results they are expected to come up with, their science becomes a caricature.[55]

Noregs Mållag also appeared to change gears in this respect, abandoning its usual steadfast line of Nynorsk as the sole Norwegian language, and its conservative leadership gave a rather grudging backing to the norm as a whole. Noregs Mållag leadership did allow for a harsh dissent to be distributed in pamphlet from a large and vocal minority.[56] Much as with the Norwegian Language Committee itself, the new textbook norm, when voted on by the Norwegian parliament, was only opposed by the entire Conservative delegation, along with two members of the Christian People's Party.

What one learns from a review of these policy conflicts adds additional weight to my general argument. These two conflicts represent cases far different from those presented in the previous chapter. First, the Liberals did not face formally organized pressure groups during its promotion of the language equality law. Additionally, once Noregs Mållag had been formed, it by and large placed its faith in the Liberals and limited its activities to making organizational preferences known to political elites. But for DNA in the 1950s, the situation was far different. It held an orientation towards language policy that was in complete opposition to the preferred stance of the organized Riksmål forces and one that was contradictory to the desires of the dominant conservative faction in Noregs Mållag. Further, in the face of increased and repeated pressure, particularly in the form of grassroots efforts in Oslo from the Riksmål forces, DNA successfully continued to implement Common Norwegian in a way that required changes in the behavior of citizens. The questions, of course, are both how and why they were able to achieve this. I maintain that the answers to these questions are in fact intertwined and that they once again lead back to electoral politics and the need to profile one's own party in opposition to that of one's opponent.

DNA was in the 1950s the undisputed hegemon of Norwegian politics. The fact that the party was quite frequently three times the size of its largest parliamentary rival often suggested that it simply did not have to be concerned about the vocal opposition from Riksmål forces to its language policies.[57] Given the close link between the conservative language organizations and the bourgeois parties, it was generally felt within the DNA leadership that the attacks on the Norwegian Language Committee and its work represented nothing more than a failed attempt to attack DNA's commitment to social democratic planning. This is evidenced in a pamphlet by DNA's then rising figure in the language question, Trygve Bull. In answering the question, "Shall We Always Have Two Languages In Norway?," Bull singled out the grassroots parents' movements that were so active in the early part of the 1950s. He conceded that, at first, they were a "partially spontaneous, democratic reaction" against the confused state of Norwegian textbooks. However, Bull argued that the political opposition was well aware that DNA could not be attacked for its economic record and thus, he saw the activities of the Riksmål parents as an attempt to successfully malign the party in some other policy area.[58] Haugen notes that other DNA figures dismissed the new Riksmål groups as nothing more than "west-end cliques," an allusion to the strongly bourgeois Oslo neighborhoods around Holmenkollen and Vinderen. Thus, in characterizing the opposition in this manner, there was little reason to take them seriously.

The opposition was also not particularly significant in terms of national vote totals. Coming from the well-to-do urban suburbs, it was not a constituency that showed signs of defection to the Labor Party. Rather, this opposition represented a constituency that DNA had never historically done well with and one whose support DNA had not been particularly eager to court. If anything, one would think that opposition from upper-class culture to the proponents of working-class culture would be a good thing. It provided ample evidence that DNA was fighting the good fight in favor of people's culture against a small group of extremists politically backed by the Conservatives and financially backed by the Norwegian business elite.[59] However, what happens when electoral fortunes are no longer as certain? And further, what happens when a social democratic party begins to emerge from the rhetoric of class struggle and turns towards the goal of becoming integrated in Europe as a modern industrial state? The answer, at least for language policy, is that what was once adopted for a mixture of electoral and ideological reasons had to be cast off in order to fulfill new objectives.

THE 1960s: RETREATING FROM COMMON NORWEGIAN

In December 1963, DNA Minister of Church and Education Helge Sivertsen gave a speech in which he stated that the time had come for the Norwegian language struggle to be "called off" and that a new committee would be appointed to replace the decade old Norwegian Language Committee.[60] That this action represented a caving-in to

Riksmål forces was suggested not only by the fact that Sivertsen appeared to be implicitly backing DNA away from the Norwegian Language Committee, but also by the fact that it was now for the first time being suggested that radical Bokmål elements be brought into the language planning process. In doing so, DNA was backing away from the Common Norwegian line that had been the hallmark of its language politics since its rise to power during the economic crises of the 1930s. That this reversal came on the heels of vocal and highly visible opposition to DNA's language policies has almost been exclusively interpreted as the success of radical Bokmål forces against a Norwegian state that was now somehow weakened in its ability to withstand pressure from language groups. Haugen refers to the shift in policy as "surprising,"[61] while the leading scholar of the Norwegian language conflict acknowledges that disentangling the forces at play in this policy reversal may simply not be possible.[62] Ultimately though, there is a general sense among some Norwegian sociolinguists that the shift in DNA language policy was the result of an increase in language group activity in opposition to the Norwegian Language Committee, arising primarily from the Riksmål camp.[63]

Implicit in the argument that the Norwegian Labor Party could not withstand the heightened pressure and calls from Riksmål forces for a retreat from the Common Norwegian line is that, at least on this one issue, societal forces had become stronger than the state capabilities in imposing their policy preferences. In a different national setting, Laitin has observed a similar discrepancy between societal and state power over language policy. Laitin raises India as a case where political elites were not able to establish the sole use of Hindi on the national level and he suggests that their inability to do so is the result of "stronger forces in society determin(ing) the outcome."[64] For Laitin, this failure at successful elite manipulation of the language issue is explained by the fact that India has had a "soft state" and that a general weakness of the state can account for its lack of success in this policy area.

The question of "soft" states and stronger societal forces helps shed some interesting light on the Norwegian case. In the past two chapters, I have repeatedly argued that successive ruling parties in modern Norway have been able to act against the preferences of organized societal opposition and to implement language policies that supported other political aims. Thus, on the basis of this investigation, one should be suspicious of a claim that the Norwegian state suddenly became "soft" on the language issue in comparison to the organized strength of language pressure groups. All things being equal, one sees little evidence that the Norwegian state should suddenly have buckled under pressure from either of the main language pressure groups.[65] But all things were not equal. Rather than just focusing on the balance of forces between the Norwegian state and the language pressure groups, one must take into account the contextual effects that electoral politics and party profiling were providing. As an alternate explanation to those that argue the Riksmål pressure groups were behind DNA's shift away from Common Norwegian, I argue in the following that changes in party ideology and political competition meant that it was no longer advantageous for DNA to maintain a stance that was at odds with the desires of its most vocal opponents on the language question.

Important changes were occurring on three fronts. First, new policy entrepreneurs on the language question had emerged in the party during the late 1950s. Second, the economic ideology of the party was increasingly centered on centralization and integration of Norway into the European economy. Finally, the break on DNA governing power in 1963 provided the necessary shock, along with the necessary window of opportunity, for a shift in language policy.

As noted earlier, Trygve Bull was a rising figure in DNA in the 1950s and had authored several key pamphlets and articles promoting the Common Norwegian line. At the same time though, his memoirs reveal that he was strongly pushing for a reevaluation of the party line on language policy. For while he publicly took part in characterizations of Riksmål forces as pawns of the bourgeois parties, his own attendance at several school meetings where parents spoke out in opposition to Common Norwegian led him to think otherwise. Bull's attendance at these parents meetings led him to believe that DNA might in fact be witnessing an Achilles heel on language policy, a weakness that could translate into a more general conservative backlash.[66] The concern that DNA's electoral position could be harmed by its policy of Common Norwegian is exceedingly clear in Bull's account. He notes that shortly after one of these meetings, he approached a cabinet member in 1950 and warned him that the Conservatives had the ability to capitalize on the issue. Further, he characterized his own fears on the matter in this fashion:

> I had been frankly concerned that a policy that had good intentions, and that while I was convinced (Common Norwegian) had a future for itself, it could simply have spelled danger for the labor movement's hard fought hegemony in Norwegian society . . .[67]

Bull's proposed alternative to the politics of Common Norwegian lay in the promotion of a norm that would allow for the "liberalization" of orthographic rules. In essence, the proposal allowed for the restoration of many Riksmål forms that had been banned in Bokmål during the 1938 reform and, by default, allowed the two written languages to continue separate development without government attempts at creating an artificial third standard. The proposed shift to a more liberal line was meant to match a "mood of the times" on language policy, one that at least in the eyes of certain DNA elites reflected deeply felt and legitimate concern over the language issue, not the posturing of a small minority.[68]

However as Kingdon notes, the mere existence of policy entrepreneurs who have compelling reasons for policy changes to be adopted does not mean that such changes will instantly (or ever!) come to pass. Rather, for policy entrepreneurs to be successful, there must be some change in the political environment or, as Kingdon refers to it, there must exist a window of opportunity.[69] For Kingdon, this can range from a change in the national feeling or mood, which one might witness in Bull's observations of opposition by "everyday Norwegians" to Common Norwegian or it might be changes in specific components of the political environment.

For DNA, backing away from Common Norwegian can in fact be attributed to concrete changes in political reality. First, the Labor Party itself had been experiencing a pronounced reshaping of party ideology, where it no longer emphasized its role as the champion of the working and farming classes to the extent that it had coming out of World War II. In what Bull describes as the party becoming "increasingly bourgeois" over time and what Esping-Andersen refers to as the "disappearance of its more socialistic features," DNA began carrying out policies of centralization that, by default, eliminated much of the support and resources that had been available for the promotion of the rural economy and culture. Particularly in the area of education, DNA opted for closing many smaller, rural school districts and reorganizing students into the larger ones. To an extent, this reflected the realities that Norwegian economic opportunities were no longer available for the younger generations in the villages, but rather were to be found in the cities and their more built-up surroundings.[70] In short, the party's goals were now being transformed. Whereas the 1930s and the immediate post-war era had seen the need to champion the underclass against the elites to bring about socialism, the late 1950s heralded the arrival of the modern, bureaucratic welfare-state party. Common Norwegian, with its heavy symbolic link to the idea of linguistic class struggle, was not a fitting counterpart to this new economic ideology.[71]

Finally, though, just as the electoral disaster of 1930 brought about a reorientation in DNA policies, the election of 1961 proved to be a similar turning point. In terms of voter percentage, DNA declined only slightly, but lost its absolute parliamentary majority as the splinter Socialist People's Party entered the Norwegian parliament with a handful of seats. On the bourgeois side of the political spectrum, the three main opposition parties overcame their historical inability to work together and forged a united front against DNA. In the summer of 1963, the bourgeois opposition, with Socialist People's Party support, managed to topple the DNA minority government. While DNA managed to regain power within a month, the effect on the power was cataclysmic. Less than ten years after reigning supreme over a fragmented right, DNA faced a new set of electoral realities. As a minority, it only managed to hold onto power through the support of a splinter socialist organization with which it vehemently disagreed over NATO. But the larger threat came from the opposite side of the political spectrum: the three main bourgeois parties stood unified and could present a real alternative to decades of social democratic rule.

Data from the 1965 Norwegian National Election Survey show not only the salience of the language conflict with the Norwegian public, but also points to a specter for DNA. In an era of decreased electoral certainty, voters strongly interested in the language question were decidedly not casting their ballots for DNA.[72] Prior to looking at how DNA was faring amongst voters on the language question, I will first look at the usage of the languages and the salience of the conflict. Table 3.3 provides figures from 1965 for the usage of the three written Norwegian languages.

The regional nature of Norwegian language usage is displayed in table 3.4, where Nynorsk is shown to have its clearest stronghold in the Western-Southern portion of the nation.[73]

Table 3.3
Use of the written Norwegian languages in 1965.
Percent. (N=1747)

Language	Percent
Nynorsk-Landsmål	.16
Riksmål-Bokmål	.83
Common Norwegian	.01
Total	100.00

Source: Norwegian National Election Survey, 1965

Table 3.4
Use of the written Norwegian languages
in 1965 by geographic region.
Percent. (N=1747)

Language	Region		
	East	West-South	Trøndelag/North
Nynorsk-Landsmål	.03	.44	.07
Riksmål-Bokmål	.97	.54	.93
Common Norwegian	.00	.02	.00
Total	100	100	100

Source: Norwegian National Election Survey, 1965

Patterns of usage, however, tell very little about whether language is strongly felt as a social and political issue. Table 3.5 deals with that concern directly, showing the figures for interest in the language conflict; whether the respondent thought the language question was nonpolitical; and whether one or more parties represented his or her view on the question. Table 3.6 provides the figures for membership in various types of organizations.

Clearly, language in Norway during the 1960s was very much a political issue and one of interest among the mass public. While only a very small percent of the respondents were members of a language pressure group, over half of the respondents considered themselves interested in the language question, and over one-third chose to identify one or more political parties that represented their view about language policy.

Table 3.5
Interest in the Norwegian language question (N=1155) and
whether respondent sees any parties as sharing his/her view on
language. (N=1192). Percent.

Interest		Political Question	
Interested	.51	One or more party named as sharing respondent's view	.34
Not Interested	.49	Issue nonpolitical	.27
		Don't Know	.39
Total	100.00		100.00

Source: Norwegian National Election Survey, 1965

Table 3.6
Respondents' membership in organizations, by type, 1965.
Percent (N=1122)

Type of Organization	Percent
Youth	.06
Sport/Leisure/Hobby	.30
Housewives	.06
Other Women's Organization	.05
Home Mission Organization	.02
Other Religious Organizations	.13
Language—Nynorsk	.01
Language—Riksmål	.02
Teetotalist	.04
Humanitarian	.29

Source: Norwegian National Election Survey, 1965

Having shown that questions over language policy was salient to a significant portion of the Norwegian population, I now turn to the question of how language was related to electoral competition. As noted earlier, Trygve Bull had expressed a fear as far back as 1950 that the language question had the potential to damage the continued electoral fortunes of DNA. By 1963, he was publicly echoing the change in course suggested by Sivertsen and urging even Riksmål adherents to assist in "taking the language issue out of politics."[74] Simply stated, was DNA out of touch with the electorate on the language question? The answer, based on data from the 1965 survey, suggests that Bull's fears were justified and that the party was in fact not closely aligned with certain segments of the electorate on the language issue. First, table 3.7 shows the survey results for the 1965 Norwegian parliamentary election by region. While the dominant party in all three regions, DNA faced a different main rival in each region, with the Conservatives being the second largest party in the East, the Liberals holding second place in the South and West, and Senterpartiet (the Center Party), the former Farmer's Party, ranked number two in Trøndelag and the North. However, when controlling for whether or not one was interested in the language question, and what written Norwegian language one used, the cross-tabulations begin to differ substantially. Table 3.8 provides the clearest picture on how language policy could adversely affect DNA at the polls. In comparing table 3.7 to table 3.8, one can see that the key difference for DNA came in the East, where the Labor Party scored dramatically worse than the Conservatives did among voters that spoke Bokmål/Riksmål and expressed an interest in the language question. By contrast, Bokmål/Riksmål speakers that were not interested in the language question split their vote for DNA and the Conservatives at roughly the same percentage as the larger general sample did. In the other two regions, DNA scored worse when looking at Bokmål/Riksmål speakers who were interested in language questions than it did in table 3.7. However, among Bokmål/Riksmål speakers who were not interested in the

Table 3.7
Parliamentary party choice by region, 1965 election. Percent.
(N=1595)

Party	East	West-South	Trøndelag/North
Communist	.01	.00	.01
Socialist People's	.06	.02	.04
DNA/Labor	.47	.35	.48
Liberal	.06	.19	.08
Christian People's	.03	.10	.04
Center	.10	.13	.16
Conservative	.23	.13	.12
Didn't vote	.04	.07	.07
Bourg. List	.00	.01	.00
Total	100.0	100.0	100.0

Source: Norwegian National Election Survey, 1965

Table 3.8
Parliamentary party choice by region for respondents that wrote
in Bokmål/Riksmål and expressed an interest in the language
question, 1965 election. N=424 (Respondents with no interest in
language question are in parentheses. (N=435) Percent.

Party	East	West-South	Trøndelag/North
NKP (Communist)	.01 (.02)	.00 (.00)	.01 (.01)
SF (Soc. People's)	.02 (.07)	.01 (.02)	.04 (.07)
DNA (Labor)	.28 (.46)	.32 (.43)	.40 (.54)
Liberals	.07 (.06)	.23 (.21)	.08 (.07)
KRF (Christian People's)	.06 (.03)	.08 (.04)	.04 (.02)
SP (Center)	.08 (.12)	.11 (.09)	.15 (.16)
Conservative	.44 (.18)	.18 (.15)	.21 (.07)
Didn't vote	.04 (.06)	.02 (.06)	.07 (.07)
Bourg. List	.00 (.00)	.05 (.00)	.00 (.00)
Total	100.0	100.0	100.0

Source: Norwegian National Election Survey, 1965

language question, DNA scored even better in these regions than it did in table 3.7.

That DNA fared so poorly in the East on the language question is of even greater interest when one considers the intensity of electoral competition between DNA and the Conservatives in the county of Oslo. Oslo is the greatest electoral prize in Norwegian elections, with 13 of 150 MPs being selected by voters in that county. While Nordland has the second largest number of MPs (12), there is an important distinction between these two counties: in Nordland, DNA has traditionally been the dominant party, taking half of the seats, with all other parties dividing the remaining seats on a roughly equal basis. However Oslo, particularly in the 1950s and 1960s, was an electoral battleground between DNA and the Conservatives. Here, DNA generally captured six of the thirteen seats, with five of the remaining MP slots going to the Conservatives. As already noted, DNA had also witnessed the defection of its small left-wing in the formation of the Socialist People's Party (SF). As SF's appeal and then-guiding principle was built around the single issue of opposition to Norwegian membership in NATO, there was little chance of DNA successfully reaching out to its left, either nationally or in Oslo. For DNA, the battle for votes in an electoral district as tightly contested as Oslo had to be waged to its political right.

Thus, the decision by DNA to rethink its stance on language politics should be thought of in this light. Backing away from the politics of Common Norwegian and seeking the alleged "de-politicization of language" was a strategy that seemed well-advised when considering both survey results and the electoral landscape. The potential benefit to DNA for this change in language strategy was that pursuing a language policy that would make the language question less visible over time and take it out of the political spotlight could strengthen its position with those Bokmål/Riksmål speakers that did not have much interest in the language question to begin with. These were the voters in the east that DNA had already been scoring well with and certainly did not wish to lose. The assumption, mirroring Bull's fears, was that if the language issue were to remain contentious, the possibility existed that Bokmål/Riksmål speakers who were not interested in the language question would sanction DNA for its Common Norwegian policies and defect to the Conservatives. More importantly though, "de-politicizing" language by bringing all sides to the table was the political strategy long favored by the Conservatives. In opting for this shift in language strategy, DNA was seeking to cast off a potentially vulnerable stance and to reduce the chance that the Conservatives would be able to use language as a way to siphon off voters from DNA.

With this in mind, the subsequent debate in the Norwegian parliament on a shift in language policy was not at all surprising. All parties concurred that the politics of Common Norwegian had gone too far, too fast, and that it was time to back away from this ideal.[75] Additionally, all parties agreed that the new goal was to be a permanent committee on language that did not have Common Norwegian as its goal and that would also have representatives from the conservative Riksmålsforbundet at its table. The data presented above suggests why DNA eventually came around to this shift in policy. However it is important to recall that for many decades, DNA did not always consider Common Norwegian a policy that was "too far, too fast." Rather, this only happened once DNA had moved on to a new set of goals as a governing party and only once it saw that its lock on the voters was no longer unchallenged.

CONCLUSION

The bulk of any investigation of Norwegian language planning must by necessity focus at length on the Norwegian Labor Party, if for no other reason than that it has been the dominant player on the political stage for much of the twentieth century. But such a detailed focus is valuable for other reasons. For in doing so, I have been able to trace the history of one party and its multiple stances on the language question. At each point, these orientations towards the language question have been determined not by the activities of pressure groups, but rather by a mixture of political forces. As a small working-class party with Comintern membership, to have held a language policy in support of one standard or the other was seen as irrelevant to the struggle at hand. As the champion of the worker-farmer coalition, DNA's promotion of Common Norwegian neatly encapsulated its role as cultural guardians of the Norwegian "underclass." And as a modern party, more bourgeois and bureaucratic than socialist, a language policy that belonged to another era and one that stood in the way of a different set of party goals, could only be an electoral liability in an era of increased competition for Norwegian voters.

Chapter 4

The Shifting Fate of the Sámi Languages in Modern Norway

INTRODUCTION

Up to now, the focus of this investigation has centered on determining the extent to which an interest group-led strategy can account for the variations in Norwegian language policy. As I have shown in the past two chapters, Norwegian language policy as a whole is best explained by the extent to which Norwegian political elites chose to create or manipulate linguistic identities in the service of other political goals.

In this chapter, I focus on the policies that Norwegian political elites have designed in regards to another linguistic culture within Norwegian borders, the Sámi people. From the mid-nineteenth century to the present, the Sámi, an indigenous ethnic minority located in northern Norway, have also been the subject of varying language policies. Just as in the case of the language policies aimed at the majority Norwegian population, these policies have had a great impact on the linguistic behavior and choices of the Sámi peoples and the historical record will easily reveal that the effects have often been far more dramatic. Generally, the policies taken towards the Sámi languages prior to World War II were ones of extreme repression. However, following World War II, Norwegian elites gradually altered course and began to promote a limited official status for the Sámi languages in certain educational and public settings.

My argument in this chapter is that the treatment of the Sámi languages by the Norwegian elites in the pre-World War II period cannot be understood apart from the broad efforts by Norwegian elites at state construction. These efforts included the establishment of a distinctly Norwegian national identity that equated the new state with one national language and the attempt to guarantee that the eastern border areas of Norway were secure from perceived threats of foreign incursion. I argue that Norwegian elites viewed Sámi ethnicity as threatening to the attainment of these goals and responded with a set of policies designed to eradicate any sense of Sámi cultural and linguistic distinctiveness.

It is important to recall that elite support for Nynorsk in the decades following parliamentary sovereignty was designed to foster a sense of Norwegian national identity that did not rest on Danish cultural heritage. Non-Norwegian ethnic minorities within the new state's borders were to suffer as a result of this effort, as Norwegian elites sought to champion only the language and the culture that was deemed sufficiently symbolic of the Norwegian people. Thus, both the language policies that promoted Nynorsk and those that oppressed the Sámi peoples were by-products of elite desire to forge national symbols and a national myth among the Norwegian people.

Of course, the shift towards limited promotion of Sámi languages in the decades following World War II requires a different explanation. In this period, I argue that Norwegian elites emerged from the wartime experience with a changed understanding regarding the role of non-Norwegian ethnic minorities in the larger Norwegian community. Questions of loyalty on the part of various ethnic groups to the Norwegian state, once a key reason in the oppression of the Sámi languages and culture, were now considered both trivial and potentially dangerous given the experience of Nazi occupation. This shift in Norwegian elite thinking was augmented by similar shifts among elites and institutions at the international level. Within the international community of states, ethnic minorities were increasingly viewed as groups that had suffered past injustices at the respective hands of the states in which they were located, and such injustices were now expected to be acknowledged and addressed.

Yet, as I will also show, the fact that the Sámi people were no longer perceived of as posing a threat to Norwegian national identity or security did not result in a complete about-face of language policies. Official support was given quite grudgingly and is still quite limited. I argue that this limited promotion of the Sámi languages on the part of Norwegian elites can be traced to the nature of Scandinavian social democratic ideology, which stresses the good of policies for society as a whole, as opposed to those that would benefit particularized groups.

However, prior to tracing the way in which elite policies towards the Sámi languages have varied over the past 100 years, some background is necessary both on the Sámi people and the specifics of the language policies that Norwegian elites have adopted towards them.

THE NORWEGIAN SÁMI

The Norwegian Sámi are the largest group of the combined Sámi peoples, who are spread out through the northern areas of Norway, Sweden, Finland, and the former Soviet Union. The Norwegian Sámi currently total approximately 20,000, only slightly greater than the 17,000 found in Sweden, and the 5,000 Finnish Sámi.[1] Even with those scholars who put the number much higher, there seems to be no disagreement that the Sámi comprise far less than one percent of the total Norwegian population.[2] While the Sámi are located throughout Norway, including a large number in the southeastern urban center of Oslo, the core areas are in the northern counties of Finnmark and Troms.[3] A review of table 4.1 shows a large downward shift in the number of Sámi in the post-war period. However, the stance of both the Norwegian government and Sámi specialists is that the census numbers for both the 1950 and 1970 period reflect an exceptionally restricted method of counting Sámi. Among these, one finds that only

Table 4.1
Sámi Population in Norway, 1850–1970.

Year	Population
1850	15,999
1865	17,187
1890	20,786
1900	19,677
1910	18,590
1920	20,735
1930	20,704
1950	8,778
1970	9,000–10,000

Source: NOU 1985:14, p. 37. Note again that the 1950 and 1970 numbers have produced controversies over counting methods employed in the census.

Sámi living in the northern core area were counted in 1950 and that individuals were only classified as having Sámi heritage if they identified themselves as having a Sámi language background.[4]

The Sámi speak a collection of dialects that are Finno-Ugric in origin and are not mutually intelligible with either of the Norwegian standards. The greatest retention of the dialects are found in the inner portions of Finnmark, with a lower level of usage on the northern coastal areas. It is estimated in the mid-1980s that in the Finnmark region, less than 10 percent of the 15,000 Sámi used Norwegian, while of the 9,000 coastal Sámi in Troms, the situation was reversed, and less than 10 percent speak Sámi.[5]

Norwegian anthropologists suggest that the continued strong usage of Sámi in the inner Finnmark region is directly related to vitality of traditional Sámi economies such as reindeer herding.[6] Alternately, as will be shown later, the strong inroads made by the Norwegian state in the northern coastal areas, both in terms of initial industrialization and then integration into the post-war welfare-state economy, can be directly linked to a decreased desire on the part of coastal Sámi to continue using their native languages.

NORWEGIAN POLICIES PERTAINING TO THE USE OF THE SÁMI LANGUAGES

While it is fair to characterize the policies taken by the modern Norwegian state toward the Sámi languages as having been initially repressive (1850s–1950s) and then more "enlightened" (1960s to the present), passing mention should be given to the way in which the Sámi were regarded in Norway prior to parliamentary sovereignty. Primarily, in the seventeenth and eighteenth centuries, Sámi was viewed by the Norwegian monarchy as an effective tool in the campaigns to further the spread of Christianity. Norwegian missionaries in the far north found that attempts to convert the indigenous people with the use of Norwegian were not producing the desired effect. However, when missionaries learned the local tongue, the ultimate aim of producing more converts came more into reach. Thus, with the spread of Christianity to the far north as a key goal, there was little difficulty in co-opting a language if it served religious interests.[7] And though Norway, pre-independence, is outside the scope of this study, observing the way in which Norwegian institutions became involved in the sanctioned use of minority languages for ulterior motives should set the stage for how modern Norway would be looking to the Sámi in a similar fashion.

Roughly four years prior to the establishment of parliamentary sovereignty in Norway, school officials in Troms issued a set of instructions for teachers in the so-called mixed districts, those where Norwegian, Sámi, and Kven (Finnish) were used. Under the new guidelines, mixed districts were gradually to be disbanded through the requirement that Norwegian be the sole language of communication in schools. Sámi and Kven were to be retained only insofar as they were necessary for explaining concepts to children that they could not grasp with their limited understanding of Norwegian. Further, teachers were required to ensure that students used Norwegian in their communication with one another even when it may not have been directly related to classes or schoolwork.[8] This policy at the local level was later codified by the newly independent Norwegian Parliament in 1889, when the Sámi and Kven languages were officially given status as "helping languages" in the mixed districts.[9] In 1898, the Norwegian Parliament issued a revision of its 1892 school law, which had established the right that a child's own spoken language could be used as much as possible within school settings. Continuing the trend begun almost ten years earlier, the Norwegian Parliament stated that this law did not apply to either the Sámi or Kven languages and reaffirmed that the two were only to be regarded as helping languages.[10]

In 1902, the Norwegian government established Finnmark as a single school district, which brought it directly under the control of the Ministry of Education. The ministry established a director for the region's schools who was to ensure that the curriculum utilized in all other Norwegian school districts was also followed to the letter in Finnmark, particularly that which pertained to the Norwegian languages. Eventually, the Norwegian state looked further to centralize its control over education in this predominantly Sámi and Kven region and, in 1905, introduced boarding schools where non-Norwegians were to be assimilated into the dominant Norwegian culture.

The final educational measure prior to World War I came in 1914, when Sámi language texts were officially banned from Norwegian schools, though it is worth noting that the actual phasing out of these books had begun years earlier.[11] The obvious consequence of these centralization measures was that Finnmark and its linguistically mixed inhabitants were just viewed as another school district, where questions of non-Norwegian minority languages were not relevant. Starting in 1920, local and national officials struck down Sámi requests for a Sámi high school, with a 1926 Norwegian Parliament committee concluding that there was not sufficient time in a school year for students to be mastering both languages and that there was a lack of teachers with sufficient training to be employed at the proposed school. Ultimately, the committee simply reasserted that Sámi served its best function as a helping language.[12] Regulations were not just limited to the arena of education. In 1902, a law forbidding the buying or selling of land in Finnmark by those who could not speak Norwegian was passed.[13]

However, as stated, Norwegian laws regarding the Sámi languages have fallen into one of two broad categories: repressive or enlightened. There is some degree of difference as to whether the seeds of change may be found in laws adopted in the late 1930s. The 1936 Education Act may have abolished the status of Kven as a helping language, but it retained that of Sámi, and it also reaffirmed the right of Sámi as a helping language. Many scholars tend to view this as a mere continuation of the previous line, but Darnell and Hoëm have interpreted this Act as the beginning of the legal claim that Sámi have the right to education in their mother tongue.[14]

Yet the post-war era has undoubtedly brought an about-face on the part of the Norwegian state towards the Sámi, even if there is disagreement among scholars over the actual significance of some of the early post-war changes. In 1948, a parliamentary report on the coordination of the Norwegian school system as a whole stated that "the Sámi people are a minority that have a natural right to be taken seriously." While the committee was charged by the Norwegian Parliament to look at the entire Norwegian school system, a subcommittee was established that focused specifically on the Sámi language question. The first piecemeal suggestions to a shift in the government line came from this committee. Among these were calls for Sámi language textbooks, a Sámi teacher's college in the north, arranging for teachers in Sámi areas to receive training in the Sámi languages, the option of Sámi children receiving Sámi language instruction in central Norway, and Nordic cooperation on language questions.[15] The concrete implementation of these suggested changes was not achieved by comprehensive parliamentary action, but rather through changes to individual policies. Roughly simultaneous to this report, the Norwegian Parliament allocated funds for the publication of textbooks with both Norwegian and Sámi in them.[16]

In 1956, the Department of Church and Education established the Sámi Committee that would "suggest concrete measures of an economic and cultural nature" to the Norwegian Parliament in an effort to better the lives of the Sámi. If the 1949 subcommittee could be criticized as being specifically limited to questions of schooling, and even then rather piecemeal, then the 1956 committee was the definitive mark of a change in the government line. The committee stated that Norway must now adopt a line of "cultural integration" toward the Sámi. The particularly Norwegian version of integration involved that the Sámi would be integrated into Norwegian society, but in such a way that the values and norms of the Sámi were respected by Norwegians.[17] While the committee dealt with many areas of emerging Sámi rights, such as the demarcation of the Sámi core area and the protection of reindeer grazing land, mention was also made of a new line that should be adopted on the language question. The committee recommended that Sámi children should have competence in both Norwegian and their Sámi standard and that Norwegian schools should play a part in the promotion of Sámi culture as a whole.[18] However, in the interim period before the government response, the 1959 School Law did specify that Sámi could be used as a language of instruction in the schools.[19] The 1969 Primary School Law better specified how Sámi could come to be used in the schools and stated that parents of children who regularly spoke Sámi could request it as a language of instruction.[20]

Most recently, a law on the use of Sámi in Norway was adopted in 1992. The law specifies that in Sámi core areas individuals have the right to use Sámi with local government bodies and to receive official responses in Sámi. Additionally, regulations were specified that allowed for the use of Sámi in the court system, in prisons, and with the police. In the schools, Sámi children were given the right to choose Sámi as a language of instruction after the seventh grade, with the option of choosing Sámi to replace either Bokmål or Nynorsk in the final two years of primary school.[21] Table 4.2 presents a summary of these policies.

Two things should be immediately clear from reviewing this table. The first is that there is a clear break between the period of repressive policies and those which began to promote the status and

Table 4.2
Norwegian Policies toward the Sámi Languages

Year Adopted	Policy	Promoted/ Repressed
1880	Abandonment of mixed language districts	Repressed
1889	Sámi/Kven as helping languages	Repressed
1898	Sámi excluded from 1892 school law	Repressed
1902	Norwegian language skills required for certain land transactions	Repressed
1902	Establishment of Finnmark as school district	Repressed
1905	Establishment of boarding schools for Sámi children	Repressed
1914	Banning of Sámi language textbooks	Repressed
1926	Sámi people denied Sámi language high school	Repressed
1936	Education Act reaffirms Sámi as helping language	————-
1948	Norwegian Parliament approves funds for Sámi texts	Promoted
1956	Bilingual competency recommended for Sámi children	Promoted
1959	Right of Sámi to be used in schools re-established	Promoted
1969	Right of parents to choose Sámi language instruction for children	Promoted
1992	Law on Sámi language use defines public usage sphere, grants usage rights to Sámi	Promoted

position of the Sámi languages, roughly simultaneous with the Second World War. The second is that when one compares the policies adopted by the Norwegian state toward Sámi with those implemented towards Nynorsk, one immediately notices a marked inconsistency in terms of the claim that political elites behaved out of a desire to support minority linguistic standards. The period of 1880 up through World War II, which saw the period of repression towards the Sámi minority, is roughly the identical period that Nynorsk was receiving its greatest level of support from Norwegian political elites. Additionally, the overview of policies toward the Sámi language minority demonstrates that there have been two basic attitudes toward the Sámi languages. Specifically, what factors can account for the shift in treatment by Norwegian elites towards Sámi languages during the twentieth century? It is to the first set of attitudes held by Norwegian elites, under the period of Norwegianization, that I now turn to.

THE PERIOD OF "NORWEGIANIZATION"

The period of repressive policies by Norwegian elites toward the Sámi minorities is generally referred to as one of *fornorskning* or

Norwegianization. As stated before, this time span roughly encompasses the period of 1880 up to the end of World War II and runs simultaneous with the period in which Norwegian political elites were promoting both the minority Nynorsk standard and the largely unrealized Common Norwegian. Three forces seem to have been at work in this phase: emerging Norwegian nationalism, security concerns about the northern border, and an elite view of minorities that assumed that no preferential treatment to protect their way of life was necessary. While each had a degree of influence on elite thinking toward Sámi language policy, we will find that nationalism and security concerns exhibited the greatest degree of influence. As the salience of nationalism and fears over the northern border area declined, so did the continued implementation of ever-more repressive linguistic policies toward the Sámi.

Nationalism

Nationalism as a driving force in the construction of language policy by Norwegian political elites should be no stranger to us at this point. As shown in chapter 2, the battle between the Liberals and the Conservatives over language policies was very much a battle to define one's own party as bearing a key symbol of the newly independent Norwegian nation. In that battle, political elites chose between written Norwegian standards to find a linguistic tool that could be easily aligned with their nationalistic rhetoric. However, despite fiery rhetoric from opposing language camps, advocates of both Nynorsk and Bokmål were considered "Norwegian" and were never genuinely considered national outsiders except by the most strident language activists. From the elite perspective, the question was instead one of which version of Norwegian best suited the nationalist aims. The relationship between the Sámi languages and Norwegian nationalism was an entirely different matter. Just as Norwegian languages were caught up in a struggle over which would be considered the dominant linguistic element of Norwegian nationalism, Sámi languages became the victims of elite views on nationalism that would exclude them from the Norwegian national identity.

To understand how nationalist thinking can account for the repression of the Sámi languages, we need to consider one of the constituent elements of nineteenth-century nationalism. Emerging political elites in the nineteenth century were strongly influenced by the idea that the unified nation was exemplified by the existence of one national language.[22] The consequence of this view would have strong significance for minority language communities that were located in newly emerging states. Specifically, the idea that only one language could officially occupy one national space directly implied that any group within a nation's borders that did not use the officially sanctioned language could not be considered part of the nation. And while nineteenth-century nationalism may have given rise to calls among minority language communities for independence, their fates were something of an entirely different matter. Almost as a rule of thumb, minority language communities in emerging nation-states faced an onslaught of assimilationist policies from their respective national rulers.[23]

In the case of Norway and the Sámi, the likelihood that Sámi languages would be viewed as a stumbling block in the process of Norwegian nationalism was compounded by an additional factor. As Hobsbawm notes, while linguistic nationalism may have been well entrenched throughout much of the nineteenth century, the rise of ethnic nationalism in the late nineteenth century precluded the chances that ethnic groups such as the Sámi could be brought into other nation-building projects with their identity intact.[24] Evidence that the ethnic version of nationalism had taken root in elite Norwegian circles can be found in statements such as those made by Admund Helland, an advisor to the Norwegian government on questions of Finnmark in the mid- and late nineteenth century. In contrasting northern Norwegians with their Sámi and Kven counterparts, Helland noted:

> (Norwegians have) all the best characteristics of the Germanic race: big, strong bone structure, powerful muscles, well-formed hands and feet, and sharply developed sense organs. Mentally, too, the Norwegian population appears to be highly talented. To this their shrewd, keen looks and swift comprehension testify.[25]

Not only do Sámi languages differ from the two Norwegian standards, but as noted previously, the two groups share a different ethnic background. In Gellner's view, language makes up only one element of ethnicity. Additionally, one needs to factor in what one ". . . wears, dances, whom he may eat with, speak with, marry, etc., and so forth. Frequently, he *is* what he does *not* eat."[26]

Thus, it is fair to say that when Norwegian political elites considered the Sámi, they had two initial reasons to engage in policies of linguistic repression and both of these were grounded in the development of European nationalist thought. On the one hand, the Sámi standards were not in any sense Norwegian and, as such, could not be used to invoke symbols of a shared Norwegian past for the new state. On the other hand, the Sámi themselves and their languages could not be left as a residual category, for there was no place for an "other" or a "second" in the concept of the monolingual state.[27] Thus, the very nationalism that forced Sámi languages to be excluded from Norwegian national identity simultaneously leads to the need on the part of elites for a separate Sámi identity to be eradicated from the modern Norwegian state. Nor should we discount the connection between Norwegianization policies and the dissolution of the union with Sweden, a period in which nationalist sentiment is generally seen as having surged.[28] Three of the more brutal Norwegianization policies come in this period. Not only do these restrict the rights of non-Norwegian speakers, but they also reshape Norwegian institutional rules in terms of property rights and the mobility of peoples within Norwegian borders.

Security Concerns

But if nationalism was the main ideological component behind the linguistic repression of the Sámi, how do external political circumstances figure into the scenario? That is, what specific events helped to shape a set of policies that sought to assimilate the Sámi people into the young Norwegian state? Fueled by the insecurities inherent in the consolidation of a newly formed nation-state, there is substantial evidence that the policies of Norwegianization were strongly dependent on a perception of a security threat from both the Finns and the Russians. This perceived threat to the new state led elites to construct language policies, not in isolation, but as part of an overall design that was to secure the northern border areas through ensuring the cultural and linguistic loyalty of all "foreigners" in the region.

The final decades of the nineteenth century witnessed four events that caused concern among political elites about the Norwegian north. What is remarkable about each of these is that the relevant minorities in each case are not the Sámi, but the Kven. First, one finds that settlements of Kven were continuing to grow in the inner regions of the north. These settlements were largely isolated and did not develop broad contacts with any of the surrounding Norwegian communities. The establishment of these pockets of immigrants in the north posed a problem for national integration by introducing a "foreign" culture and tongue. However, there was a related concern purely in terms of resources. While the northern regions of Norway were still sparsely populated, increasing numbers of Norwegians were moving from the central and southern regions of the country to Troms and Finnmark. As they moved north, they discovered that their attempts to locate suitable land was being made all the more difficult by groups of Kven that were simply relocating westward from Finland, Sweden and Russia.[29] Thus, not only was the fluid border situation posing problems in terms of consolidating national identity, it also had the potential to lead to conflict over the allocation of arable land.

Second, this period witnessed a rise in an extreme variant of Finnish nationalism. The advocates of this nationalism stressed a pan-Finnism which pointed to the need for all Finnish people in the northern Arctic areas to unite as one people. While these calls first occurred late in the nineteenth century, they intensified throughout the early twentieth century and reached their height following the Finnish civil war. Extremist organizations such as the *Akademiske Karelie-Selskapet* formed and sent contacts across the border into northern Norway. Among other things, these activists frequently wrote articles in Kven newspapers attempting to gain support for their "Greater Finland" project. There is little evidence that Norwegian Kven responded to these calls, but their efforts did serve to perpetuate suspicions on the part of Norwegian authorities toward the Kven.[30]

Third, the Finnish authorities tacitly challenged the sovereignty of the Norwegian state in the north by establishing schools along the border areas in 1890. In a move that was understandably provocational to the elites of a new nation, Finnish authorities allowed for Norwegian citizens to cross the border and to attend these schools, thus raising the question of whether loyalty could be expected among a group of peoples that resided in one nation, but were partly socialized by the institutions of another.

Finally, concerns about consolidating the northern border need to take into account the relationship between the Finns and Imperial Russia. Eriksen and Niemi tacitly point to a type of early "domino theory" mentality that prevailed among Norwegian elites. At the time of Norway's independence, Finland was an autonomous state joined in a union with Tsarist Russia. The expansionist desires of the Russian state, particularly in terms of acquiring ice-free ports, were well-known.[31] Thus, the source of the threat was ultimately the much more threatening Russian state, which had in essence annexed Finland and where Finnish authorities and extremists were now using both institutions and propaganda to stir up sentiment in other Scandinavian nations. Fears of Finland were at this point strongly equated to fears of Russia. Nor was this fear limited solely to the Norwegians. Neighboring Swedish elites also expressed concern at the rise of a joint Russian/Finnish threat, particularly in their own northern border area of Tornedalen, an area where Sweden and Russia had drawn a border, thus dividing a community of Finns. Swedish authorities feared that Russia was using this area as "a potential object of Russian infiltration, hostility and annexation." Thus, this shared concern on the part of the Swedes provided their Norwegian counterparts with confirmation that the northern border areas could become difficult to consolidate and control.[32]

The question remains, however, as to how fears of Russian expansionism and continued Kven settlement should apply to the development of Sámi language policies. The answer is relatively simple. There exists no real evidence that Norwegian elites differentiated between Sámi and Kven in terms of linguistic repression. Rather, the historical record demonstrates that as the perception of the vulnerable northern border emerged, repressive language policies were aimed at all northern minorities and they did not differentiate between a "Kven threat" and a "Sámi threat."[33]

While it is plausible to suggest that the combination of a non-Norwegian population in the north and security concerns from the East may have produced policies of Norwegianization, some degree of evidence that this was the case should be expected. As stated earlier, Finnmark had been brought directly under the Department of Education and Church Affairs control in 1902 via the appointment of a director of schools for the region. Two of the clearest pieces of evidence that Norwegian elites linked the policies of Norwegianization to these perceived threats comes from reports filed by the then director of schools for Finnmark.

In terms of the concern over the "foreign" population in the north, Director Bernt Thomassen's five-year report for 1901–1905 evaluates the priorities and successes of northern Norwegian schools in light of whether or not they had increased the percent of the population speaking Norwegian. Thomassen's charts pay particular attention to a division of students into Norwegian, Sámi, and Kven categories. He also noted with satisfaction the more heavily populated areas of the north where Norwegian came to dominate. Still, he expressed concern over those regions where Sámi or Kven were still widely used and couched all optimistic predictions on whether or not any "mass migrations" from Finland to northern Norway will take place.[34]

Five years later, Thomassen wrote to the Department of Education and Church Affairs about a trip he had taken to observe Russian schools along the Norwegian border. The majority of Thomassen's account centers around what languages were officially allowed in these border schools and he notes the strict use of Russian by the instructors, when students that can only comprehend Sámi or Kven. Thomassen notes that as schooling in Russia and Finland is not mandatory, these schools most likely represent a Russian response to Norway's own stepped up efforts at border schools. He concludes by pointing to two ways that the presence of these schools will affect Norway. First, he suggests that the establishment of Russian schools will decrease the amount of border traffic by Russian Kvens, a comment that can be considered in light of the Norwegian goal to decrease the fluidity of the border region. However, in a comment telling of the prevailing attitude taken by the Norwegian state towards indigenous peoples, Thomassen observes that the strict reliance on Russian in these schools may serve to decrease the likelihood that Norway's own linguistic minorities will complain about the language policies in education.[35]

Thus, both the ongoing ambiguous border situation and concerns of further large scale immigration into the north combined to produce a certain border fear among Norwegian elites. These elites felt that Norwegian language and culture had to be consolidated in the north in order for there to be border security, a sentiment that is perhaps best expressed by the candid statement of the Norwegian foreign minister in 1905, "A national population, a population of Norwegian farmers who are tied by their livelihood to where they live and who have an emphatic sense of Norwegian nationhood, that is our best protection against the threat from the East."[36]

The Enlightenment of Minority Peoples

As noted in chapters 2 and 3, the first Liberal prime minister, Johan Sverdrup, was frequently portrayed as having a great deal of sympathy for the emerging Nynorsk movement. But we should not be surprised that this alleged sympathy for one minority language did not extend to the others that inhabited Norway. Jernsletten notes that both

Sverdrup and Johannes Steen, another early Liberal elite that was critical in the adoption of Nynorsk for strategic purposes, were strong advocates of the policies of Norwegianization.[37] Sverdrup was in fact rather open about the desire to see the success of Norwegianization, stating that, ". . . for the Lapps, the only salvation lies in their assimilation into the Norwegian nation."[38] Similarly, Thomassen, in one of his first annual reports to the Department of Church Affairs and Education, ends on a note of hope for better times in the "work of enlightenment" that northern Norwegian authorities are engaged in.[39]

But is there anything uniquely Norwegian about this view of indigenous peoples as groups that could only be "saved" if they were given the culture that dominated in the rest of society? While rhetorical, such elite attitudes need to be considered in terms of the dominant views held by European elites as a whole toward minorities. In fact, comments such as Sverdrup's seem to differ little from those made in France during the previous century, when elites began the unification of the various French provinces into one state via language. Influential advocates of the French language were prone to rhetoric that championed the beneficial nature of their spoken tongue: "Let us crush ignorance! Let us send teachers of French into the countryside!" and, "The peasant whose ideas are very restricted will be continually cut off from education so long as he does not know the language spoken by educated persons."[40]

Such comments are representative of Gellner's description of how "High Culture" pervades European societies in the nineteenth-century, with the emphasis being largely on the assimilation of marginal populations into the community via a single chosen tongue and culture.[41] Advantages are expected to accrue to those who adopt the tongue of the "High Culture," for they will then be able to share in the modernization process inherent in state-building. Those who reject the language associated with enlightenment are seen not only as turning their back on the nation, but also on the progress that the national elites wish to provide to all members of the community.

Implicit in this "path to progress" for minorities is the assumption that their own language and culture is somehow contradictory to notions of progress and that enlightenment can only derive from the language of the dominant elites. Such views are closely intertwined with nationalist thinking and obviously allowed for a consistent approach to be developed towards minorities. Nationalist ideology stated that there could only be one linguistic community within a given border.

Related to this, the politics of linguistic enlightenment spoke in the seemingly incontrovertible logic of progress to justify the need for that one linguistic community. An extension of this argument is provided by scholars that take a decidedly pro-Sámi stance. Jernsletten argues that Norwegian attitudes towards the Sámi are consistent with the general trend of European colonialism.[42] From this perspective, though on a smaller scale, Norwegians were not simply unifying the outlying provinces, but were going into foreign lands, spreading their language and culture, all under the colonial banner of "the white man's burden."

FROM REPRESSION TO PROMOTION

The previous section has shown how Norwegianization has been the result of the combined effects of nationalist ideology, security concerns, and the belief that spreading the Norwegian language would allow for the improvement of ethnic minorities. However, as table 4.2 shows, the repressive policies of Norwegianization come to a close with the Second World War. In this section, I will account for this shift in policies toward the Sámi by focusing attention on the effects of World War II. As an event, the war appears to have exhibited great mediating effects on the both the nationalist projects and the security concerns that were prevalent under Norwegianization. These changes were augmented by shifts in the ideological, institutional, and legal makeup of the international political arena in such a way that a rethinking of language policies toward the Sámi was necessary. In some cases, initial traces of the shift in international attitudes towards the rights of minorities can be found in the pre-World War II years.

At the same time as these factors are responsible for the "loosening up" of policy toward the Sámi languages, attention must also be given to the attitudes among Norwegian elites that prevented a full policy reversal. That is, when push came to shove, even though Norwegian political elites were now cautiously promoting the rights of Sámi speakers, there existed certain ideological and policy-oriented goals that prevented Sámi speakers from immediately and fully being given the same linguistic rights as all other Norwegians.

The Second World War and Norwegian Political Culture

Darnel and Hoëm point out that Norwegian political elites experienced a "remarkable shift" in attitude towards the Sámi shortly after World

War II. That decades of Norwegianization policies were to be slowly undone without pressure from the affected groups in society is remarkable. Yet, the role of the war in this change of perspective is rather straightforward and influenced the policy shift in one key manner. Primarily, the Second World War provided Norwegian elites with an empirical test for their fears about the alleged lack of national loyalty on the part of the Sámi. Much of the foundation for the repression of the Sámi in the first half of the twentieth century rests in the elite perception that the northern border area was not fully secure and that the combination of nomadic people and immigrant populations could provide ample fodder for foreign interventionist efforts. Opportunities certainly abounded during the occupation for the Sámi to display a "lack of loyalty" to the Norwegian government in exile, but there is no evidence that such was the case. Rather, to the extent that the Sámi did engage in treasonous activity, it was not systemic and therefore did differ from the scope of collaborationist efforts found in the Norwegian population.[43] As Jahr and Trudgill observe, World War II was a time when "Norwegians had proven themselves to be equally good or equally bad national patriots during the occupation."[44]

Closely related to this is Katzenstein's discussion of Austria's own wartime experience and the role of *Angstgemeinschaft* after the war.[45] Though used as part of an argument to explain the rise of corporatist social policy, there does seem to be an appropriate linkage here. Katzenstein notes that Austria's post-war corporatism was not built on the existence of a pre-war consensus, but rather through the shared fear of ever having to experience traumatic national upheavals again, such as civil war and foreign occupation. In the Norwegian case though, and as witnessed by the broad ideological consensus toward the rebuilding process and the establishment of the modern welfare state, *Angstgemeinschaft* would appear to have produced a realization that earlier claims of "Norwegian nationhood" associated with certain groupings (e.g., Bokmål or Nynorsk speakers) were not only counterproductive, but that they also had the potential to produce the most awful of consequences.[46]

Changes in the International Political Environment

The other main factor in the shift of Sámi language policies stems from the way in which the international political environment was changing immediately after the war and into the following decades.

New ideas on minority rights came into existence, both independently and as we have seen, as a result of World War II. Additionally,
increased Norwegian involvement in international bodies and treaties
frequently required that Norway alter its domestic policies so as to be
in line with international regulations. At the same time, increasing
Nordic cooperation on the Sámi issue is for our purposes a distinct
subset of the increased international cooperation. Here, the emphasis
is less on the legal need to alter policies and more on the way in
which Norway followed the lead of its Finnish and Swedish neighbors
in terms of language policy toward the Sámi.

Ole Henrik Magga, the first president of the Norwegian Sámi
Parliament, suggests that the shift can be traced to the decades immediately preceding the war, when new ideas on minority rights were
being aired in such arenas as the League of Nations, and that the war
may have simply delayed them from being adopted in Norway.[47] Norway had certainly engaged in lip service by advocating minority rights
in the League of Nations prior to the war, despite its extensive repression of the Sámi and Kven.[48] However, there is evidence that as the
1930s drew to a close, this lip service was in the process of being
transformed into concrete policy changes and that the Department of
Church Affairs and Education had intended to implement some measure of Sámi language reforms in the school system, only to be delayed by the outbreak of war.[49] In the main government report on
Sámi culture and education, Niemi concurs with this "time-lag" view
of a change in minority policy and also points to pre-war international
settings such as the League of Nations for the new ideas that would
slowly come to dominate following the war.[50] In fact, if one accepts
that the groundwork for the shift is established prior to the war, then
the extensive Norwegian involvement in the United Nations' Universal Declaration on Human Rights is merely fitting evidence that the
Norwegians were in keeping with the new global line on minorities.[51]

Additionally, it is this strong involvement with the UN that brings
us to the second of our international factors, the increasing role of
Norway in terms of international bodies and treaties. In a 1984 Norwegian Justice Department report, the legal status of the Sámi in
Norway was reviewed and an embarrassing admission in terms of the
past was made. Namely, the report conceded that regardless of the
rationale that previous governments had used to justify Norwegian-

ization, the simple truth was that the policy had been in sharp contradiction to guidelines for the treatment of minorities as established
by the League of Nations.[52] The authors point to the shift in international attitude toward minority rights following the war and note that
the new international norm was the idea of certain basic and equal
rights for all citizens. Thus, while they only go so far as to suggest that
Norway responded to the change in the post-war international environment regarding minorities, I maintain that it is the large role of a
small state in post-war international bodies that partially necessitates
the shift in policies. From its involvement in the UN Universal Declaration on Human Rights, Norway was frequently in the spotlight at
the UN, not on questions of the Cold War, but rather on humanitar-
ian issues such as refugee questions, racial conflicts, and opposition to
colonial rule in Southwest Africa. As Helge Pharo notes, starting with
its involvement at the UN, Norway was required to take a stance on
matters that may have seemed quite peripheral for a small state in
northwestern Europe. However, while peripheral in terms of geography, these international questions of social policy had domestic par-
allels, and credibility and leadership could not be established on these
questions until similar changes were made at home.[53]

But if general involvement in international institutions was
influencing the Norwegian approach to minorities, how did the Nordic arena affect the changes in policy? The answer appears to be that
the relationship between Norway and its eastern Nordic neighbors
had been transformed by the war. Norway's membership in NATO
afforded it sufficient confidence in terms of its border relationship
with Finland, and the latent hostility that existed with Sweden after
the dissolution of the union and throughout the first few decades of
the twentieth century had fully dissipated. Thus, Sweden and Finland
were no longer potential adversaries on the Sámi question, but rather
became valuable external resources for the Norwegian government to
draw upon as it tried to fashion a new approach that was in keeping
with post war attitudes.

There are two examples that demonstrate the way in which
Norwegian policy toward the Sámi languages in the immediate post-
war period was influenced by contacts with Sweden and Finland.
First, one of the immediate post-war tasks of the Norwegian government was to revamp the nation's education policy. Einar Boyesen, the

chair of the parliamentary committee charged with this task, made a trip to Sweden in early 1947 to visit Swedish "nomad" schools and to gain an understanding of how Swedish authorities were coping with the Sámi. Information obtained on this trip was used as a starting point for meetings in the north of Norway among the relevant experts that would eventually lead to a parliamentary subcommittee dealing with Sámi language and education questions. Following these meetings, Boyesen proposed that Norwegian and Swedish authorities cooperate to find common solutions to the "Sámi questions."[54]

As we have seen earlier in this chapter, the 1948 parliamentary committee resulted in piecemeal suggestions for changes in language policy toward the Sámi. More comprehensive suggestions at change in the language policy came from the 1956 Sámi Committee. In fact, Norwegian government documents confirm that two events in 1951 influenced both the timing and scope of this committee. In the official history of Norwegian policy toward the Sámi, Niemi observes that a more comprehensive approach was made necessary by the Finnish parliament's own detailed report on Sámi relations and by an international conference in northern Sweden that stressed a pan-Nordic perspective to dealing with Sámi related questions.[55] That Nordic cooperation was a factor in the new approach should not be of surprise. The post-war period, particularly with the new international emphasis on the bipolar order, saw the Nordic states attempting to mark their identity through the creation of several institutions that allowed for the cooperation and sharing of resources on the full range of policy areas. Thus, in some senses, whereas Sámi language policy had once been conceived as a tool in marking out a national identity separate from that of other Nordic states, it was now transformed into one of many issues that the Nordic states cooperated on to share material and intellectual resources. This joint approach continues to be the case, as in the mid-1980s, the Norwegian government began work on a Sámi language law and drew heavily on the policies already adopted in Sweden and Finland.[56]

The Limits of Promotion

None of the preceding is to suggest that Norwegian elites simply followed the lead of other nations or international opinion without any autonomy. Scholars of the Sámi question have made much of the fact that while Norwegian elites did shift their thinking on the language question in the 1940s and 1950s, it was not a fully decisive shift. Moreover, it seemed to be limited to moves that were less than comprehensive. Certainly one of the better examples of the limits of change on the part of the Norwegian government was its refusal to ratify the 1957 ILO Convention No. 107.

ILO-107 required that signatory nations would guarantee, among other things, the language and property rights of indigenous peoples. States were expected to honor this guarantee through "respect and promotion" of the relevant resources. While Norway had signed other international agreements dealing with minority issues, to sign ILO-107 would require that Norway acknowledge the Sámi as an indigenous group and afford it special treatment. The Norwegian representative at the ILO conference signed the treaty, but the government denied that any such indigenous groupings existed in Norway and the issue was put on ice for several decades.[57]

How can one explain that the Norwegian government was quite willing to begin loosening up Sámi language policy through the printing of Sámi texts and the reintroduction of the language into the classrooms, but that it would quite stridently deny that any indigenous peoples existed within its own borders? Specifically, what factor limited the willingness of DNA to promote the Sámi languages and other related cultural traits? To answer that, attention needs to be focused on the ideology of Scandinavian social democracy in the effort literally to rebuild Norwegian society following the Second World War.

Esping-Andersen observed that the cornerstones of Scandinavian social democracy's welfare policy are a universalization of benefits, in which all individuals and groups in society are eligible to take advantage of benefits provided by social welfare policy; that benefits should "immunize" workers from market forces; and that social democratic welfare policy should further equality. In noting the interrelation between these three elements, Esping-Andersen states that, "The political risk for a social democratic welfare state is considerable. If social services are allowed to follow occupational or other social demarcations, broader loyalties are readily sacrificed at the expense of narrower corporate identities."[58] Of course, such social demarcations are precisely what the Sámi people were seeking in their effort to be recognized as an indigenous people, meriting special benefits different from those received by all other groups in Norwegian society.

Additionally though, the promotion of Sámi culture was limited by post-war Norwegian policies that by and large sought to consolidate economic and administrative resources into a smaller number of largely urban settings. In terms of ethnic Norwegians, this process brought about resentment from Nynorsk activists in the affected areas, as they lost the institutional bases that would maintain the percent of the population that used Nynorsk. In terms of the Sámi, this process began far earlier, with the reconstruction of the north following the scorched earth policy of the retreating Nazis.[59] While the overall intention of centralization may have been to streamline administration and to better guarantee that an equality of services was provided, the merging of smaller Sámi municipalities into larger surrounding urban and Norwegian ones inevitably diluted the independence of Sámi culture.

As Olsson and Lewis observe, Scandinavian social welfare policy offered the Sámi the opportunity to participate in the same standard of living and culture enjoyed by the dominant ethnic groups. However, this welfare policy was focused on equality, egalitarianism, and promoting the social "wholeness" of the nation. Claims put forth by the Sámi to have their cultural autonomy recognized and to receive special benefits as a result of this cultural difference were not easily consistent with the goals of the modern Scandinavian welfare state.[60]

Thus for the Sámi, the consequence of the increasingly centralized welfare-state was that while recognition of past injustices was now present, they were to be rectified through a combination of small-scale changes in language policy and the accelerated integration into the mainstream Norwegian culture. In terms of language policy, an ambiguous dual standard was arrived at in terms of the Sámi languages. To fulfill the new prevailing attitude towards the Sámi as minorities, various educational policies were implemented that did permit the increased use of Sámi languages in educational settings. However, the overarching goal of centralization required that there still be an emphasis on Norwegian as the language of economic opportunity. Thus, any calls for the recognition of the Sámi as indigenous peoples with full control over their own linguistic fate were rejected as being out of line with this goal.

A NOTE ON THE ROLE OF SÁMI PRESSURE GROUPS

Prior to concluding, it is necessary to raise an additional question. Could Sámi pressure groups, both language and otherwise, have been responsible for the language policies in the more recent period of promotion? Advocates of an interest group approach would have a difficult time substantiating their case in the period of Norwegianization. There are sufficient historical accounts to suggest that some level of Sámi activism did occur in this period in an effort to sway Norwegian elites away from the repressive linguistic policies, though by all accounts, these groups and efforts had no impact whatsoever.

Among the failed efforts during the period of Norwegianization, we find the following: The establishment of Sámi language newspapers in northern Norway that ran frequent editorials calling for equal rights to be given to the Norwegian Sámi; repeated efforts by Southern Sámi activists to obtain separate Sámi schools; and attempts at founding a national Sámi organization that would have served to provide a common front against the Norwegianization activities. One interesting case of attempted Sámi pressure was the election of Sámi Isak Saba to the Norwegian Parliament for the period 1906–1912 on a pro-Sámi platform. However, despite Saba's attempt to make something of his pro-Sámi election platform, the result was that he faced strong opposition both at the local level and from the Norwegian state bureaucracy. Additionally, in the Norwegian Parliament, he was fully isolated from all other members to the point where he did not set forth any proposals for the reduction of Norwegianization policies.[61]

The shift to promotion of the Sámi language after World War II would appear to be a bit more contentious in terms of an interest group argument. Nevertheless, an interest group argument also falls short here for a number of reasons. While Sámi activity did emerge in this period, such as the Sámi Council for Finnmark in 1953, these small groups of Sámi elites not only had difficulties in establishing any type of common agenda for political action, but also did not do so until the discussion around the 1948 Education Reform Committee was well under way. It appears that the sole Sámi pressure group active at this time was limited to questions of reindeer herding and did not have an active interest in the reshaping of educational policy. Thus, it is fair to state that this initial shift came about solely as a result of Norwegian elite activities and without any systematic, discernible, or broad input from Sámi pressure groups. Similarly, as Sámi organizations and local pressure groups grew in the 1960s, their work was eased considerably by the fact that frequently their demands had already received official support from the Norwegian Parliament.[62]

The point that Sámi "pressure" activities in the post-war era have been largely dependent on windows of opportunity created by Norwegian elites is made quite clearly by Paine. He notes that in the first decades after the war, non-Sámi (i.e., Norwegian elites) were not only the spokespeople for increased Sámi rights, but they were also the policy architects of these changes.[63] Quite simply, the legacy of Norwegianization, which destroyed the organizational base of the Sámi in the pre-war era, meant that they did not have the ability to bring about the shift in language policy on their own. It is only after Norwegian elites began to reshape language policies in consultation with other Nordic states and provide organizational resources to the Sámi that we see the emergence of Sámi pressure groups who have the ability to expand on the promotion/reform work started by a handful of Norwegian elites in the 1940s and 1950s.

A final note is necessary regarding the Alta-Kautokeino Hydroelectric Conflict of 1979–1981. While the controversy surrounding Alta directly resulted in Sámi hunger strikes in the center of Oslo that were in opposition to plans to dam the Alta river in northern Norway, the end result had ramifications that touched all areas of Sámi politics, including those of language policy. While the Sámi activists lost the immediate battle to prevent the construction project, it is generally felt that they won a much larger victory in terms of "forcing" the government to establish the Sámi Rights Committee, which would be instrumental in gaining autonomy for the Sámi in a number of policy areas, including that of language. It is certainly fair to say that this is an instance where crisis produced opportunity and change, but did it produce change that was in opposition to the overall orientation of the Norwegian government to the Sámi?

The answer, as is often the case, depends on how one wishes to define influence. If one is concerned about the timing of the change, then there is little doubt that the activities of the Sámi activists in the Alta controversy are directly responsible for changes in Norwegian Sámi policy that began in the 1980s. Sámi activists pursued a clever strategy whereby their hunger strike was conducted in Oslo, easily visible not only to everyday Norwegians, but also to the Oslo representatives of the international broadcast media.[64] Both the world and Norway were made aware of claims of unjust treatment by the "fourth-world" inhabitants of northern Norway.

However, if the question is one of whether Alta produced a change in the policy orientation of Norwegian elites that was either drastic or forced them to sacrifice other political goals, then the answer is far less certain. As already stated, the small group of Sámi activists failed in their immediate goal to halt the construction, as after a series of stops and starts in which both sides were able to temporarily save face, the government ultimately prevailed over the Sámi activists and the dam was built. But, as is easily seen in regards to the larger victory of the Sámi Rights Committee, the end result was a very limited Sámi autonomy, for Norwegian elites had the initial right to appoint the relevant "experts and representatives" to the committee. As such, Thuen correctly notes that the Norwegian government was able to regain control over the situation after the immediate crisis had passed. Further, while the Norwegian government accepted the Sámi proposal of establishing a Sámi Parliament, it has quite limited control over Sámi affairs and is ultimately dependent on the approval of the Norwegian state.

Ultimately, the crisis of Alta, often portrayed as a clear-cut victory for Sámi pressure groups, may have been something quite different. Norwegian elites were able to respond to the outrage of a small group of counterelites, while not ceding any broad control over Sámi affairs and all the while making sure that Sámi activists did not deter them from their main objective of increased economic development. Thus, even in the more recent years of the promotion phase, and even in its more dramatic events, one can see that the Norwegian government has been able to resist pressure or to cleverly respond to it such that control is ultimately maintained.

CONCLUSION

In this chapter, I have explored the historical development of Sámi language policies in Norway and shown how these policies have their roots in the Norwegian elite desire to construct a national identity based around a purely Norwegian ethnicity and language. Given this, the culture and language of the Sámi people were not only excluded from the nation-building project, but also Norwegian elites took extreme measures to eliminate symbols of the Sámi people. Additional reasons were shown to contribute to the policies of Norwegianization. These include the perceived threat that the Sámi people posed to the security of the northern Norwegian borders, and the prevailing attitudes among Europeans toward questions of minority rights.

Most critical in the establishment of the post-war promotion phase has been the experience of World War II. The war, much as it did for other European nations, reshaped the idea of national community, such that linking claims on patriotic values to various societal groups no longer seemed particularly relevant. As well, the war also demonstrated that the fears Norwegian elites had about Sámi loyalty towards the nation were clearly unjustified. Also of importance was the change in international thinking towards ethnic minorities. This shift has some roots in the pre-World War II years, but was greatly strengthened by the wartime experience itself. Finally, successive post-war Norwegian governments developed closer ties with their Nordic neighbors on a number of issues, including the Sámi language question, which allowed them to share in the construction of possible solutions.

The post-war period of promotion was not a blank check for Sámi language activists, as DNA governments walked an uneasy and ambiguous line between enhancing the rights of ethnic linguistic minorities and promoting the economic centralization of the nation through the expansion and modernization of the Norwegian welfare state. Norwegian elites were also able to maintain control over the Sámi language question throughout the post-war period of promotion, having initiated the debates and the first round of reforms well prior to the establishment of post-war Sámi pressure groups. In more recent times, events show that Norwegian elites have still been able to limit the extent to which Sámi activities have forced Norwegian governments to deviate from their key goal of increased economic development.

Chapter 5

Norway Compared: The Case of Belgian Language Politics

INTRODUCTION

The previous chapters have demonstrated that Norwegian language policy has not been the result of interest group mobilization. Rather, I have shown that policies toward the written Norwegian languages are best accounted for by the desire of political elites to manipulate linguistic identities as they sought to achieve other political goals. Additionally, I have shown how Norwegian policy towards the Sámi languages was largely motivated by shifting concerns among Norwegian elites about the extent to which Sámi languages posed a threat to the establishment and maintenance of a Norwegian identity.

In this chapter, I present a contrast to the Norwegian case and investigate the development of language policies in Belgium. I argue that Belgian language policies do not primarily reflect the desires of political elites. I will show that the salience of language in Belgium is the result of ethnoregional groups who have employed language as a symbol in their efforts to gain increased amounts of economic and political power.

Thus, I argue that the Belgian case and that of the Norwegian Sámi are different in at least one key regard. In the case of the Sámi, pressure on Norwegian elites was not the determining factor in bringing about an increased official recognition for the Sámi languages. On the other hand, I argue that ethnoregional groups within Belgium have had more success in their efforts to attain linguistic rights. In comparison to their Sámi counterpart, I would maintain that the success of ethnoregional groups within Belgium can largely be attributed to questions of ethnic-group size and changes in the electoral rules. As will be shown in this chapter, the sheer number of Flemings, once enfranchised, made them a force that political elites had no choice but to acknowledge if they wished to be successful in the newly expanded electoral arena. Enfranchisement will also be shown to have produced another factor that forced Belgian elites to respond to ethnolinguistic demands. Specifically, the increase in the franchise led entrepreneurs within the ethnic groups to establish ethnic-based political parties that sought to challenge the role of the traditional parties in the electoral arena. In an effort to stave off the electoral prospects of these ethnic-based parties, the traditional Belgian parties adopted many of the demands from the ethnic-based parties, thus depriving them of their distinguishing characteristic.

The Belgian case also differs from that of the Norwegian language conflict in a number of respects. First, whereas the conflict between the two standards of written Norwegian takes place within the confines of the same ethnic group, the Belgian language conflict involves two distinct ethnic groups, the Flemings and Walloons. Additionally, while Nynorsk has consistently been employed by only a minority of Norwegians, the Flemings and Walloons have had rough numerical parity since the nineteenth century.[1]

Perhaps the key difference between the Norwegian and the Belgian language conflict has to do with the difference in whether or not language was complementary to the political goals that elites in each nation were attempting to attain. As I have shown in Norway, elites viewed language as a tool that was symbolically important and that could be drawn upon and emphasized as they sought to engage in a number of political projects. However, as I will show in the case of Belgium, language presented elites with no such opportunity throughout much of the past 150 years. Instead, language was an issue that cut across the traditional lines of cleavage that centered around religion and ideology.

Thus, for much of modern Belgium's history, language has only been seen as a political threat by Belgian elites. The traditional response by Belgian elites to the introduction of the language issue has been to either attempt to ignore it or to offer piecemeal reforms. By the 1960s, this strategy had clearly failed. Faced with the realization that ethnoregional demands needed to be seriously dealt with, Belgian elites responded with a series of creative measures that allowed them to substantively deal with the language issue, while at the same time maintaining control over the party system.

A short exploration of the Belgian case will reveal that Belgian political elites have sought to craft language and related ethnoregional policies so as to maintain their controlling position in the party system. That is, Belgian elites did not initialize the placement of language on the political agenda, but merely sought to ensure that this new dimension of cleavage did not excessively damage their control of the party system.

HISTORICAL BACKGROUND IN THE BELGIAN CASE

If for political scientists, Norway constitutes a little-known example of language conflict, then Belgium quite certainly figures as the complete opposite. From the late 1960s to the present, the conflict between the Flemish-speaking north and Wallonia has resulted in a dramatic reshaping of Belgian political institutions. Decisions concerning most "regional" issues are no longer made at the central government level, but instead at the regional level. The institutional effects of this language conflict have not just been limited to governing institutions. The "traditional" Belgian political parties—Catholic, Socialist and Liberal—have also been affected by the continued presence of the language question on the political agenda. In the late 1960s and early 1970s, each of the major parties split into two smaller parties, one to represent Flemish-speakers and one to represent the Walloons. Finally, in the past thirty years, the Belgian party system has witnessed the rise and subsequent decline of ethnonationalist parties that sought to alter the ethnolinguistic policies of the traditional parties.

Historically, the language border in Belgium runs roughly along a straight line from Aachen to Calais, with Flemish/Dutch dialects taking precedence north of that line and Walloon-related dialects dominating south of the line.[2] Ethnolinguistic identity was not an initial factor among the Flemings and Walloons when the Belgian state first emerged from its forced union with the Netherlands in the 1830s. As a number of scholars have observed, to the extent there was group identity in the new Belgium, such identity was only found at the national level.[3] For several decades prior to independence, Belgium was a province first of France and then of the Netherlands. Belgian nationalism was partially a result of rule from the Netherlands. During this period, Belgian elites opposed the imposition of the new Dutch constitution on Belgium and the formal linkage between Belgian schools and the Dutch state. This opposition eventually led to the Belgian revolution of 1830. Quite simply, the Belgian revolution of 1830 was not the result of any internal conflict between Flemings and Walloons, but rather represented the desire of the southern half of the Dutch empire (Belgium) to break free of the northern half, which was seen as a foreign ruler.

The two ethnolinguistic regions also possessed different resource advantages that had great implications for their fortunes during Belgium's industrialization. Prior to independence, the Flemish portion of the nation had importance in the international trade arena in terms of linen production. Flanders' linen sector's advantage over its chief competitor, the British, derived from the significantly lower wages, generally half of that paid to the British workforce. However, northern Belgium declined as an economic force in the nineteenth century as cheaper prices from other nations, particularly in the agricultural arena, made it less competitive.[4] Contrasted to the north, Wallonia displayed great economic growth in the mid- and late nineteenth century, as it developed industries in mining, metal working, arms, and glass.[5] The Flemish portion of the nation was further disadvantaged in comparison to the south in the mid-nineteenth century when it was struck by a potato famine. The central government's response to this was to provide relief to the region, but not any alteration in investment that might have shifted the north away from a declining agricultural sector.[6]

During the first decades of an independent Belgium, language had hardly developed sufficient weight among Belgian elites to constitute a divisive or even defining issue. Whereas Norwegian elites were divided early on by language and political ideology, elites in Belgium in 1830 were solidly behind the sole use of the French language as the new official standard. According to Zolberg, the heavily pro-French nature of Belgian elites could be explained by two factors. The anti-Dutch nature of the Belgian revolution had unified the Belgians and with it opposition to the Dutch language. But, more importantly, the desire to see the French language as the sole language of the state stemmed from the simple reality that it had been the common language of Belgian elites for several decades, particularly as a result of French rule.[7]

The near universal use of French by the Belgian elites contrasted with the language usage patterns of the Belgian population as a whole. As Lorwin notes, within Flanders, the mass of peasants, workers and the lower-middle classes employed the various, and often mutually incomprehensible, Flemish dialects as their chief tongue.[8] Walloons for that matter, while using a series of dialects that were related to the French standard, did not use French per se and were viewed by the French as speaking an "abominable patois."[9]

As Stengers observes, the fact that the Flemish elite already used French in commerce, education, and in the legal system suggested that they had a vested interest in the perpetuation of French as the sole official language. Thus, he points out that despite their ethnic identity, any support for Flemish-based linguistic nationalism from the Flemish elite would not be forthcoming in the period that immediately coincided with the Belgian revolution.[10] The support for the French language as the sole Belgian standard was also mirrored in the new Belgian parliament, where despite the fact that the new constitution stated that "the use of language shall be optional," a decree was issued stating that French was the only official Belgian language.

FROM NONISSUE TO A NONTHREATENING ISSUE

Key in the transformation of language to a political issue was the role of industrialization in Belgium. According to Huyse, industrialization influenced the emergence of language as a salient political issue in the mid- and late nineteenth century in two manners. First, industrialization created a tertiary sector of management positions that had the potential to be filled by those who sought to move up the economic ladder. Access to the new management positions created under industrialization was dependent upon "manipulating symbolic rather than physical objects."[11] Therefore, with French as the official language, those who were not elites and used their everyday Flemish dialect as the language of communication were greatly disadvantaged as they looked to their chances to move into this new economic class. Second, and as noted earlier, the pace of industrialization played an important factor. Flanders received far less investment than did

Wallonia and was generally relegated to a backwards position that was dependent upon a declining agricultural sector. Thus, the dependence on agriculture and related "household" economies meant that survival was insured by keeping the Flemish youth close to the home and denying them the educational opportunities necessary to eventually move up the economic and class ladder.

The emergence of a Flemish movement in the 1830s and 1840s follows the pattern well-known from Anderson's *Imagined Communities*, already discussed in relation to the Norwegian case. Just as in Norway, the Belgian counterelites that came to rally behind the idea of promoting a language of low social status were precisely those groups that had the most to gain from seeing the language obtain a more privileged societal footing. In terms of the Flemish dialects, those who attempted to draw attention to the importance of using Flemish in Belgian society were by and large the middle-class and the intelligentsia.[12] Changes in the laws requiring the use of French as the sole official standard at higher levels of education and in government service would allow these Flemish groups to access greater societal and economic capital without having to suffer the costs of forced bilingualism. Starting with a petition to the Belgian parliament that was signed by 30,000 people in 1840, the Flemish movement demanded specifically "the use of Dutch in the conduct of official affairs in the Flemish provinces and in correspondence between the central government and the Flemish provinces, the establishment of a Flemish academy, and the elevation of Dutch to a position equal to that of French at the University of Ghent."[13]

However, the initial demands put forth by the Flemish movement, derisively known as the *Flamingants* by the French-speaking elites, can be summed up as centering around the desire to see official status extended to the Flemish language in the Flemish provinces. Additionally, in seeking the use of Flemish between the central government and Flemish provinces, the movement attempted to shift some of the burden for bilingualism to elites at the political center.

As stated in the introduction to this chapter, my contention is that language has proved to be less of an overall political opportunity to Belgian elites than it has been to their Norwegian counterparts. The initial demands put forth by the Flemish movement offer part of the answer as to why Flemish was understandably less suitable as a candidate for political opportunism in the Belgian case than it was in Norway. In the Norwegian case, language first emerged onto the political landscape as a symbol that could be linked to a mythical national and uniquely Norwegian past that predated the centuries long occupation by Denmark. While Nynorsk may have largely stemmed from one region of Norway, its adoption as a political symbol was intended to be such that all ethnic Norwegians could look to it as an expression of their nationhood.

In Belgium, the symbol of language was promoted by a regionally based ethnic group that was seeking official advancement for the Flemish language on the subnational level. Confined by its own advocates to a regional arena, Flemish as a regional political issue stood in sharp contrast to the efforts of Catholics and Liberals who were seeking to build parties with national appeal. Whereas Norway's Liberals had been able to integrate limited support for Nynorsk into a overall platform that portrayed them as the standard-bearers of liberalism and an independent Norway, no such natural fit existed between the Flemish language and either the Catholics or the Liberals. Catholics were wary towards the official advancement of Flemish out of fear that its membership in the Germanic family of languages would facilitate the spread of the Protestant Church in the northern counties.[14] At the same time, the largest bloc of Belgian Catholics was located in the Flemish north.

As for the Liberals, while individual members of the Liberal party could be found in the Flemish movement, the party as a whole championed the independence and sovereignty of the Belgian state. Promotion of a newly independent state was at odds with the subnational demands of the Flemish movement, particularly when the language in question had historical attachment to the decades of Dutch rule. Socialists too had their reason for initial distance from the Flemish question. The formation of the Belgian Socialist party in 1885 was largely directed at capturing the vote of the growing working class in the increasingly industrialized and French-speaking Wallonia.

Finally, there was an electoral reality relevant to each of these traditional parties, but particularly to the Catholics and the Liberals. In 1884, only 2 percent of the Belgian population had the vote, with the overwhelming majority of those who were enfranchised coming from elite classes and therefore using French. Basing electoral appeals on the need to increase the official space for Flemish simply did not make electoral sense when the targeted audience had little to gain from the advance of Flemish.[15]

Yet, despite the fact that the three major parties each had reasons for not promoting the demands of the Flemish language movement, the period from 1873 to 1898 witnessed a series of language laws passed by the Belgian parliament that gave certain advances to the Flemish language. This apparent contradiction is easily reconciled when one takes into account that the laws did not require significant changes in the linguistic behavior of the overwhelmingly French elites. This is not to argue that the first round of Belgian language laws were simply for show. Far from being merely symbolic in effect, the laws did in fact grant Flemish a foothold in official life. Among these were an 1873 law that called for the use of Flemish in criminal trials held in Flemish counties unless the defendant requested that the trial be held in French. Also, an 1876 law allowed for degrees to be awarded in Flemish literature from the University of Ghent. An 1878 law required that "notices and communications" aimed at the general public be either bilingual or in Dutch. An 1883 law mandated that Dutch be used in Flemish public secondary schools; and an 1898 law required that all laws adopted by the Belgian parliament be published in both French and Dutch.[16]

In looking at this first round of policies as a whole, one notes that while they were largely in keeping with the demands of the early Flemish movement, they also did not have any impact outside of the Flemish counties. Dutch-speakers in the North were being given limited rights to use their language in official settings, but the rights of Walloons and French-speaking elites were not being challenged in any meaningful way. Moreover, even with these laws being adopted, they carried with them broad protection for French-speakers, such as allowing for judges to communicate amongst themselves in French and allowing for separate secondary school classes to be organized for students who could not understand Dutch. Finally, even in the Flemish north, only 20 percent of Belgian youth attended public secondary schools. The remainder attended private Catholic schools, which were exempt in the Flemish counties from having to provide instruction in Dutch.[17] Given the noncontroversial and limited nature of these first language laws, they were not politically dangerous steps for Belgian political elites to take. Belgian language laws that had an influence on the entire nation would have to wait until the electorate had been expanded to include the majority Flemish community.

MASS ENFRANCHISEMENT AND ITS EFFECT ON THE LANGUAGE QUESTION

Changes in enfranchisement came in 1893 when the vote was expanded to provide for universal manhood suffrage, although with plural voting. Under the new constitutional provisions, all males over the age of twenty-five were eligible to vote. Additional votes were allocated to those who were over thirty-five, the head of households, property owners, and those with certain educational credentials. No one person was to be allowed more than three votes.[18] The dramatic recasting of the franchise, such that inhabitants of the Flemish provinces now comprised a significantly larger share of the Belgian electorate, was not lost on the traditional political parties. Recognizing that a numerical majority could not be obtained by simply relying on the Walloon industrial class, the Socialist Party expanded its efforts to attract new voters by reaching out to Flemish workers in the North.[19]

While the Socialists centered their appeal to Flemish workers around class issues, the Catholics looked to language as a way of defending their share of the Flemish vote. With a far stronger base in the North than that of the Socialists, the Catholics partially cast off earlier fears about the link between the Flemish language and Protestantism. Looking to block the advances of the Socialists into the Flemish counties, northern Catholics that were not among the party's hierarchy reached out to Flemish voters via the language issue and sought to integrate certain Flemish demands into their party profile.[20]

The period following this expansion of the electorate also brought the first language-related change in Belgium's constitution. Comparable to Norway's largely symbolic language equality law, the new constitutional stance toward language declared that both Dutch/Flemish and French were the official languages of Belgium. Of course, such a declaration did not require any specific changes in the linguistic behavior of the French-speaking elites or the Walloons. However, this law set the formal groundwork for much of the subsequent legislation that would increase the status of Dutch.

The timing of this constitutional change, following the expansion of the electorate, is significant. As early as the 1860s, a Flemish member of parliament had proposed a modification in the constitution that would have granted Dutch/Flemish status alongside French. A similar modification was also proposed during the discussions that eventually led to universal male suffrage. However, in granting the constitutional change after the expansion of the electorate, the Belgian parties, and particularly the Catholics, were simply witness to the writing on the wall. If definitive proof was needed that the Catholics had their primary electoral audience in the north, it came in the next parliamentary election. The 1894 election saw the Catholics send an overwhelming 114 members to the 162-seat parliament.[21] This landslide win was directly attributed to the fact that the Flemish provinces had thrown their support behind the Catholics, while the Liberals and the Socialists wound up dividing the Walloon counties. Thus, the Flemish electorate had demonstrated that they had political clout on two related fronts. On one front, their sheer size in the electoral mix meant that they had the power to alter national election outcomes. On another front, their heavily pro-Catholic orientation was a trait that the Catholic Party wished to make use of in future elections cycles. Adopting one of the more radical Flemish demands, that of making Flemish an official national language, was a relatively low-risk way of providing a symbolic benefit to this emerging political force. For Catholics, it signaled that they were quite aware who was sending them to parliament. For the support that came from other parties, it implied the recognition that Belgian politics could no longer be waged only with the interests of the French-speaking minority in mind.

The influence of the Flemish majority was further strengthened in 1919 when the one-person, one-vote principle was introduced. The upper-class had been the primary beneficiary of the multiple vote system. With the removal of this automatic advantage at the ballot box, the French-speaking elite of the Belgian nation now had to confront the full political force of both the Flemish community and the Belgian working class.[22]

One immediate legislative response to this change in the composition of the electorate was the decision to make Dutch/Flemish the official language of the northern counties and French/Walloon the official standard in the south. Municipalities where a majority of those used a different standard than that of the region were free to designate their own language as the official choice for administration. However, this measure was largely symbolic in nature given that the Belgian legislature added no method of enforcement or sanctions for violation.[23]

The change in electoral laws opened the door for the growth of small Flemish nationalist parties. These parties by and large were born from the Flemish backlash against seeing members of their ranks prosecuted for collaboration with the Germans during World War I. While not questioning the actual collaboration, the active participation of Walloon elites in this process led many Flemish activists to feel that the trials were in fact a general cultural assault on the Flemish people.

Divided largely into two groups, the Minimalists and the Maximalists, these Flemish nationalists saw eye-to-eye on the question of extending additional linguistic rights to the North. However, they differed substantially on the question of the future of Belgium as a whole. The Maximalists were also calling for the partitioning of the Belgian state along linguistic lines.[24] An additional difference was that the Minimalist groups did not directly opt for the electoral arena. Rather, it was the Maximalists who first began fielding candidates for the Belgian lower house in 1919.

Table 5.1 shows the steady growth of these small parties in their first decade. As the 1919 and 1921 election cycles coincide with the introduction of "one-person one-vote," they can be used as a benchmark to show how Flemish nationalist support more than doubled in terms of votes and members elected to the lower house in the election cycles that followed this shift in the franchise.

Mughan notes that the response of the traditional parties, who feared the sudden growth of a linguistic cleavage that was at odds with

Table 5.1
Electoral Support for Flemish Maximalist Parties, 1919–1929

Year	Number of Votes	MP's Elected
1919	57,422	5
1921	58,769	4
1925	84,143	6
1929	132,962	11

Source: Shepard B. Clough, A History of the Flemish Movement in Belgium, (New York: Octagon Books, 1968). pp. 229–230.

their national party organizations, responded by preempting the demands of the Flemish nationalists. Thus, in 1932, the major parties introduced two major laws that redefined the official linguistic stature of Belgium.[25] Primarily, these laws recast language usage in Belgium such that it was no longer a matter of personal choice, but a matter of the region in which one lived. In terms of both the government administration and the educational system, there was to be "complete regional administrative unilingualism, reorganization of the central administration in accordance with the country's linguistic duality, equal respect for the national languages, and obligatory bilingualism of public officials in Brussels."[26]

Given that these new laws were designed to halt the progress of the Flemish movement and prevent the language conflict from having a negative impact on the electoral fortunes of the traditional parties, one has to wonder why the language question not only persisted in the coming decades, but why it continued to grow dramatically in terms of intensity. Huyse refers to these new laws as "legal fictions," claiming that once again, because of the lack of specific sanctions for those who chose to violate them, they were largely symbolic in nature.[27] Mughan points out that these laws were "badly written" and that the Flemish movement did not have the strength to enforce them in the more Francophone urban areas where they were intended to have made a difference.[28] However, one additional language related measure adopted in 1932, calling for a national language census to be taken every ten years, would not be implemented until the immediate post-war era. As we will see in the following, while all components of the 1932 language laws were designed to defuse the potential destabilizing effects of language on the power of the traditional parties, the first (and only!) language census would contribute to an outcome that was just the opposite.

THE INCREASED SALIENCE OF LANGUAGE
IN THE POST-WAR YEARS

It is tempting to argue that the persistence of the language issue on the political agenda is a consequence of weak and unenforceable language laws, but such an account does not consider the shifting demographic and economic fortunes within the two regions in the post-war era. The presence of language on the political agenda is a result of both the 1947 language census and the strong economic decline of the Walloon counties resulting from shifting patterns of investment. Whereas earlier language demands had been divorced from questions of regional economic policy, calls for regional autonomy in determining cultural and economic policies placed increasing strains on the party system in the post-war era. The threat presented to the traditional parties by these new demands was very straightforward. National parties would face the risk of being literally torn apart as the salient lines of political cleavage came to emphasize ethnoregional issues, not the ideologies represented by the traditional parties.

The 1947 census revealed that Flemish-speakers comprised a much greater portion of the nation than most had expected. According to the census, 51.3 percent of the population spoke Dutch/Flemish, 32.94 percent spoke French, and 15.7 percent used both in Brussels. However, it was the territorial distribution of the population that had a greater impact on sharpening the conflict. The population in Flanders was shown to have grown by 385,000, giving the northern counties three more lower-house seats and one more upper-house seat. Conversely, with the Walloon population declining by 60,000, the South lost four lower-house seats and one upper-house seat.[29] By default, competition for votes was being further shifted to the north. With a greater percentage of the vote being sought in Flemish territory, the Flemish movement obtained yet another clue regarding their importance in the national arena.

The role of economic development was also critical in the initial appearance of the language question on the Belgian political agenda. The post-war era demonstrated once again the connection between economic change and ethnolinguistic conflict. Whereas the first round of industrialization had benefited the Walloons and contributed to the call for linguistic rights by the Flemish, the post-war era witnessed an interesting reversal. Along with a slowly declining population, Wallonia was also suffering from a declining industrial base, particularly in terms of one of its traditional economic strengths—the steel and coal industries.[30]

As Wallonia was entering an economic decline, Flanders was experiencing an economic boom, partly for reasons attributed to the changing face of the European economy, but also for external political reasons. Not only was Flanders home to the growing port at

Antwerp, an important shipping point for commercial traffic through-out Europe, but the increased economic fortunes of Flanders were also tied to increased investment from the Americans. Americans looked favorably upon the tradition of lower wages, lower strike rates, and a weak socialist party, all of which figured prominently in the North.[31] Covell argues that both the Walloon economic decline and the increased political power of the Flemish led to a heightened sense among Walloons that the Belgian center was no longer responding to their economic needs as a distinct region, and that autonomy for the two ethnic regions ought to be considered.[32]

No one incident better illustrates the link between language and economic factors within Belgian politics than the austerity package proposed by the Belgian government in 1960. The chief elements of the package included elimination of government subsidies for the south and a new investment plan aimed at creating 20,000 jobs an-nually. The heavily Walloon Socialist Trade Union openly suspected that the plan was the result of a central government that was blatantly pro-Flemish and seeking to use the new investments to shift industry to the Flemish north. When the bill was approved by both houses of the legislature, the Socialist Trade Union declared a general strike. Their northern counterpart, the Catholic Trade Union, refused to throw their support behind the strike, maintaining that the package did in fact provide benefits for the Belgian working class in the long run. The perception of the austerity package as being anti-Walloon and the subsequent lack of support from the Flemish-based union led several Walloon politicians to form the separatist Walloon Popular Front and to petition the Belgian king for institutional reforms that would lead to a federalist state.[33]

In what would be a final attempt by the traditional parties to maintain a completely unitary state, the joint Catholic-Socialist gov-ernment adopted a series of laws in the early 1960s that permanently fixed the language border such that each region was as linguistically homogenous as possible. It also gave both Dutch and French speakers increased protection for the use of their respective language in and around Brussels. However, while the laws were successful in carving out hard and fast language boundaries, they also strengthened the perception on the part of both Flemish and Walloon activists that the political elites at the central government level were willing to commit "injustices" against both ethnic groups to maintain control over gov-erning institutions. As Zolberg notes, the compromises that had been necessary to achieve the new boundaries had involved the movement of territory back and forth across the proposed language border. While the intent of these shifts was to come up with an acceptable compromise to politicians at the parliamentary level, the perception for each community of ethnic activists was that the central government had engaged in policy-making that implied "a discrete set of losses" for both the Flemings and the Walloons.[34]

At the same time as a coalition of Catholics and Socialists was attempting to contain the language issue yet again, Flemish and Walloon nationalist parties were making gains in the political arena. Their increased strength provided further evidence that the traditional parties were increasingly unable to control ethnoregional demands and to channel them into the existing party system. In 1961, the Flemish *Volksunie* (VU) sent five members to the lower house and saw this number more than double to eleven in 1965. Additionally, a pro-French party in Brussels (FDF) sent two members to the lower house in 1965, while pro-federalist Walloons (RW) sent three members. Table 5.2 shows the figures for percent of parliamentary vote

Table 5.2
Percent of parliamentary vote for Belgian parties by region, 1958–71

Year	Communist	Socialist	Catholic	Liberal	VU (Flemish)	FDF/RW (Walloon)
		Flanders				
1958	.001	.292	.566	.106	.034	–
1961	.010	.297	.509	.116	.060	–
1965	.017	.247	.438	.166	.116	–
1968	.014	.260	.390	.162	.169	–
1971	.016	.245	.378	.164	.188	–
		Brussels				
1958	.027	.424	.335	.182	.011	–
1961	.036	.416	.280	.170	.016	–
1965	.041	.263	.196	.334	.024	.100
1968	.024	.200	.276	.263	.043	.186
1971	.028	.206	.201	.135	.056	.345
	Wallonia					
1958	.046	.485	.342	.115	–	–
1961	.065	.471	.301	.118	–	–
1965	.098	.367	.233	.258	–	.033
1968	.070	.351	.203	.265	–	.106
1971	.060	.350	.201	.173	–	.212

Source: Zolberg (1977), op. cit., p. 119.

given to each party within the regions of Flanders, Wallonia and Brussels. While the data show that the Liberals were the main beneficiary at the polls in 1965, table 5.2 also shows that the ethnonationalist parties were engaged in dramatic growth all throughout the 1960s, halting the growth of the Liberals and contributing to the decline of the two other traditional parties in their respective regional strongholds.

Ethnic-based pressure was not just coming from outside of the traditional parties, but also from unofficial linguistic wings with each of the major three parties. Most notably, this pressure arose in the Catholic Party during the 1968 crisis over the University at Louvain. The French portion of the university maintained that its facilities were stretched to capacity and needed to expand into surrounding Flemish territory. When the Prime Minister initially refused to block the expansion, the eight Flemish members of the Catholic cabinet resigned, stating that, "We will not have peace in this country as long as the French-speaking community refuses to adapt itself to the reality of Belgium as it is today . . ."[35] Having brought about the collapse of one government, the new officeholders signaled that ethnic conflict had now reached such a pitch that constitutional revisions were unavoidable: "The unitary state . . . has now been outpaced by events . . . the communities and the regions must now takes their place among the renovated structure of the state."[36]

The constitutional reform that followed in 1970 provided for limited cultural autonomy. Members of the Belgian parliament were divided along linguistic lines and they formed Cultural Councils that in essence served as regional parliaments with decision-making authority over "cultural, educational, and linguistic matters."[37] In this round of constitutional revisions, regional economic matters were still controlled at the central government level. Preceding the establishment of the Cultural Councils, each of the traditional parties split into separate language wings. For the Catholics, the language wings attained the status of two fully independent organizations, while for the Socialists and the Liberals, the language wings had their independence checked by central oversight from the national party structure.[38] Murphy notes that the adoption of the 1970s constitutional changes suggested that few questioned whether Belgian political and economic life ought to be restructured along ethnoregional lines; the question was simply how.[39] Over the following decade, discussions led to an additional series of revisions that extended the federal direction of the Belgian nation, particularly in the area of finances. While the central government remains in firm control of much of the state's industrial policy, policy areas such as social services have been handed over to the regional level.[40]

One has to wonder whether there was any advantage for the traditional parties in bringing about the institutional devolution of the Belgian state. Were they simply backed into a corner by the growing chorus of ethnoregional complaints about poor treatment on cultural and economic matters? While the timing of the start of the constitutional revisions may have been dictated by the salience of the language issue, the question of traditional elite support for constitutional revision had also taken on linguistic overtones. Specifically, elite support for the gradual devolution of Belgian political institutions hinged on a very simple mixture of forces: the party one represented and the region one was elected in.

Using the Socialist party in the post-1970 era as an example, Covell argues that members of the Flemish Socialist Party (BSP) have opposed efforts at devolution, given the historical strength of the Catholics in the North. Members of the French wing of the Socialist Party (PSB), however, have thrown their support behind efforts at decentralization, being aware that they would most likely be the dominant player in any regional-based Walloon government.[41] Further, Newman observes that embracing the constitutional reform process and inviting the ethnonational parties to join in the efforts allowed the major parties to blur the lines of distinction between the traditional parties and their linguistic-based rivals.[42] Flemish and Walloon nationalist parties were obtaining their programmatic goals by partaking in the restructuring of Belgium's institutions. At the same time, though, the support they were receiving from the major parties meant that there was increasingly less of an issue to differentiate the traditional parties from the newer language-based ones.

In short, the electoral uncertainty produced by the rise of the nationalist parties allowed specific Belgian elites to opt for constitutional reform. Doing so had two distinct advantages. First, jumping on the reform bandwagon, regardless of how necessary it actually was, deprived the nationalist parties of their chief issue. At the same time though, it offered certain elites the chance to obtain increased electoral security for themselves and their parties at the regional level, while they gave the well-being of the national party organizations far less consideration.

CONCLUSION

In exploring the case of language conflict in Belgium, one consistently reoccurring theme has emerged. Whereas the Norwegian case allowed for the conscious choice of language as a tool by political elites, no such choice existed in Belgium. Rather, when language appeared on the Belgian political agenda, it was first forced upon Belgian elites by economic and demographic forces. However, it was just as frequently perpetuated as a political issue by a lack of elite ability to deal decisively with the issue. Paradoxically, the bulk of the measures adopted appeared to have only heightened ethnonationalist demands.

That language in Belgium was less of an effective political tool for elites, and that elites appeared to have dealt so poorly with the issue for much of Belgium's history, can ultimately be traced to one factor. Unlike Norway, language in Belgium existed as an issue that was not complementary to the cleavage structure around which the traditional parties had organized. Language in Belgium had ethnic overtones in a party system where the organizing principles were ideological and religious values. As such, elites were understandably wary about integrating an issue that ran so counter to their own defining issues. Uncertain about how to manage an issue that cut across so much of each party's membership, elites responded with partial solutions that only exacerbated Flemish and Walloon demands. Once nationalist parties had made themselves a sufficient specter on the political horizon, traditional elites were forced to confront the language issue and to abandon defense of the old institutional and political order.

Belgium may not be a case where the general pattern has been one of party elites seeking to mobilize constituents on the basis of language. However, it is worth recalling that even while containment of language as a political issue has been a recurring theme of this chapter, there were professional politicians that viewed the language-based ethnoregional conflict as a way to increase their power share in a situation of changing electoral laws and institutional design. Specifically, one should recall that upon mass enfranchisement in the late nineteenth century, northern Catholics made the linkage between their strong regional base in the north and the salience of Flemish as an issue of concern to many voters by incorporating Flemish demands. Moreover, it is important to reemphasize that support for institutional devolution in the 1970s was not just a reflexive re-sponse to the "weight" of cultural issues. Rather, ethnoregional conflict produced a devolution of powers that benefited political parties likely to play a leading role in the regions.

Language has also served as an effective political tool in the arsenal of regional and ethnic activists. Specifically, it has been shown that the Flemish movement, in the early and mid-nineteenth cen-tury, stood to gain a great deal in terms of access to more favorable career opportunities if less restrictive language laws were adopted. In the post-World War II era, the ethnoregional consciousness of Wallonia, along with calls for regional autonomy, became increas-ingly visible. Yet, this growth in regional consciousness cannot be understood apart from the broader economic transformations that were weakening Wallonia's position when compared to Flanders. Thus, even in Belgium, where language policies primarily figured as a defensive response against the power of cultural cleavage, the "right" mix of institutional and socioeconomic context allowed some actors to view language and ethnoregional conflict as a helpful addition to the political toolbox.

Chapter 6

Conclusion

The principal argument in this book has been that the choice of language policies by Norwegian political elites can be best explained by considering the electoral and ideological goals of the elites who make those policies. As Bull has noted, scholars of Norwegian language policy have by and large avoided confronting the question over causality in their studies. To the extent that the question has been raised as to why Norwegian language policy looks the way it does, the dominant explanation that appears in the literature has emphasized the role of pressure groups.

The evidence regarding the role of pressure groups as the main determinant of Norwegian language policy is less than convincing. Without a doubt, there is a rich body of literature that illuminates the history of Norwegian language pressure groups. However, I have shown that a focus on changing party profiles, parties' electoral goals, and the related need by parties to attract specific voter constituencies, has a greater ability to account for Norwegian language policy than do the pressure group arguments that center around a correlation between certain group demands and policy outcomes.

In this conclusion, I have three chief areas of focus. First, I consider the implications that this case study has for the use of rational choice in comparative politics. Second, I will argue that the chief contribution made by the Norwegian case is that it allows for an extension of Anderson's argument concerning the role of language in the construction of identity. Finally, I briefly address the relevance of this historical study for other situations of contemporary language conflict, and how language has, once again, become a contentious issue in Norwegian cultural politics.

THE LIMITED ROLE FOR RATIONAL CHOICE

As David Laitin has noted, the use of rational choice in studying the relationship between culture and politics does have distinct advantages. Drawing mainly on Abner Cohen's definition of culture, Laitin emphasizes how rational choice largely views cultural symbols in terms of their ability to serve as resources, and in terms of their ability to be manipulated by various groups seeking an increase in political and economic power.[1] For Laitin, the advantage to this "modified rational-choice approach" is that it allows one to see why culture is of interest to various political actors. In this case, culture "provides a plethora of shared symbols" that can be used to create and enhance group cohesion, as well as to maintain political communication.[2]

Yet, Laitin does have criticism for the way in which cultural symbols are viewed by practitioners of rational choice. Primarily, while rational choice can identify which cultural symbols and identities may be salient for a given group, it has less potential in explaining specifically *why* a given set of cultural identities have become salient.[3] As Laitin notes, "Certain aspects of identity become crucial at certain times and politically irrelevant at others."[4]

The focus within rational choice on the availability of identities that can be manipulated appears to leave two significant questions unanswered. In the first place, why is it even desirable for political elites to manipulate cultural identities? Secondly, why are some cultural identities ripe candidates for manipulation when others are never given serious consideration?

As shown in the case study chapters, different Norwegian linguistic identities were fostered, maintained and discarded at various critical points during the course of the language conflict. Understanding why political elites found it initially desirable to manipulate linguistic identities required that substantial attention be given to the manner in which elite goals were shaped by broader forces in both the national and international arena. I have shown that these forces included the level of consolidation of the Norwegian state, the impact of industrialization, the World War II experience, and the post-war economic boom. As I have shown, each of these forces helped shape a set of political goals that Norwegian elites sought to address through a broad range of policies, including those pertaining to language.

While these broader forces necessitated that elites develop creative policy responses, they did not in and of themselves determine what linguistic identity elites would choose to manipulate. Here, I maintain that the choice of the specific linguistic identity to be adopted was shaped by the fit between the larger political objective and the symbolic meaning of a given linguistic identity within the polity. Thus, while I argue that the choice of language policies in the Norwegian case primarily reflects an elite desire to manipulate linguistic identities to achieve other ends, I also argue that this elite use of language is situated inside a larger grouping of social, political, and economic forces.

Thus, if one accepts Laitin's critique that culture has simply been portrayed within rational choice as a tool that is already given, then it becomes apparent that exploring the fit between a larger political objective and the symbolic meaning of a given linguistic identity moves beyond the traditional scope of rational choice investigations. In the following, I offer a summary of how the link between linguistic identities and political goals came to shape the choice of language policies in the Norwegian case.

As is clear from each of the case study chapters, language can be attractive to policy makers because of its function as an indicator of group identity. While group identity based on language is frequently presented as being linked to either the nation as a whole or a specific ethnic group that occupies a given nation,[5] identities based on language can also serve to mark other types of group membership. Two examples of how language can reflect nonethnic or nonnational identity are of course Nynorsk, which is linked to the territorial identity of coming from the rural western areas of Norway, and Common Norwegian, the Norwegian Labor Party's vision of a fused worker-farmer series of dialects. In this case, language would serve not as a regional indicator, but rather as that of a class that was moving from cultural oppression to cultural acceptance.

Yet, language as an indicator of a certain group identity is only important insofar as this identity can be employed to mobilize a targeted group that political elites believe necessary for obtaining a certain electoral or programmatic end. Many distinct linguistic identities are possible in any society (ethnic, regional, class, even disability-based identities such as sign-language communities), yet not all of them have significant political use to elites. However, languages as identities do become useful to elites when they are able to integrate the symbolic nature of the language's identity into a broader political agenda. Table 6.1 provides a clear presentation of this argument in the case of the Norwegian language planning conflict.

Table 6.1
The Relationship between Language
and Norwegian Political Parties

Party	Language	Characteristic of language	(Dis)advantage to party
Liberals	Nynorsk	Rural-based, Mythology of being truly Norwegian	Aided party in profiling against urban elites linked to foreign powers
Conservatives	Bokmål/Riksmål	Urban, used by commercial elite and civil service	Privileged position of Bokmål hand-in-hand with privileged status of urban elite
DNA (pre-1930s)	Any	Identities based on regional and national issues	Language detracts from centrality of class struggle
DNA (1930s–1960s)	Common Norwegian	Worker-farmer alliance	Symbol of "people's party" against urban bourgeoisie
DNA (post-1960s)	Common Norwegian	Worker-farmer alliance	Evokes resentment in competitive electoral districts

One of the key points derived from this table is that while a given language may possess certain characteristics that make it politically useful at a given point, it is no guarantee that a language will always retain its favorable position among policymakers. Specifically, the political context may alter itself in which elites make decisions about what language activates desired constituencies. Whether or not a language does retain its favorable position among elites appears to be contingent on the interplay between demographic, economic and electoral forces, and the symbolic meaning of a given linguistic identity.

But how does this discussion of the meaning of linguistic identities and their relationship to broader political forces pertain to the question of an appropriate role for rational choice in investigating cultural phenomena? The answer is relatively clear. In essence, focusing on the symbolic meaning associated with different languages, and in looking at the influential role of larger political forces, has also meant focusing on the context in which elites shaped their strategies for obtaining goals. In making political and social context critical to my analysis, I argue that it would not have been enough to limit myself to a rational choice perspective solely focused on how elites acted upon their strategic preference to manipulate Norwegian linguistic identities. Rather, I have sought to illuminate the conditions under which those preferences first arose, and how they were altered throughout the course of the language conflict. My earlier discussion of the logic that would be employed in locating evidence for elite manipulation of the language question is crucial in this regard. Given that for some, a rejection of the pressure group hypothesis may not constitute sufficient evidence to confirm my research hypothesis, I outlined two points that served as guidelines in the search for evidence that elite manipulation of language policies was occurring. The first of these two points, that a plausible linkage between the language question and other elite political goals must be observable bears most strongly on why I maintain that a standard rational choice explanation would have been insufficient in the case of Norwegian language policy.

To fulfill this methodological guideline, my investigation of Norwegian language policy needed to show that the broader political context provided issues and other political goals that served as potential candidates for linkage to the language question. As standard rational choice explanations have not generally set out to account for the origins of preferences, limiting myself to this approach would have prevented me from demonstrating why Norwegian political elites found the language question to be a salient issue in the first place.

Quite simply, reliance on a standard rational choice approach would have provided me only with an assumption that elites considered language to be of great political use. In going beyond a traditional rational choice framework and exploring why elite preferences on the language issue have emerged, I am better able to demonstrate the validity of my overall claim, particularly for those that may be less than satisfied by a conclusion that rests simply on rejecting the alternative hypothesis.

The sentiment that rational choice ought to be employed alongside of more traditional forms of analysis is echoed by Margaret Levi. She suggests that rational choice should not be considered the sole tool for comparativists, as "(rational choice) tends to rely on stylized facts rather than on the observations and details that enrich both the narrative and our confidence that we have explained an actual occurrence."[6] Rather, Levi suggests that rational choice needs to be augmented by efforts at research that include "a far more detailed knowledge of the case than was previously expected of rational choice scholars," with a particular emphasis not just on actors and interests, but also on the "relevant technological, social, political or economic constraints . . ."[7] Thus, self-interest and acting upon preferences are an important part of any story, but they form only one part. The manner in which elites come to define their self-interest, and why they wind up with a given set of preferences is equally important for giving a meaningful account of any case within comparative politics.

LANGUAGE AND THE CONSTRUCTION OF IDENTITY

This study has primarily been directed towards showing how political elites have engaged in a careful dance with language, both tapping its political potential and remaining cognizant of language's ability to eventually threaten the same political ends that it once served. However, an additional point has emerged, suggesting that the traditional linkage of language to questions of ethnicity and nation-building in political science literature may only be telling a partial story regarding the importance of language.

In this investigation, language has not only emerged as a powerful symbolic force that can be used to support the nation-building goals of political elites, or to aid in the aspirations of resource-deprived ethnic groups. Instead, I have also shown that language has remained politically useful well after the consolidation of the state, and for purposes divorced from the demands of ethnic groups. Specifically, I have presented the case of the Norwegian Labor Party and Common Norwegian as an instance where language policy was embraced to aid the rise of social democracy.

The case of the Norwegian Labor Party and Common Norwegian should be viewed as a complementary extension to the arguments offered by both Hobsbawm and Anderson regarding the role of language in the construction of identities. As discussed in chapter 1, Anderson and Hobsbawm's arguments can briefly be summarized as portraying language in highly instrumental terms. Language was of service to emerging nineteenth-century political elites that sought to tap its potential as a way to provide the masses with a collective identity that conceived of the nation in terms of a commonly held language.

In most European cases, the establishment and consolidation of the modern nation-state marked the high point for the salience of language to political elites. The case of Norway differed in two regards.

First, while Norwegian elites were no different than their European counterparts in tapping the nation-building potential of language, their strategy was not to impose a single national language on Norway. Language activists on both sides of the debate sought to portray their written version of Norwegian as the only standard that could truly express a distinct sense of being uniquely Norwegian. However, political elites opted to give both standards official recognition. Thus, as opposed to states where the emergence of one national standard led to the decreased salience of language, the initial set of language policies themselves ensured that language would continue to have a place on the political agenda.

Second, the overlap of linguistic cleavage with class and regional cleavage allowed for additional opportunities for language to appear on the political agenda. Social Democratic elites were most adept at exploiting this overlap to their political advantage.

An initial difficulty existed in that the urban working class did not speak a Nynorsk based dialect, and did not appear to be an immediate candidate for linguistic alliance with the rural farmer. However, working class dialects were heavily maligned by the urban elite, allowing the Labor party to reshape linguistic identities such that they meshed perfectly with the class divide.

Despite these differences of the Norwegian case from the more typical European case, it is worth noting that the case of the Norwegian Labor Party mainly differs from that of earlier linguistic nationalism in that a cross-class identity, as opposed to a national identity, was being fostered. Thus, my analysis of the Norwegian case in the 1920s and 1930s is strongly influenced by the insight and logic offered in Anderson and Hobsbawm. More generally, the Norwegian case differs from many other instances of language conflict in that it has been entirely nonviolent. While some may view this as surprising, recent research by Laitin suggests that the Norwegian case, one where language conflict centered on official standards and language legislation for schools and other public settings, would not be expected to have been anything other than peaceful. Drawing upon data from the "Minorities at Risk" database, covering 268 "politically active communal groups" in 148 countries, one of his findings is that "language grievances held by the minority, in regard to the official language of the state or in regard to medium of instruction in state schools, are not associated with group violence . . ."[8]

It is also worth observing that the case of the Norwegian Labor Party and Common Norwegian is not an isolated example. Greece provides a fitting historical example of a case where political elites have employed language to foster group identity in the service of larger political aims. Similar to Norway, two standards of Greek, Dimotiki and Katharevousa, have had varying levels of support from political elites throughout the twentieth century. With each of these standards, an ideological association developed that was fostered by political activists on both the left and the right.

Katharevousa resulted from an effort in the eighteenth century by linguistic purists to come up with a national language that would rid the commonly spoken dialects of any foreign loan words and merge them with certain forms of ancient Greek. The result was a standard that "was a mixed, archaic form of language, full of hypercorrections and false archaisms."[9]

Despite the fact that this artificial standard had no native speakers, it was adopted as the sole official language by the newly independent Greek government. In the mid-nineteenth century, it underwent repeated revisions, all of which were designed to further "purify" the language of any foreign influence. This factor strongly contributed to a perception of Katharevousa as being aligned with highly nationalistic and conservative forces in Greek society.

Dimotiki emerged in the late nineteenth century as a response to the artificial nature of Katharevousa, and was based largely on the common dialects that had been increasingly mixed since the War of Independence earlier in the century.[10]

If Katharevousa had an explicit association with conservative political forces, Dimotiki gained the opposite association at the start of the twentieth century, when a left-wing political activist wrote a pamphlet calling for a linkage of the language question with broader questions of social policy. In subsequent decades, the Communist Party adopted Dimotiki as their official standard.[11]

Throughout much of the twentieth century, education at the secondary level has only been offered in Katharevousa, leading left-wing forces to view the language question as a class issue in which common people were being denied access to official recognition and prestige for their spoken dialects. Similarly, conservative forces feared that Dimotiki was too closely aligned with the Communist movement, and sought to implement language reforms that would prevent the Communists from making political use of the language issue.

This overt linking of political ideology with language use is most clear during the military dictatorship of 1967–1974, in which the junta forbade the use of Dimotiki in educational and other official settings, explicitly making the argument that Dimotiki was linked to communism.[12] The language issue in Greece has also undergone marked depoliticization in the decades since the fall of the military dictatorship, with broad agreement existing for a "Standard Modern Greek," that draws on the more commonly used forms of Dimotiki. Thus, in both the Greek and the Norwegian case, language became intimately linked with issues other than national identity, and served as a tool for political elites to mobilize supporters and define the opposition in terms of language/class-based identities.

CONTEMPORARY LANGUAGE CONFLICT: NORWAY AND BEYOND

An in-depth case study about the political history of a small, peripheral European state might leave some wondering how to make the link between the findings of this book and contemporary cultural politics. Specifically, while the Norwegian conflict may have similarities to other recent historical cases, what does it tell us about contemporary language conflict? While this study has primarily addressed the history of one European state, there is little question that the language politics is presently of great concern in many societies. Some of these contemporary instances have strong similarities to chapter 2's discussion of language and the construction of nation-states. Csergo's work on Slovakian language policy reveals an instance of policy exploitation that takes place "against the backdrop of a state-building (or state-consolidating) process designed by a dominant political elite." In this case, majority Slovakian elites implemented a state language act in 1995 that required the use of one Slovakian standard throughout the state, and thereby "institutionalized second-class citizenship for speakers of other languages."[13] Other cases, while seemingly worlds away from the specifics of the Norwegian language conflict, share profound institutional similarities. India, with at least thirteen major languages, has a number of official directives that mirror the complex language regulations of Norway: citizens are allowed to address union or state officials in any of the official languages, and states are required to make adequate provision for mother tongue instruction to linguistic minorities. Further, a "Special Officer for linguistic minorities" reports directly to the Indian president on all matters relating to the safeguarding of minority language rights. Mitra observes that the broad outlines of Indian language policy, which can be summarized as "Hindi + English + official regional languages" represents the recognition by political elites of "the compulsions of mass democracy and the imperative of coalition-building."[14]

In the current battle over language in the United States, recent research has shown that the institutional structure of states can play a role in whether advocates of English as an official language will have success with their state legislators. As Schildkraut notes, the salience of the debate over English as an official language has been on a steady rise since 1980. English has been declared the official language in twenty-six of the fifty states, with twenty-one of those declarations occurring since 1980. Half of the remaining twenty-four states have seen debates in the past decade as to whether English ought to be made the official language.[15] However, Schildkraut's key point is that the institutional possibility to bypass state legislators via an initiative increases the likelihood that a given state will designate English as the official language, stating that, "Not every state that has English as its official language and a direct initiative process has used the method to pass the law, but the mere existence of the opportunity makes passage more likely . . ."[16] The availability of direct initiatives on language policy, a factor lacking in the Norwegian case, is yet another reminder that institutional context shapes the response of relevant actors.

Thus, the Norwegian case has value for considering a wide range of contemporary situations where language plays a salient role: in Europe, Asia, and North America. However, this is not to suggest that language conflict in Norway is relegated to the history books. Recent events have shown that the language issue can still wind up on the front burner of Norwegian political debates. In 2000, the Conservative-led Oslo city council proposed removing the obligatory alternative norm instruction from Oslo schools,[17] claiming that a significant number of students had reading and writing difficulties in the dominant Bokmål standard, and that as such, the time spent on Nynorsk could be better spent on shoring up skills in Bokmål.[18] Critics of the proposal, particularly from Noregs Mållag, pointed out that exempting Oslo school-students from obligatory alternative norm instruction requirements would impact one-third of all Norwegian students.[19] Moreover, arguments were raised as to how this proposal would affect language requirements associated with being employed as either a teacher or as a civil servant, where competency of Nynorsk is often a requirement.[20] Trond Giske, the then DNA minister of education who had jurisdiction over the request, surprised many by not immediately dismissing the idea. In October of 2000, he suggested a possible alternative, wherein it was possible that Nynorsk would not be removed from the Oslo schools, but that students would no longer have to take exams in Nynorsk. Giske alleged that this might make Nynorsk a better-taught and more interesting subject.[21] Despite what many saw as an ambivalent stance, DNA eventually came out strongly in favor maintaining the alternative norm instruction at its November 2000 convention as part of its platform on culture, stating that "Nynorsk, as an administrative language, must be strengthened such that a minimum usage of 25 percent is attained. Mandatory instruction in the alternative norm must be maintained."[22] Noreg Mållag greeted the new platform plank warmly, noting that while it would need to be followed up with a series of concrete action points, "it was clearly a stronger formulation than in previous programs."[23] Thus, over thirty years after the major parties backed away from a hardened conflict over language, there is still sufficient controversy over the issue that old friendships can be rekindled, if only for matters of convenience.

As I have shown in this study, elites have chosen among different language policy orientations with their own electoral and ideological agendas as primary considerations. Yet, it cannot be overemphasized that even while a subsidiary concern to political elites, language policy outcomes are by no means trivial. In multilingual societies, the official rights accorded to various languages will have great day-to-day meaning for members and nonmembers of those linguistic communities. In these societies, what we speak determines how others view our status, what our educational options are, what our career choices may be, and perhaps even ultimately, our ability to take part in politics as a whole. Language is certainly used by elites to gain political resources, but it is also a resource in and of itself that shapes how everyday citizens will have access to all types of societal resources. Thus if in politics, looking to answer "who gets what, when, how and why" is the key focus of our investigations, then answering the question of "who speaks and writes what, when, how and why" may be just as important.

Notes

CHAPTER 1: LANGUAGE, POLITICS, AND MODERN NORWAY

1. Norwegian political elites have directed considerable efforts towards both limiting and partially promoting the use of the Sámi languages, spoken by the indigenous people of northern Norway. These efforts are the focus of chapter 4, The Shifting Fate of the Sámi Languages in Modern Norway.

2. Ludwig Wittgenstein, *Philosophical Investigations* (New York: MacMillian Publishing, 1953) 3e.

3. Karl Marx and Frederick Engels, *The German Ideology* (New York: International Publishers, 1963) 16–18.

4. Marx and Engels, 19.

5. Marx and Engels, 19.

6. Karl Marx. *Grundrisse: Foundations of the Critique of Political Economy* (New York: Vintage Books, 1973) 104.

7. Marx, 105.

8. Antonio Gramsci, *Selections from Prison Notebooks* (New York: International Publishers, 1971) 238–243, as cited in Martin Carnoy, *The State & Social Theory* (Princeton: Princeton University Press, 1984) 68–83.

9. Carnoy, *State & Social Theory* 83.

10. David Forgacs and Geoffrey Nowell-Smith, eds., *Antonio Gramsci, Selections from Cultural Writings* (Cambridge: Harvard University Press, 1985) 166–167.

11. Gramsci writes, "I hope that you will let him speak Sardinian and will not make any trouble for him on that score. It was a mistake, in my opinion, not to allow Edmea to speak freely in Sardinian as a little girl. This harmed her intellectual development and put her imagination in a straightjacket. You mustn't make this mistake with your children. For one thing Sardinian is a not a dialect, but a language in itself, even

though it does not have a great literature, and it is a good thing for children to learn several languages, if it is possible. Besides, the Italian that you teach them will be a poor, mutilated language made up of only the few sentences and words of your conversations with him, purely childish; he will not have any contact with a general environment and will end up learning two jargons and no language." See Frank Rosengarte. *Antonio Gramsci, Letters From Prison, Volume One* (New York: Columbia University Press, 1994) 89.

12. See Richard Harker, "Bourdieu—Education and Reproduction," In Richard Harker, Cheleen Mahar and Chris Wilkes, eds., *An Introduction to the Work of Pierre Bourdieu* (New York: St. Martin's Press, 1990) 87–90, and Pierre Bourdieu, *Distinction: A Social Critique of the Judgement of Taste* (Cambridge: Harvard University Press, 1984) 387.

13. Pierre Bourdieu, "What Makes a Social Class? On the Theoretical and Practical Existence of Groups," *Berkeley Journal of Sociology* vol. 32 (1987) 3–4, as cited in Craig Calhoun, "Habitus, Field, and Capital," Craig Calhoun, Edward LiPuma and Moishe Postone, eds., *Bourdieu: Critical Perspectives* (Chicago: University of Chicago Press, 1993) 69–70.

14. Pierre Bourdieu and Loïc J. D. Wacquant, *An Invitation to Reflexive Sociology* (Chicago: University of Chicago Press, 1992) 142.

15. Pierre Bourdieu, "Economics of Linguistic Exchanges," *Social Science Information* vol. 16, no. 6 (1977), 652.

16. James Collins, "Bourdieu on Language and Education," in Craig Calhoun, Edward LiPuma and Moishe Postone, eds., *Bourdieu: Critical Perspectives* (Chicago: University of Chicago Press, 1993) 132.

17. Brian Weinstein, *The Civic Tongue: Political Consequences of Language Choices* (New York: Longman, 1983).

18. David Laitin, "Language Games," *Comparative Politics* vol. 20, no. 3 (1988).

19. Ernest Gellner, *Nations and Nationalism* (Ithaca: Cornell University Press, 1993).

20. Weinstein, *Civic Tongue*.

21. For examples, see Benedict Anderson, *Imagined Communities* (London: Verso, 1991), Elie Kedourie, *Nationalism* (London: Hutchinson, 1985), E. J. Hobsbawm, *Nations and Nationalism Since 1780* (New York: Cambridge University Press, 1992), and Gellner, *Nations and Nationalism*.

22. David Laitin, *Politics, Language and Thought: The Somali Experience* (Chicago: University of Chicago Press, 1977) and David Laitin, *Language Repertoires and State Construction in Africa* (New York: Cambridge University Press, 1992).

23. Jonathan Pool, "The Official Language Problem," *American Political Science Review* vol. 85 (1991).

24. William Safran, "Language, Ideology, and State-Building: A Comparison of Policies in France, Israel, and the Soviet Union," *International Political Science Review* (1992), vol. 13, no. 4 397–414.

25. For examples, see Kenneth D. McRae, *Conflict and Compromise in Multilingual Settings* (Ontario: Wilfred Laurier University Press, 1983), Arend Lijphart, *Conflict and Coexistence in Belgium: The Dynamics of a Culturally Divided Society* (Berkeley: University of California Press, 1981), and David Laitin, et al., "Language and the Construction of States: The Case of Catalonia in Spain," *Politics & Society* vol. 22, no. 1 (1994) 5–29.

26. As in Christina Bratt Paulston, *Linguistic Minorities in Multilingual Settings* (Philadelphia: John Benjamins Publishing Company, 1994). I consider ethnicity to be a reference to a shared biological past and common ancestors (factual or fictional).

27. Eckstein (like so many of his Norwegian counterparts) identifies the Norwegian language conflict as one that perfectly encapsulates the series of geographical and cultural cleavages that have had the potential to divide the Norwegian polity. Harry Eckstein, *Division and Cohesion in Democracy: A Study of Norway* (Princeton: Princeton University Press, 1966) 18, 44–47. Additionally, Eckstein quips on p. 55 that "During my stay in Norway I found that any flagging conversation, any tepid interview, could be warmed up by the mere mention of Nynorsk."

28. For extensive treatment on the language conflict in Belgium, see Kenneth D. McRae, *Conflict and Compromise in Multilingual Settings*, and Alexander B. Murphy, *The Regional Dynamics of Language Differentiation in Belgium* (Chicago: University of Chicago's Committee on Geographical Studies, 1988).

29. See Anderson, *Imagined Communities*, Chapter 5, Hobsbawm, *Nations and Nationalism*, Chapter 2, and John Breuilly, *Nationalism and the State* (Chicago: University of Chicago Press, 1993) 145.

30. Anderson, *Imagined Communities* 80–82.

31. Hobsbawm, *Nations and Nationalism* 104.

32. Anthony Smith, "Culture, Community and Territory: The Politics of Ethnicity and Nationalism," *International Affairs* vol. 72, no. 3 (1996) 446.

33. This is similar to the first step in Weinstein's typology of the formation and implementation of language policy, which he refers to as the coalescence of language ideology or attitudes.

34. John W. Kingdon, *Agendas, Alternatives and Public Policies*. Boston: Little, Brown and Company (1984) 208–209. It should be observed

that the distinction between these groups may be far less clear-cut in Norway than in the American context. An example directly relevant to this study is the University of Oslo's Department of Scandinavian Studies and Comparative Literature, Section of Lexicography and Dialectology. While the staff here is certainly among the chief group of academics consulted in language questions, many of them are also hold visible leadership positions in language interest groups on all sides of the controversy. Additionally, some of these individuals also sit on the Norwegian Language Council. Thus, in this one workplace, we find overlapping memberships between three categories that are certainly not as easily traversed in the United States.

35. See Bryan D. Jones, *Reconceiving Decision-Making in Democratic Politics* (Chicago: University of Chicago Press, 1994) 84–85 for a discussion of Arrow and "issue cycling."

36. William Riker, *Liberalism Against Populism* (San Francisco, W. H. Freeman, 1982).

37. Riker.

38. William Riker, "Implications from the Disequilibrium of Majority Rule for the Study of Institutions," *American Political Science Review* vol. 74 (1980).

39. Robert Cooper, *Language Planning and Social Change* (New York: Cambridge University Press, 1989).

40. Cooper.

41. Weinstein, *Civic Tongue* 190.

42. Laitin, *Language Repertoires* (1992).

43. See Ernst Håkon Jahr, *Innhogg i nyare norsk språkhistorie* (Oslo: Novus Forlag, 1992).

44. Olaf Almenningen (a), "Ny arbeidsdag og mellomkrigstid," in Olaf Almenningen, Thore A. Roksvold, Helge Sandøy, and Lars S. Vikør, eds., *Språk og samfunn gjennom tusen år* (Oslo: Universitetsforlaget, 1981), and Arne Torp and Lars S. Vikør, *Hovuddrag i norsk språkhistorie* (Oslo: Ad Notam Gyldendal, 1993).

45. Ole Dalhaug, *Mål og meninger* (Oslo: Noregs forskningsråd, 1995).

46. Endre Brunstad, *Nasjonalisme som språkpolitisk ideologi* (Oslo: Noregs forskningsråd, 1995).

47. Lars S. Vikør, *The New Norse Language Movement* (Oslo: Novus Forlag, 1975).

48. Ernst Håkon Jahr, *Innhogg i nyare norsk språkhistorie etter 1814* (1989).

49. Jahr (1989).

50. Åsmund Lien, "Nynorsken i skuleverket," in *Målreising i 75 år: Noregs Mållag 1906–1981* (Oslo: Fonna Forlag, 1981).

51. Einar Haugen, *Language Conflict and Language Planning* (Cambridge: Harvard University Press, 1966).

52. Frank R. Baumgartner and Bryan D. Jones, *Agendas and Instability in American Politics* (Chicago: Chicago University Press, 1993).

53. Robert Dahl, "Further Reflections on 'The Elitist Theory of Democracy,' " *American Political Science Review*, vol. 60, no. 2 (June 1966) 297.

54. See Robert Dahl, "A Critique of the Ruling Elite Model," *American Political Science Review*, vol. 52, no. 2 (June 1958) 463–469.

55. James A. Bill and Robert L. Hardgrave, *Comparative Politics: The Quest for Theory* (Lanham, MD: University Press of America, 1981) 168.

56. Jack L. Walker, "A Critique of the Elitist Theory of Democracy," *American Political Science Review*, vol. 60, no. 2 (June 1966) 286.

57. Dahl, Further Reflections on 'The Elitist Theory of Democracy,' " note 7, 298.

58. Ezra Suleiman, *Elites in French Society* (Princeton: Princeton University Press, 1978) 12–13.

59. Robert D. Putnam, "Studying Elite Political Culture: The Case of Ideology," *American Political Science Review*, vol. 65, no. 3 (September 1971) 651.

60. Robert D. Putnam, *Making Democracy Work* (Princeton: Princeton University Press, 1993). In one of the early articles carried out under the same research program that led to Making Democracy Work, Putnam emphasizes again that his use of elites is roughly synonymous with that of "professional politicians." See Robert D. Putnam, "Attitude Stability among Italian Elites," *American Journal of Political Science*, vol. 23, no. 3 (August 1979) 465.

61. Jonathan Pool, "Language Regimes and Political Regimes," in Brian Weinstein. ed., *Language Policy and Political Development* (Norwood, NJ: Ablex Publishing Corp., 1990) 240–242.

62. Another possible value, though never one opted for by a Norwegian government, would be language policies that exclusively promoted the value of regional dialects.

63. An in-depth overview of the various activities that interest groups can engage in may be found in chapter 8 of Kay Lehman Schlozman and John T. Tierney's *Organized Interests and American Democracy* (New York: Harper & Row, 1986).

64. Gary King, Robert O. Keohane, Sidney Verba, *Designing Social Inquiry* (Princeton: Princeton University Press, 1994) 109–110.

CHAPTER 2: NATIONAL IDENTITY, PARTY IDENTITY,
AND THE ROLE OF NYNORSK IN THE
NEW NORWEGIAN STATE

1. In ranking the various Scandinavian societies' degree of language consciousness, Danish linguist Jørn Lund places the Norwegians at number two, just below the Færoese. See Jørn Lund, "Det sprogsociologiske klima i de nordiske lande," Språk i Norden (Oslo: Nordiske Språkråd, 1986) 37.

2. Ernst Håkon Jahr, "A Rationale for Language-Planning Policy in Norway," in Ernst Håkon Jahr, Innhogg i nyare norsk språkhistorie (Oslo: Novus Forlag, 1991) 45.

3. Aarebrot and Urwin concluded that in the period of initial party formation in modern Norway that "language was the most significant element of cultural dissent." See Frank H. Aarebrot and Derek Urwin, "The Politics of Cultural Dissent: Religion, Language, and Demonstrative Effects in Norway" Scandinavian Political Studies vol. 2, (1979) 75.

4. Stein Rokkan, Derek Urwin, Frank H. Aarebrot, Pamela Maleba and Terje Sande, Centre-Periphery Structures in Europe (Frankfurt: Campus Verlag, 1982) 26.

5. Rokkan, Urwin, Aarebrot, Maleba, and Sande, 41.

6. Rokkan, Urwin, Aarebrot, Maleba, and Sande, 41.

7. Rokkan, Urwin, Aarebrot, Maleba, and Sande, 191. Rokkan states that this is "one of the central themes of modern Norwegian political science." See also Henry Valen and Stein Rokkan, "Norway: Conflict Structure and Mass Politics in a European Periphery," in Richard Rose, ed., Electoral Behavior: A Comparative Handbook (New York: The Free Press, 1974) 315–370.

8. See pp. 51–60 of T. K. Derry's, A History of Modern Norway (Oxford: Oxford University Press, 1973) for an account of the events that led to parliamentary sovereignty.

9. As Kjell Haugland notes, at the turn of the century, it was a minority of teachers from southern Norway that could not be placed into the category, "teacher, Liberal, and Landsmål-man." See Kjell Haugland, "Mål og makt i Venstre," in Ottar Grepstad and Jostein Nerbøvik, eds., Venstres hundre år (Oslo: Gyldendal Norsk Forlag, 1984) 91.

10. See chapter 13, "Oversikt over utviklingen fra 1842 til 1913," in Gunnar Jahn, Alf Eriksen and Preben Munthe, eds., Norges Bank gjennom 150 år (Oslo: Norges Bank, 1966).

11. Fedraheimen, June 28, 1884.

12. Kjell Haugland, "Ei pressgruppe tek form: Målrørsla og Venstrepartiet 1883–1885," *Historisk Tidskrift* vol. 53, no. 2 (1974) 157.

13. Haugland 158.

14. *Dagbladet*, October 10, 1884, here cited after Tove Bull, "1885 enda ein gong," *Maal og Minne* (1987–88) 116.

15. Haugland, *Ei pressgruppe tek form*, 159.

16. These numbers are based on Haugland's study of Landsmål-friendly resolutions announced in the Norwegian press from 9/23/1884 to 6/1/1885. See Haugland, *Ei pressgruppe tek form* 1974, Appendix.

17. Kjell Haugland, "Organisasjonsgjennombrotet i målarbeidet ved hundreårsskiftet," *Historisk Tidskrift* (1977) vol. 56, no. 2 19–52.

18. A geographic breakdown of support for the thirty-seven rural sponsors is provided in Haugland, *Ei pressgruppe tek form* 168.

19. Tove Bull, *1885 enda ein gong*, 115–116.

20. Ernst Håkon Jahr, *Utsyn over norsk språkhistorie etter 1814* (Oslo: Novus Forlag, 1989) 9.

21. Lars S. Vikør, "Den nasjonale revolusjen (1814–1905)" in Olaf Almenningen, Thore A.Roksvold, Helge Sandøy, and Lars S. Vikør, ed., *Språk og samfunn gjennom tusen år* (Oslo: Universitetsforlaget, 1981) 60.

22. Jahr, *Utsyn over norsk språkhistorie*, 13–20. As those familiar with the language situation in Norway will note, it is an exaggeration to claim that Aasen was representing all dialects in his constructed language. Notably absent were the dialects of the eastern part of the nation. Far from historic trivia, it is the absence of these dialects that will lead to DNA's fusion of people's spoken languages (both western and eastern) in the twentieth century as part of the effort to construct a distinct third line in the language conflict.

23. Anderson, *Imagined Communities*, 74.

24. Jahr, op. cit. p. 31. This discussion can also be viewed from a more explicitly sociolinguistic emphasis in Ernst Håkon Jahr, "Kor gammalt er Noreg? Eit sosiopolitisk perspektiv på skriftspråknormeringa i Noreg på 1800-tallet," in *Innhogg i nyare norsk språkhistorie* (Oslo: Novus, 1992) 9–17.

25. Haugland, *Ei pressegruppe tek form*, 150.

26. Bull, *1885 enda ein gong*, 112.

27. Lars S. Vikør, "Jamstillingsvedtaket i 1885: Ein replikk," *Norsk Lingvistisk Tidsskrift* (1990) vol. 8, 75.

28. This debate has played itself out in a variety of settings over the years. In the Riksmål press of the late 1960s, and as a result of the Vogt Committee report, see Einar Lundeby, "Språksaken i Stortinget," *Ordet*

1969, 380–387, Johannes Elgvin, "Politikk, taktikk og realiteter i Stortinget," *Ordet* 1969, 407–421. Following the 100-year anniversary of the language equality law, is Bull's 1987 article and by Ernst Håkon Jahr, "Jamstillings-vedtaket i 1885—forstår vi det nå?" in *Innhogg i nyare norsk språkhistorie* (Oslo: Novus, 1992) 18–27.

29. Vikør, *Jamstillingsvedtaket i 1885* 76.

30. Bull, *1885 enda ein gong* 109.

31. For a discussion of this, see Kjell Haugland, *Striden om skulespråket* (Oslo: Det Norske Samlaget, 1985) 95–109.

32. *Dagbladet*, May 5, 1885.

33. See Derry, *A History of Modern Norway* 143–147.

34. E. E. Schattschneider, *The Semi-Sovereign People* (Hinsdale: ILL: The Dryden Press, 1960) 66.

35. Bull, *1885 enda ein gong*.

36. For an account of the Conservatives' language policies from the 1880's until the mid-1970s, see Asbjørn Lind, *Partiet Høyre og norsk språkstrid*. Unpublished M.A. thesis (Oslo: Institut for Nordistikk, Universitetet i Oslo, 1975).

37. Leiv Mjeldheim, *Folkerørsla som vart parti* (Oslo, Universitets-forlaget, 1984) 391–392.

38. Kjell Haugland, *Striden kring sidemålsstilen* (Oslo: Det Norske Samlaget, 1971) 133.

39. Olaf Almenningen, *Målstrev and Målvokster* (Oslo: Det Norske Samlaget, 1984).

40. Trond Nordby, *Venstre og samlingspolitikken, 1906–1908: en studie i partioppløsning og gjenreisning* (Oslo: Novus Forlag, 1983) 13.

41. Alf Kaartvedt, Rolf Danielson and Tim Greve, *Det norske storting gjennom 150 år* vol. III (Oslo, Gyldendal, 1964) 2–3.

42. Kent Weaver and Bert Rockman, "Assessing the Effects of Insti-tutions," in Weaver and Rockman, eds., *Do Institutions Matter?* (Washing-ton, DC: The Brookings Institution, 1993, 18).

43. Leiv Mjeldheim, *Parti og rørsle : ein studie av Venstre i land-krinsane 1906–1918* (Bergen: Universitetsforlaget, 1978) 177–178.

44. Mjeldhelm 180.

45. One member of parliament lamented that "Local interests, class interests and village patriotism threaten to overshadow the larger common interest of the county and the state." Mjeldhelm, 176.

46. Stein Rokkan et al. *Party Systems* 198–201.

47. Almenningen, *Målstrev and Målvokster*, 13.

48. Nordby, *Venstre*, 29.

49. David Mayhew, *Congress: The Electoral Connection*. New Haven, CT: Yale University Press, 1974, pp. 61–62.

50. Haugland *Striden kring sidemålsstilen* 56.

51. Haugland 59.

52. *Den 17de Mai*, February 8, 1906, here cited after Haugland *Striden kring sidemålsstilen* 60.

53. *Valgprogrammer—1906*, Norwegian Parliamentary Archives, Oslo, Norway.

54. Nordby, *Venstre* 27.

55. Haugland, *Striden kring sidemålsstilen* (1971) 62.

56. Unlike the Liberals, the Conservatives did not issue an election platform that was distinct from the governing coalition during this Norwegian parliamentary election cycle.

57. Nordby, *Venstre* 28.

58. Lind, *Partiet Høyre* 82.

59. Haugland (1971), *Striden kring sidemålsstilen* 83–84.

60. Haugland 80–84.

61. For the text of the government proposal, see *Stortings Forhandlinger* (1906–07), Ot. prp. nr. 11. The Liberal proposal is cited in, among other places, Haugland *Striden kring sidemålsstilen* 98.

62. Lind, *Partiet Høyre* 84, 87.

63. Haugland (1971), *Striden kring sidemålsstilen* 125.

CHAPTER 3: LANGUAGE AND SOCIAL DEMOCRACY IN TWENTIETH-CENTURY NORWAY

1. Gøsta Esping-Andersen, *Politics Against Markets: The Social Democratic Route to Power* (Princeton: Princeton University Press, 1985) 81.

2. Peter Katzenstein, *Small States in World Markets* (Ithaca: Cornell University Press, 1985) 177.

3. DNA Chairman, Christian Knudsen, in Social-Demokraten, August 10, 1912, as cited in Åshild Rykkja, *Det Norske Arbeiderparti og språkstriden, 1903–1937*. Unpublished M.A. Thesis, University of Oslo, Department of Scandinavian Studies, 1978, p. 152.

4. Knudsen 152.

5. Halvdan Koht, *Historikar i lære* (Oslo, Grøndahl & Son, 1951) 159.

6. Ernst Håkon Jahr, "Halvdan Koht og språkstriden," in Jahr's *Innhogg i nyare norsk språkhistorie* (Oslo: Novus Forlag, 1992) 78.

7. This section is based exclusively on Halvdan Koht, *Arbeidarreising og målspørsmål* reprinted in E. Hanssen & G. Wiggen, eds., *Målstrid er klassekamp* (Oslo: Pax Forlag, 1973).

8. Koht 38.

9. Chief among these were gun clubs, teetotalist groups, and civilian groups in support of the Norwegian military. See Jahr, *Innhogg i nyare norsk språkhistorie* 76–78.

10. Ernst Håkon Jahr, "Arbeidarpartiet og samnorskpolitikken," in Jahr's *Innhogg i nyare norsk språkhistorie* (Oslo: Novus Forlag, 1992) 118.

11. Noregs Mållag, *Målreising i 75 år: Noregs Mållag 1906–1981* (Oslo: Fonna Forlag, 1981) 107–108.

12. Statistisk Sentralbyrå, *Statistisk årsbok* (Oslo: SSB, ongoing series).

13. Edvard Os, cited in *Norsk Ungdom* in 1918 and quoted in Noregs Mållag, *Målreising i 75 år* 108.

14. Derry, *A History of Modern Norway* 292.

15. Statistisk Sentralbyrå, *Historisk statistikk* Table 9.2 (Oslo: SSB, ongoing series).

16. Det Norske Arbeiderparti, *Sprog og andre kulturspørsmål* (Oslo: Det Norske Arbeiderparti, 1933).

17. Hans Fredrik Dahl, *Fra klassekamp til nasjonal samling: Arbeiderpartiet og nasjonale spørsmål i 30-årene* (Oslo: Pax Forlag, 1971). Unless otherwise noted, material for this section is based on Dahl, 32–67.

18. It should be noted that on the stump party elites did try to play down the revolutionary stance and declare other issues, such as disarmament, tax questions, and unemployment to be the real concerns. However, the rather conspicuous nature of the platform far overshadowed any efforts at backpedaling.

19. Esping-Andersen, *Politics Against Markets* 80.

20. Strengthening the need to rethink a party line that was seen as antinational and antireligious is Grønvik's observation that when one compares DNA parliamentary members by rural or urban representation, seven of the twelve seats that DNA lost came in the rural areas, with four of those coming from strongly Nynorsk counties. See Oddrun Grønvik, *Målbruken i offentleg teneste i tida 1930–1940* (Oslo: Det Norske Samlaget, 1987) 76.

21. Gunnar Jahn, Alf Eriksen and Preben Munthe (eds.) *Norges Bank gjennom 150 år* (Oslo: Norges Bank, 1966) 287.

22. Esping-Andersen, *Politics Against Markets* 81.

23. Dahl, *Fra klassekamp til nasjonal samling* 58.

24. Esping-Andersen, *Politics Against Markets* 76–77.

25. See footnote 43 in Sheri Berman, "Civil Society and the Collapse of the Weimar Republic," *World Politics* (1997) vol. 49, no. 3, 401–429.

26. Esping-Andersen, *Politics Against Markets* 8.

27. Dahl, *Fra klassekamp til nasjonal samling* 60.

28. See footnote 8.

29. Rykkja, *Det Norske Arbeiderparti* 176.

30. *Sprog og andre kulturspørsmål* 42.

31. *Sprog og andre kulturspørsmål* 46–47.

32. Anthony Downs, *An Economic Theory of Democracy* (New York: Harper Collins, 1957) 100–101.

33. Rykkja, *Det Norske Arbeiderparti* 177.

34. *Stortings Forhandlinger.* Innst. S. nr. 216 (1937) 441.

35. A more detailed, if not diplomatic, account of the differences between these two groups can be found in the 50th anniversary commemorative for Noregs Mållag. See Ivar Eskeland, *I strid for norske mål* (Oslo: Noregs Mållag, 1956) 122–126.

36. Lars S. Vikør, *The New Norse Language Movement* (Oslo: Novus, 1975) 58.

37. Per Ivar Vaagland, *Målrørsla og reformarbeidet i trettiåra* (Oslo: Det Norske Samlaget, 1982) 42. No reliable membership records exist for Noregs Mållag in the early 1930s, thus the 1929 numbers of approximately 10,000 are the best benchmark for organizational size.

38. *Valgprogrammer—1933*, Norwegian Parliamentary Archives, Oslo, Norway.

39. Einar Haugen, *Language Conflict and Language Planning*, 120.

40. See Haugen, *Language Conflict and Language Planning* 120–127 as an example.

41. Haugen, *Language Conflict and Language Planning* 122.

42. Carl Keilhau, *Krigen mot riksmålet* (Oslo: H. Aschehoug & Co., 1955) 33.

43. Almenningen et al., *Språk og samfunn* 108. Noregs Mållag's official response to the committee proposal, issued in the same year, contains a rather stinging critique of what was seen as both highly subjective and nonscholarly approach to an issue that most thought to require precision. See pp. 49–63 of Rettskrivingsnemndi åt Noregs Mållag, *Merknader til tilråding frå den departementale rettskrivingsnemnd av 1934* (Oslo: Noregs Boklag, 1936).

44. Riksmålsvernet, *Rettskrivningen. Uttalelse av Riksmålsvernets og Riksmålsforbundets komiteer om tilrådningen fra den departementale rettskrivningsnevnd av 1934* (Oslo: H. Aschehoug & Co., 1936) 22.

45. Haugen, *Language Conflict and Language Planning* 146.

46. Jahr *Innhogg I nyare* norsk språkhistorie 121–122.

47. For the story of Nazi attempts to alter the Norwegian language, see chapter 10 of Almenningen et. al, *Språk og samfunn* and pp. 158–162 of Haugen, *Language Conflict and Language Planning*.

48. Plank twelve of thirteen in DNA's 1945 election platform stated that the party supported, "continued work to achieve a Common Norwegian language based on the people's language." Koht himself continued to push the Common Norwegian line to language activists, using DNA's famous election slogan "By og land—hand i hand!" (City and country-side—hand in hand!) as an analogy for the goals of a Common Norwegian strategy. See Halvdan Koht, "By og land," *Syn og Segn* (1950) no. 2., 49–61.

49. Data for tables 3.2 through 3.10 was obtained from the Norwegian National Election Study Series (Henry Valen, Principal Investigator), 1957 and 1965. The 1957 data set was made available through the Norwegian Social Sciences Data Services, while the 1965 data set was made available through the Inter-University Consortium for Social and Political Research.

50. See André Bjerke, "Foreldreaksjonen i Oslo," *Ordet* (1950) nr. 2, 27–31, Ernst Sørensen, "Foreldreaksjonene mot sproget i lærebøkene," *Ordet* (1951) nr. 2, 27–31 and Ernst Sørensen, "Hvorfor får vi ikke lærebøker med moderate former?" *Ordet* (1951) nr. 4, pp. 83–87, as examples.

51. Alf Hellevik, "Norsk språknemnd blir til," in Alf Hellevik and Einar Lundeby, eds., *Skriftspråk i utvikling* (Oslo: Cappelens, 1964) 15.

52. Øistein Parmann, "Det alvorligste angrep på landets åndsfrihet," *Ordet* (1951) nr. 10, 267–270.

53. Almenningen et al., *Språk og samfunn* p. 123. Eskeland's account of the organizational history also states that Noregs Mållag defined Nynorsk as the equivalent of the Norwegian people's language and that the new language committee could be content with the mere promotion of Nynorsk instead of searching for a people's language. See Eskeland, *I strid* p. 145.

54. Haugen, *Language Conflict and Language Planning* 198–199.

55. Riksmålsvernet et al., *Kritikk av "Framlegg til læreboknormal 1957. Fra Norsk språknemnd"* (Oslo: No publisher listed, 1958) 26. When the final version of the textbook norm was produced, Riksmål elites were far less forgiving, noting that the new norm indicated that, "Riksmål has been forbidden."

56. Haugen, *Language Conflict and Language Planning* 249.

57. This electoral dominance was made all the more pronounced by an inability of the bourgeois parties to come up with a mutually agreed upon strategy to oppose DNA at the ballot box.

58. Trygve Bull, *Skal vi alltid ha to språk i Norge?* Oslo: Fram Forlag (1953) 12. Similar to Hellevik, Bull saw the war as being critical for the language struggle. To him though, the Nazi orthographic reform partially explains why parents emerged from the years of the occupation willing to fight against the politics of Common Norwegian.

59. A common criticism of *Ordet* from the social democratic side was that its many advertisements from large Norwegian companies were simply ways of passing corporate money to a group that would be a thorn in the side of DNA.

60. "Foran en hel revisjon av norsk sprogpolitikk?" *Aftenposten* (December 21, 1963) 1.

61. Haugen, *Language Conflict and Language Planning* 272.

62. Lars S. Vikør, private communication.

63. See Oddrun Grønvik, "Fra stridsemne til språkforum," in Leif Mæhle, Einar Lundeby, Oddrun Grønvik, eds., *Fornying og tradisjon* (Oslo, Cappelen, 1987) 9; Asbjørn Lind, *Partiet Høyre og norsk språkstrid* 174; Almenningen et. al. *Språk og samfunn* 126; and Tove Bull, 'Conflicting Ideologies in Contemporary Norwegian Language Planning,' in Ernst Håkon Jahr, ed., *Language Conflict and Language Planning* (New York: Mouton de Gruyter, 1993) 25, as examples.

64. David Laitin, "Language Policy and Political Strategy in India," *Policy Sciences* (1989) vol. 22, 421.

65. Additionally, other investigations of Norwegian state strength in general have found it to be quite high. See Thorvald Gran, *The State in the Modernization Process* (Oslo: Gyldendal, 1995).

66. Trygve Bull: *For å si det som det var* (Oslo: Cappellen, 1981) 203–206. An attack on Bull's account is presented in Alf Hellevik, "Trygve Bull's private språkhistorie," *Syn og Segn* (1981) vol. 87, no. 5.

67. Bull, *For å si det som det var* 206.

68. Haugen cites articles in the DNA press where writers warned the party that the parents movement was far larger than many thought, and that it was not epihenomenal of the ideological battle between the Conservatives and DNA. Additionally, Løberg spoke out in the Norwegian parliament, warning the government that it should take opposition to its policy of Common Norwegian seriously. See Haugen, *Language Conflict and Language Planning* 202, 214.

69. See Kingdon, *Agendas, Alternatives and Public Policies.*

70. Esping-Andersen, *Politics Against Markets* 101

71. DNA's drive to combine smaller rural school districts with those of nearby towns, contributed to the pronounced decline in Nynorsk usage. Nynorsk usage fell from 28 percent of the population in the early 1950s to just over 20 percent in the early 1960s.

72. The 1965 Norwegian National Election Study, under the direction of Henry Valen, was the second in the series, with no survey having been conducted in 1961. While the 1957 survey included one question directly related to language politics, the 1965 survey featured seven chief language-related questions: the form of spoken Norwegian used by the respondent during the interview; the written form of Norwegian used by the interviewer; which language the respondent prefers to use; whether or not the efforts to build Common Norwegian should be continued; whether or not Nynorsk will remain an independent language; which political parties the respondent viewed as being close to their own views on the language question; and the degree to which the respondent was interested in the language question.

73. The *fylker*, or counties, included in each region are as follows. East: Østfold, Akershus, Oslo, Hedmark, Oppland, Buskerud, Vestfold and Telemark. West and South: Aust-Agder, Vest-Agder, Rogaland, Hordaland, Bergen, Sogn og Fjordane and Møre og Romsdal. Trøndelag and North: Sør-Trøndelag, Nord-Trøndelag, Nordland, Troms and Finnmark.

74. Ernst Sørensen, "Riksmålsbevegelsen i året som gikk," *Ordet* (1964) no. 10, 360.

75. Lars S. Vikør, "Rettskrivingsvedtaka i Språkrådet: ei oppsummering og ei vurdering," *Mål og Makt* (1979) vol. 9, no. 3 24.

CHAPTER 4: THE SHIFTING FATE
OF THE SÁMI LANGUAGES IN MODERN NORWAY

1. *Stortings Forhandlinger* (1989–90), Ot. prp. nr. 60., Samisk språk., p. 8, and *Stortings Forhandlinger* (1986–87), Ot. prp. nr. 33., p. 205.

2. Trond Thuen, *Quest for Equity: Norway and the Saami Challenge* (St. John's, Newfoundland: ISER, Memorial University of New Foundland, 1995) 24.

3. Dag Finn Simonsen, "Sámigiella—almmolas giella. En sammenlikning mellom lovregler for bruk av samisk i Norge, Sverige og Finland," *Språk i Norden* (Oslo: Gyldendal, 1992) 100–101.

4. Ot. prp. nr. 33., 37.

5. Robert Paine, "Norwegians and Saami: Nation-State and the Fourth World," in Gerald C. Gold, ed., *Minorities and Mother Country Imagery* (St. John's, Newfoundland: ISER, Memorial University of New Foundland, 1984) 216.

6. Nils Jernsletten, "Språket i samiske samfunn," in Tove Bull and Kjellaug Jetne, eds., *Nordnorsk: Språkarv og språkforhold i Nord-Noreg* (Oslo: Det Norske Samlaget, 1982) 102.

7. Harald Eidheim, *Aspects of the Lappish Minority Question* (Oslo: Department of Social Anthropology, University of Oslo, 1987) 70.

8. Helge Dahl, "Norsk målpolitikk i Finnmark," *Syn og Segn* (1950) no. 6, 277, and *Norges Offentlige Utredninger: Samisk kultur og utdanning* (NOU 1985:14) 50.

9. Dahl 280.

10. Jernsletten, op. cit., 102.

11. Frank Darnell and Anton Hoëm, *Taken to Extremes: Education in the Far North* (Oslo: Scandinavian University Press, 1996) 100.

12. Dahl, *Norsk målpolitikk i Finnmark* 283–284.

13. Dahl, *Norsk målpolitikk i Finnmark* 280 and Eidheim, *Aspects of the Lappish Minority Question* 73.

14. Knut Einar Eriksen and Einar Niemi, *Den finske fare: Sikkerhetsproblemer og minoritetspolitikk i nord 1860–1940* (Oslo: Universitetsforlaget, 1981, 360, NOU 1985:14, 52, and Darnell and Hoëm, *Taken to Extremes* 170.

15. Dahl, *Norsk målpolitikk i Finnmark* 284, NOU 1985:14, 123.

16. NOU 1985: 14, 55.

17. *Stortings Forhandlinger* (1959), Instillingen fra Samekomiteen.

18. *Stortings Forhandlinger* (1959), Instillingen fra Samekomiteen.

19. *Stortings Forhandlinger* (1959), Lov om folkeskolen, paragraph 37, point 8.

20. *Stortings Forhandlinger* (1969), Lov om grunnskolen, paragraph 41, point 7.

21. *Stortings Forhandlinger* (1989–90), Ot. prp. nr. 60., Samisk språk., 52.

22. See Anderson, *Imagined Communities*, pp. 72–76 for examples of the link between the national ideal and that of one national language.

23. Michael Keating, "Minority Nationalism and the State: The European Case," in Michael Watson, ed., *Contemporary Minority Nationalism* (New York: Routledge, 1990) 175–180 gives an overview of the attempts at assimilation by several European states and the mixed results.

24. Eric Hobsbawm, *Nations and Nationalism since 1780* 182.

25. Eriksen and Niemi, *Den finske fare* 358.

26. Ernest Gellner, *Encounters with Nationalism* (Cambridge, MA: Blackwell, 1994) 35.

27. Thuen, *Quest for Equity*, p. 30, makes this point differently, viewing the Sámi less from the perspective of Norwegian elites and more from the perspective of the Sámi themselves, referring to them as a "second nation."

28. Eriksen and Niemi, *Den finske fare* 358.

29. NOU 1985:14, 52.

30. Marjut Aikio and Anna-Ritta Lindgren, "Den finske minoriteten i Nord-Noreg," in Tove Bull and Kjellaug Jetne, eds., *Nordnorsk: Språkarv og språkforhold i Nord-Noreg* (Oslo: Det Norske Samlaget, 1982) 122.

31. Concerns among Norwegian elites about Russian expansionist designs first surface in the mid 1820s, when Russians conceded a number of points on northern frontier settlement, thus raising fears that this was done to detract attention from their ultimate plans of an ice-free harbor. See Derry, *A History of Modern Norway*, pp. 82–84, for how this fear continued throughout the nineteenth century.

32. On the Swedish fears of Russia/Finland, see Harald Runblom, "Ethnic Minorities in Sweden, 1500–1980," *L'image de l'autre: Étrangers—Minoritaires—Marginaux*. Stuttgart: Congrés International des Sciences Historiques (1985) vol. 2, 507–508. On the connection between Norwegian and Swedish security concerns, see Eriksen and Niemi, *Den finske fare* 353–354 and Dahl, *Norsk målpolitikk i Finnmark* 280.

33. If one is to locate preferential treatment for the Sámi during this period vis-à-vis the Kven, it can only be found in the 1936 Education Act, which did not offer any concessions to Sámi speakers, but did eliminate Kven as an official helping language.

34. "Utdrag fra femårsberetningen," Excerpt no. 47 in Anton Höem and Arild Tjeldvoll, *Etnopolitikk som skolepolitikk: Samisk fortid, norsk framtid?* (Oslo: Universitetsforlaget, 1980) 104–111.

35. "Rapport fra Russegrensen," Excerpt no. 76, in Anton Höem and Arild Tjeldvoll, 166–167.

36. Paine, *Norwegians and Saami* 219.

37. Jernsletten, *Språket i samiske samfunn* 102.

38. Carsten Smith, "The Sámi Rights Committee: An Exposition, "in *Self-Determination and Indigenous Peoples* (Copenhagen: IWGIA, 1987) 16.

39. "Utdrag av skoledirektørens årsmelding for 1902," Excerpt no. 11, Hoëm and Tjeldvoll 53.

40. R. D. Grillo, *Dominant Languages.* Cambridge: Cambridge University Press, 1989, 32, 39.

41. Gellner, *Encounters with Nationalism*, 42.

42. Jernsletten, *Språket i samiske samfunn* 103.

43. Ole Henrik Magga, "The Sámi Language in Norway, " in Dirmid R.F. Collis, ed., *Arctic Languages: An Awakening* (Paris: UNESCO, 1990) 424.

44. Ernst Håkon Jahr and Peter Trudgill, "Differences and Similarities Between the Development of Written Greek and Norwegian" in Ernst Håkon Jahr, ed., *Language Conflict and Language Planning* (New York: Mouton de Gruyter, 1993) 88.

45. Katzenstein, *Small States in World Markets*, 188–189.

46. It is also possible to make the argument that Norway's *Angstgemeinschaft* was not just limited to the horror of foreign occupation, and could be linked to the strong pre-war Norwegian movement, as discussed in Ulf Lindström, *Fascism in Scandinavia, 1920–1940.* Stockholm: Almqvist & Wiksell International, 1985.

47. Magga, *The Sámi Language in Norway* 424.

48. Eriksen and Niemi, *Den finske fare* 371.

49. It is the timing of this change prior to the war that gives elite exposure to outside ideas credence as a force independent of World War II. Had we not witnessed any shifts in minority rights attitudes on the part of elites prior to the war, it would not be necessary to draw attention to the role of Norwegian involvement in international bodies, as we could then assume that they were simply derivative of the general cultural impact of the war as previously discussed.

50. NOU (1985:14) 54.

51. Eidheim, *Aspects of the Lappish Minority Question* 43.

52. Norges Offentlige Utredninger: Om samenes rettsstilling (NOU 1984:18) 17.

53. Helge Ø. Pharo, "Norge og den tredje verden," in Trond Bergh, ed., *Vekst og velstand: Norsk politisk historie 1945–1965* (Oslo, Universitetsforlaget, 1977) 279.

54. NOU (1985:14), 55.

55. Pharo 58.

56. Pharo 172–175.

57. NOU (1984:18) 302.

58. Esping-Andersen, *Politics Against Markets* 149.

59. One of the intital major post-war objectives was to rebuild the northernmost portion of the nation, which had been gutted in the final

months of the war by the retreating Nazi army. See Fritz Hodne, *The Norwegian Economy 1920–1980* (New York: St. Martin's Press, 1983) 127.

60. Sven E. Olsson and Dave Lewis, "Welfare Rules and Indigenous Rights: The Sámi People and the Nordic Welfare States," in John Dixon and Robert P. Scheurell, eds., *Social Welfare with Indigenous Peoples* (New York: Routledge, 1995) 177–178.

61. For detailed examples of attempts at Sámi pressure activities in this period, see NOU (1985:14) 54; Jernsletten, *Språket i samiske samfunn* 106–107; and *The Sámi Language in Norway* 423.

62. In fact, Niemi notes that in the first fifteen to twenty years after the war, there was remarkably little engagement at the mass level by the Sámi for any policies that would have promoted Sámi culture.

63. Paine, *Norwegians and Saami* 424.

64. See chapter 10 of Thuen, *Quest for Equity*, for a detailed account.

CHAPTER 5: NORWAY COMPARED: THE CASE OF BELIGAN LANGUAGE POLITICS

1. In 1846, the first official Belgian census revealed that 57 percent of the population spoke a Flemish dialect, while 42.1 percent used French. The number of French speakers has stayed roughly constant over the past 150 years, while the Flemish speaking community marginally declined to 53 percent by the post-war era.

2. Aristide Zolberg, "Transformation of Linguistic Ideologies: The Belgian Case," in Jean Guy Savard and Richard Vegneault, *Les Etats multilingues: Problems et Solutions* (Quebec: Presses de l'Universite Laval, 1974) 446.

3. Reginald de Schryver, "The Belgian Revolution and Emergence of Biculturalism," in Arend Lijphart, ed., *Conflict and Coexistence in Belgium* (Berkeley: Institute of International Studies, 1981) 22.

4. A. J. Baron Vlerick, "Flanders Socio-Economic Emancipation Since the Industrial Revolution," *Plural Societies* vol. 17, no. 3 (1987) 10–11.

5. Vlerick 10.

6. Aristide Zolberg, "The Making of Flemings and Walloons: 1830–1914," *Journal of Interdisciplinary History* vol. 5, no. 2 (1974) 198.

7. See Aristide Zolberg, *Transformation of Linguistic Ideologies* (1974).

8. Val R. Lorwin, "Belgium: Religion, Class and Language in National Politics," in Robert Dahl, ed., *Political Opposition in Western Democracies* (New Haven, CT: Yale University Press, 1966) 158.

9. Aristide Zolberg, *The Making of Flemings and Walloons* 204.

10. Jean Stengers, "Belgian National Sentiments," in Arend Lijphart, ed., *Conflict and Coexistence in Belgium* (Berkeley: Institute of International Studies (1981) 57.

11. Luc Huyse, "Political Conflict in Bicultural Belgium," in Arend Lijphart, ed., *Conflict and Coexistence in Belgium* (Berkeley: Institute of International Studies, 1981) 109.

12. Aristide Zolberg, (1974b), *The Making of Flemings and Walloons* 206.

13. Murphy, *The Regional Dynamics of Language Differentiation in Belgium*, 64.

14. Murphy 50.

15. David M. Rayside, "The Impact of the Linguistic Cleavage on the 'Governing' Parties of Belgium and Canada," *Canadian Journal of Political Science* vol. 11, no., 1, 1978, 66.

16. For a detailed account of all laws adopted in this period, see Murphy, *Regional Dynamics of Language Differentiation* 70–74.

17. Murphy 72.

18. See Lorwin, *Belgium* 156, 156n.

19. Zolberg, *The Making of Flemings and Walloons* 207.

20. Rayside, *The Impact of the Linguistic Cleavage* 66.

21. Vernon Mallinson, *Belgium* (New York: Praeger, 1970) 82. The national vote share for the Catholics had actually decreased from 54 percent in 1892 to 51 percent.

22. James A. Dunn, Jr., "The Revision of the Constitution in Belgium: A Study in the Institutionalization of Ethnic Conflict," *Western Political Quarterly* vol. 27, no. 1 (1974) 146.

23. Murphy, *Regional Dynamics of Language Differentiation* 110.

24. Murphy 107–108.

25. Anthony Mughan, "Modernization and Ethnic Conflict in Belgium," *Political Studies* vol. 27, no. 1 (1979) 24.

26. Murphy, *Regional Dynamics of Language Differentiation* 114–116.

27. Huyse, *Political Conflict in Bicultural Belgium* 112.

28. Mughan, *Modernization and Ethnic Conflict in Belgium* 24.

29. Murphy, *Regional Dynamics of Language Differentiation* 129.

30. Dunn, *Revision of the Constitution in Belgium* 148.

31. Saul Newman, *Ethnoregional Conflict in Democracies: Mostly Ballots, Rarely Bullets* (Westport, CT: Greenwood Press, 1986) 62, and Mughan, *Modernization and Ethnic Conflict in Belgium* 25.

32. Maureen Covell, "Ethnic Conflict and Elite Bargaining," *West European Politics* vol. 4, no. 3 (1981) 208.

33. Mallinson, *Belgium* 164–165, and Lorwin, *Belgium* 171–172.

34. Aristide Zolberg, "Splitting the Difference: Federalization without Federalism in Belgium," in Milton J. Esman, ed., *Ethnic Conflict in the Western World* (Ithaca: Cornell University Press, 1977) 121.

35. Mallinson, *Belgium* 189.

36. Zolberg, *Splitting the Difference* 127.

37. Els Witte, "Belgian Federalism: Towards Complexity and Asymmetry," *West European Politics* vol. 15, no. 4 (1992) 98, and Jean Ellen Kane, "Flemish and Walloon Nationalism: Devolution of a Previously Unitary State," in Uri Ra'anan, ed., *Ethnic Resurgence in Modern Democratic States* (New York: Pergamon Press, 1980) 138–139.

38. Kane, *Flemish and Walloon Nationalism* 139.

39. Murphy, *Regional Dynamics of Language Differentiation* 145.

40. Maureen Covell, "Regionalization and Economic Crisis in Belgium: The Variable Origins of Centrifugal and Centripedal Forces," *Canadian Journal of Political Science* vol. 19, no. 2 (1986), 267.

41. Covell, (1981), *Ethnic Conflict and Elite Bargaining* 208–209.

42. Newman, *Ethnoregional Conflict in Democracies* 99–100.

CHAPTER 6: CONCLUSION

1. David Laitin, *Hegemony and Culture* (Chicago: The University of Chicago, 1986) 13.

2. Laitin 15.

3. Laitin 150.

4. Laitin 102.

5. As an example, see Thomas Hylland Eriksen, "Language in Identity Politics," in Unn Røyneland, ed., *Language Contact and Language Conflict: Proceedings of the International Ivar Aasen Conference* (Volda, Norway: Volda University College, 1997) 25–49.

6. Margaret Levi, "A Model, A Method, and A Map: Rational Choice in Comparative and Historical Analysis," in Mark Lichbach and Alan Zuckerman, eds., *Comparative Politics: Rationality, Culture, and Structure* (New York: Cambridge University Press, 1997) 33.

7. Levi 30.

8. David Laitin, "Language Conflict and Violence: Or the Straw That Strengthened the Camel's Back," Estudio/Working Paper 1999/137, (June 1999) 3

9. Jahr and Trudgill, *Differences and Similarities* 90.

10. Jahr and Trudgill 90.

11. Geoffrey Horrocks, *Greek: A History of the Language and its Speakers* (New York: Longman, 1997) 358–359.

12. Horrocks 361.

13. Zsuzsa Csergo, "Language Policy as a Question of Polity in Europe," paper presented at the 95th Annual Meeting of the American Political Science Association, Atlanta, GA, September 2–5, 1999. 16–17.

14. Subrata K. Mitra, "Language and Federalism: The Multi-Ethnic Challenge," *International Social Science Journal*, vol. 53, no. 1 (March 2001) 55–57.

15. Deborah J. Schildkraut, "Official-English and the States: Influences on Declaring English the Official Language in the United States," *Political Research Quarterly*, vol. 54, no. 2 (June 2001) 445.

16. Schildkraut 455.

17. Ottar Fyllingness, "Kompromiss om sidemål i Oslo," *Dag og Tid* (August 31, 2000).

18. "Elever bør slippe nynorsk," *Bergens Tidende* (August 6, 2000) and Heidi Larssen, "Tvungen sidemålsopplæring?" *Aftenposten* (August 18, 2000).

19. Kjell-Erik Kallset, "Målfolk slår tilbake," *Dagsavisen* (August 26, 2000).

20. Hilde Charlotte Solheim, "Nynorskfritak kan gi utdanningsforbud" and "Må beherske nynorsk i statlige stillinger" *Dagsavisen* (August 25, 2000).

21. Hilde Lundgaard, "Ikke nynorsk-fritak i Oslo," *Aftenposten* (October 3, 2000).

22. Atle Faye, "Ap. er for obligatorisk opplæring," *Aftenposten* (December 11, 2000).

23. Noregs Mållag, "Mållaget rosar Arbeidarpartiet," http://www.nm.no//side.cfm/1660/28785, December 11, 2000.

Bibliography

Aikio, Marjut, and Anna-Ritta Lindgren. "Den finske minoriteten i Nord-Noreg," in Tove Bull and Kjellaug Jetne, Eds. *Nordnorsk: Språkarv og språkforhold i Nord-Noreg.* Oslo: Det Norske Samlaget, 1982.

Almenningen, Olaf. "Ny arbeidsdag og mellomkrigstid," in Olaf Almenningen, Thore A. Roksvold, Helge Sandøy, and Lars S. Vikør, Eds. *Språk og samfunn gjennom tusen år.* Oslo: Universitetsforlaget, 1981.

Almenningen, Olaf. *Målstrev and Målvokster.* Oslo: Det Norske Samlaget, 1984.

Anderson, Benedict. *Imagined Communities.* London: Verso, 1991.

Aarebrot, Frank H., and Derek Urwin. "The Politics of Cultural Dissent: Religion, Language, and Demonstrative Effects in Norway." *Scandinavian Political Studies.* Vol. 2, 1979.

Baumgartner, Frank R., and Bryan D. Jones. *Agendas and Instability in American Politics.* Chicago: Chicago University Press, 1993.

Berman, Sheri. "Civil Society and the Collapse of the Weimar Republic," *World Politics.* Vol. 49, No. 3, (1997) 401–429.

Bill, James A., and Robert L. Hardgrave. *Comparative Politics: The Quest for Theory,* Lanham, MD: University Press of America, 1981.

Bjerke, André. "Foreldreaksjonen i Oslo," *Ordet.* 1950, Nr. 2.

Bourdieu, Pierre. "Economics of Linguistic Exchanges." *Social Science Information.* Vol. 16, No. 6. (1977), 645–668.

Bourdieu, Pierre. *Distinction: A Social Critique of the Judgement of Taste.* Cambridge, MA: Harvard University Press, 1984.

Bourdieu, Pierre, and Loïc J. D. Wacquant. *An Invitation to Reflexive Sociology.* Chicago: University of Chicago Press, 1992.

Paulston, Christina Bratt. *Linguistic Minorities in Multilingual Settings.* Philadelphia: John Benjamins Publishing Company, 1994.

Breuilly, John. *Nationalism and the State.* Chicago: University of Chicago Press, 1993.

Brunstad, Endre. *Nasjonalisme som språkpolitisk ideologi.* Oslo: Noregs forskningsråd, 1995.

Bull, Tove. "1885 enda ein gong," *Maal og Minne.* 1987–88, 98–136.

179

Bull, Tove. "Conflicting Ideologies in Contemporary Norwegian Language Planning," in Ernst Håkon Jahr, Ed. *Language Conflict and Language Planning*. New York: Mouton de Gruyter, 1993.

Bull, Trygve. *Skal vi alltid ha to språk i Norge?* Oslo: Fram Forlag, 1953.

Bull, Trygve. *For å si det som det var*. Oslo: Cappellen, 1981.

Calhoun, Craig. "Habitus, Field, and Capital," Craig Calhoun, Edward LiPuma and Moishe Postone, Eds. *Bourdieu: Critical Perspectives*. (Chicago: University of Chicago Press, 1993.

Carnoy, Martin. *The State & Social Theory*. Princeton: Princeton University Press, 1984.

Collins, James. "Bourdieu on Language and Education," Craig Calhoun, Edward LiPuma and Moishe Postone, Eds. *Bourdieu: Critical Perspectives*. Chicago: University of Chicago Press, 1993.

Cooper, Robert. *Language Planning and Social Change*. New York: Cambridge University Press, 1989.

Covell, Mauren. "Ethnic Conflict and Elite Bargaining," *West European Politics*. Vol. 4, No. 3, 1981, 197–218.

Covell, Maureen. "Regionalization and Economic Crisis in Belgium: The Variable Origins of Centrifugal and Centripedal Forces," *Canadian Journal of Political Science*. Vol. 19, No. 2, 1986.

Csergo, Zsuzsa. "Language Policy as a Question of Polity in Europe," paper presented at the 95th Annual Meeting of the American Political Science Association, Atlanta, GA, September 2–5, 1999.

Dagbladet. May 5, 1885.

Dahl, Helge. "Norsk målpolitikk i Finnmark," *Syn og Segn* 1950, No. 6, 277–285.

Dahl, Hans Fredrik. *Fra klassekamp til nasjonal samling: Arbeiderpartiet og nasjonale spørsmål i 30-årene*. Oslo, Pax Forlag, 1971.

Dahl, Robert. "A Critique of The Ruling Elite Model," *American Political Science Review*, Vol. 52, No. 2, June 1958, 463–469.

Dahl, Robert. "Further Reflections on 'The Elitist Theory of Democracy,'" *American Political Science Review*, Vol. 60, No. 2, June 1966, 296–305.

Dalhaug, Ole. *Mål og meninger*. Oslo: Noregs forskningsråd, 1995.

Darnell, Frank, and Anton Hoëm, *Taken to Extremes: Education in the Far North*. Oslo: Scandinavian University Press, 1996.

Derry, T. K. *A History of Modern Norway*. Oxford: Oxford University Press, 1973.

Deschouwer, Kris. "Patterns of Participation and Competition in Belgium," *West European Politics*. Vol. 12, No. 4, 1989, 28–41.

de Schryver, Reginald. "The Belgian Revolution and Emergence of Biculturalism," in Arend Lijphart, Ed., *Conflict and Coexistence in Belgium*. Berkeley: Institute of International Studies, 1981. 13–33.

Det Norske Arbeiderparti, Sprog og andre kulturspørsmål. Oslo: DNA, 1933.

Downs, Anthony. *An Economic Theory of Democracy*. New York: Harper Collins, 1957.

Dunn, Jr., James A. "The Revision of the Constitution in Belgium: A Study in the Institutionalization of Ethnic Conflict," *Western Political Quarterly*. Vol. 27, No. 1, 1974. 143–163.

Eckstein, Harry. *Division and Cohesion in Democracy: A Study of Norway*. Princeton: Princeton University Press, 1966.

Eidheim, Harald. *Aspects of the Lappish Minority Question*. Oslo: Department of Social Anthropology, University of Oslo, 1987.

Elgvin, Johannes. "Politikk, taktikk og realiteter i Stortinget," *Ordet*. 1969, 407–421.

Einar Eriksen, Knut, and Einar Niemi. *Den finske fare: Sikkerhetsproblemer og minoritetspolitikk i nord 1860–1940*. Oslo: Universitetsforlaget, 1981.

Eskeland, Ivar. *I strid for norske mål*. Oslo: Noregs Mållag, 1956.

Esping-Andersen, Gøsta. *Politics Against Markets: The Social Democratic Route to Power*. Princeton, Princeton University Press, 1985.

Faye, Atle. "Ap. er for obligatorisk opplæring," *Aftenposten*, December 11, 2000. *Fedraheimen*.

Forgacs, David, and Geoffrey Nowell-Smith, Eds. Antonio Gramsci, *Selections from Cultural Writings*. Cambridge: Harvard University Press, 1985.

Fyllingness, Ottar. "Kompromiss om sidemål i Oslo," *Dag og Tid*, August 31, 2000.

Gellner, Ernest. *Nations and Nationalism*. Ithaca: Cornell University Press, 1993.

Gellner, Ernest. *Encounters with Nationalism*. Cambridge, MA: Blackwell, 1994.

Gramsci, Antonio. *Selections from Prison Notebooks*. New York: International Publishers, 1971.

Gran, Thorvald. *The State in the Modernization Process*. Oslo: Gyldendal, 1995.

Grillo, R. D. *Dominant Languages*. Cambridge: Cambridge University Press, 1989.

Grønvik, Oddrun. *Målbruken i offentleg teneste i tida 1930–1940*. Oslo: Det Norske Samlaget, 1987.

Grønvik, Oddrun. "Fra stridsemne til språkforum," in Leif Mæhle, Einar Lundeby, Oddrun Grønvik, Eds. *Fornying og tradisjon*. Oslo, Cappelen, 1987.

Harker, Richard. "Bourdieu—Education and Reproduction," In Richard Harker, Cheleen Mahar and Chris Wilkes, Eds. *An Introduction to the Work of Pierre Bourdieu*. New York: St. Martin's Press, 1990.

Haugen, Einar. *Language Conflict and Language Planning*. Cambridge: Harvard University Press, 1966.

Haugland, Kjell. "Ei pressgruppe tek form: Målrørsla og Venstrepartiet 1883–1885," *Historisk Tidskrift*. 1974, Vol. 53, No. 2, 148–182.

Haugland, Kjell. "Organisasjonsgjennombrotet i målarbeidetved hundreårsskiftet," *Historisk Tidskrift*. 1977, Vol. 56, No. 2, 19–52.

Haugland, Kjell. "Mål og makt i Venstre," in Ottar Grepstad and Jostein Nerbøvik, Eds. *Venstres hundre år*. Oslo: Gyldendal Norsk Forlag, 1984, 90–104.

Haugland, Kjell. *Striden kring sidemålsstilen*. Oslo: Det Norske Samlaget, 1971.

Haugland, Kjell. *Striden om skulespråket*. Oslo: Det Norske Samlaget, 1985.

Hellevik, Alf. "Norsk språknemnd blir til," in Alf Hellevik and Einar Lundeby, Eds. *Skriftspråk i utvikling*. Oslo: Cappelens, 1964.

Hellevik, Alf. "Trygve Bull's private språkhistorie," *Syn og Segn*. 1981, Vol. 87, No. 5.

Hobsbawm, E. J. *Nations and Nationalism Since 1780*. New York: Cambridge University Press, 1992.

Hodne, Fritz. *The Norwegian Economy 1920–1980*. New York: St. Martin's Press, 1983.

Höem, Anton, and Arild Tjeldvoll. *Etnopolitikk som skolepolitikk: Samisk fortid, norsk framtid?* Oslo: Universitetsforlaget, 1980.

Horrocks, Geoffrey. *Greek: A History of the Language and its Speakers*. New York: Longman, 1997.

Huyse, Luc. "Political Conflict in Bicultural Belgium, in Arend Lijphart, Ed. *Conflict and Coexistence in Belgium*. Berkeley: Institute of International Studies, 1981, 107–126.

Hylland Eriksen, Thomas. "Language in Identity Politics," in Unn Røyneland, Ed. *Language Contact and Language Conflict: Proceedings of the International Ivar Aasen Conference*. Volda, Norway: Volda University College, 1997, 25–49.

Jahn, Gunnar, Alf Eriksen, and Preben Munthe, Eds. *Norges Bank gjennom 150 år*. Oslo: Norges Bank, 1966.

Jahr, Ernst Håkon. *Utsyn over norsk språkhistorie etter 1814*. Oslo: Novus Forlag, 1989.

Jahr, Ernst Håkon. *Innhogg i nyare norsk språkhistorie*. Oslo: Novus Forlag, 1992.

Jahr, Ernst Håkon, and Peter Trudgill. "Differences and Similarities Between the Development of Written Greek and Norwegian," in Ernst Håkon Jahr, Ed. *Language Conflict and Language Planning*. New York: Mouton de Gruyter, 1993.

Jernsletten, Nils. "Språket i samiske samfunn," in Tove Bull and Kjellaug Jetne, Eds. *Nordnorsk: Språkarv og språkforhold i Nord-Noreg*. Oslo: Det Norske Samlaget, 1982, 101–117.

Jones, Bryan D. *Reconceiving Decision-Making in Democratic Politics*. Chicago: University of Chicago Press, 1994.

Kaartvedt, Alf, Rolf Danielson and Tim Greve, *Det norske storting gjennom 150 år*. Vol. III Oslo, Gyldendal, 1964.

Kallset, Kjell-Erik. "Målfolk slår tilbake," *Dagsavisen*, August 26, 2000.

Kane, Jean Ellen. "Flemish and Walloon Nationalism: Devolution of a Previously Unitary State," in Uri Ra'anan, Ed. *Ethnic Resurgence in Modern Democratic States*. New York: Pergamon Press, 1980.

Katzenstein, Peter. *Small States in World Markets*. Ithaca: Cornell University Press, 1985.

Keating, Michael. "Minority Nationalism and the State: The European Case," in Michael Watson, Ed. *Contemporary Minority Nationalism*. New York: Routledge, 1990, 174–194.

Kedourie, Elie. *Nationalism*. London: Hutchinson, 1985.

Keilhau, Carl. *Krigen mot riksmålet*. Oslo: H. Aschehoug & Co., 1955.

Keilhau, Carl. *22 år og en skjebnetime*. Oslo: H. Aschehoug & Co., 1956.

King, Gary, Robert O. Keohane, Sidney Verba, *Designing Social Inquiry*. Princeton, NJ: Princeton University Press, 1994.

Kingdon, John W. *Agendas, Alternatives and Public Policies*. Boston: Little, Brown and Company, 1984.

Koht, Halvdan. *Arbeidarreising og målspørsmål*, (1921) reprinted in E. Hanssen & G. Wiggen, Eds., *Målstrid er klassekamp*. Oslo: Pax Forlag, 1973.

Koht, Halvdan. "By og land," *Syn og Segn*, 1950, No. 2., 49–61.

Koht, Halvdan. *Historikar i lære*. Oslo, Grøndahl & Son, 1951.

Laitin, David. *Politics, Language and Thought: The Somali Experience*. Chicago: University of Chicago Press, 1977.

Laitin, David. *Hegemony and Culture*. Chicago: The University of Chicago, 1986.

Laitin, David. "Language Games," *Comparative Politics*. Vol. 20, No. 3, 1988.

Laitin, David. "Language Policy and Political Strategy in India," *Policy Sciences*. 1989, Vol. 22.

Laitin, David. *Language Repertoires and State Construction in Africa*. New York: Cambridge University Press, 1992.

Laitin, David, et al. "Language and The Construction of States: The Case of Catalonia in Spain," *Politics & Society*. Vol. 22, No. 1, 1994. 5–29.

Larssen, Heidi. "Tvungen sidemålsopplæring?" *Aftenposten*, August 18, 2000.

Lehman Schlozman, Kay, and John T. Tierney, *Organized Interests and American Democracy*. New York: Harper & Row, 1986.

Levi, Margaret. "A Model, A Method, and A Map: Rational Choice in Comparative and Historical Analysis," in Mark Lichbach and Alan Zuckerman, Eds., *Comparative Politics: Rationality, Culture, and Structure*. New York: Cambridge University Press, 1997, 19–41.

Lien, Åsmund. "Nynorsken i skuleverket," in *Målreising i 75 år: Noregs Mållag 1906–1981*. Oslo: Fonna Forlag, 1981.

Lijphart, Arend. *Conflict and Coexistence in Belgium: The Dynamics of a Culturally Divided Society*. Berkeley: University of California Press, 1981.

Lind, Asbjørn. *Partiet Høyre og norsk språkstrid*. Unpublished M.A. thesis, Oslo: Institutt for Nordistikk, Universitetet i Oslo, 1975.

Lindström, Ulf. *Fascism in Scandinavia, 1920–1940*. Stockholm: Almqvist & Wiksell International, 1985.

Lorwin, Val R. "Belgium: Religion, Class and Language in National Politics," in Robert Dahl, Ed. *Political Opposition in Western Democracies*. New Haven, CT: Yale University Press, 1966.

Lund, Jørn. "Det sprogsociologiske klima i de nordiske lande," *Språk i Norden*. Oslo: Nordisk språkråd, 1986.

Lundeby, Einar. "Språksaken i Stortinget," *Ordet*, 1969, 380–387.

Lundgaard, Hilde. "Ikke nynorsk-fritak i Oslo," *Aftenposten*, October 3, 2000.

Magga, Ole Henrik. "The Sámi Language in Norway," in Dirmid R.F. Collis, Ed. *Arctic Languages: An Awakening*. Paris: UNESCO, 1990.

Mallinson, Vernon. *Belgium*. New York: Praeger, 1970.

Marx, Karl, and Frederick Engels, *The German Ideology*. New York: International Publishers, 1963.

Marx, Karl. *Grundrisse: Foundations of the Critique of Political Economy*. New York: Vintage Books, 1973.

McRae, Kenneth D. *Conflict and Compromise in Multilingual Settings*. Ontario: Wilfred Laurier University Press, 1983.

Mayhew, David. *Congress: The Electoral Connection.* New Haven, CT: Yale University Press, 1974.

Mitra, Subrata K. "Language and Federalism: The Multi-Ethnic Challenge," *International Social Science Journal,* Vol. 53, No. 1, March 2001. 51–60.

Mjeldheim, Leiv. *Parti og rørsle : ein studie av Venstre i landkrinsane 1906–1918.* Bergen: Universitetsforlaget, 1978.

Mjeldheim, Leiv. *Folkerørsla som vart parti.* Oslo: Universitetsforlaget, 1984.

Mughan, Anthony. "Modernization and Ethnic Conflict in Belgium," *Political Studies,* Vol. 27, No. 1, 1986. 21–37.

Murphy, Alexander B. *The Regional Dynamics of Language Differentiation in Belgium.* Chicago: University of Chicago's Committee on Geographical Studies, 1988.

Newman, Saul. *Ethnoregional Conflict in Democracies: Mostly Ballots, Rarely Bullets.* Westport, CT: Greenwood Press, 1986.

Nordby, Trond. *Venstre og samlingspolitikken, 1906–1908: en studie i partioppløsning og gjenreisning.* Oslo: Novus Forlag, 1983.

Noregs Mållag. *Målreising i 75 år: Noregs Mållag 1906–1981.* Oslo: Fonna Forlag, 1981.

Noregs Mållag. "Mållaget rosar Arbeidarpartiet," http://www.nm.no//side.cfm/1660/28785, December 11, 2000.

Norges Offentlige Utredninger: Om samenes rettsstilling. (NOU 1984:18).

Norges Offentlige Utredninger: Samisk kultur og utdanning. (NOU 1985:14).

Norwegian National Election Study Series, 1957, 1965.

Ny rettskrivning 1941. Oslo: Blix, 1941.

Olsson, Sven E., and Dave Lewis, "Welfare Rules and Indigenous Rights: The Sámi People and the Nordic Welfare States," in John Dixon and Robert P. Scheurell, Eds. *Social Welfare with Indigenous Peoples.* New York: Routledge, 1995, 141–185.

Paine, Robert. "Norwegians and Saami: Nation-State and the Fourth World," in Gerald C. Gold, Ed. *Minorities and Mother Country Imagery.* St. John's, Newfoundland: ISER, Memorial University of New Foundland, 1984.

Parmann, Øistein. "Det alvorligste angrep på landets åndsfrihet," *Ordet,* 1951, Nr. 10.

Pharo, Helge Ø. "Norge og den tredje verden," in Trond Bergh Ed., *Vekst og Velstand: Norsk politisk historie 1945–1965.* Oslo: Universitetsforlaget, 1977, 279–330.

Pool, Jonathan. "Language Regimes and Political Regimes, in Brian Weinstein Ed., *Language Policy and Political Development.* Norwood, NJ: Ablex Publishing Corp., 1990.

Pool, Jonathan. "The Official Language Problem," *American Political Science Review.* Vol. 85, 1991.

Putnam, Robert D. "Studying Elite Political Culture: The Case of Ideology," *American Political Science Review,* Vol. 65, No. 3, September 1971, 651–681.

Putnam, Robert D. "Attitude Stability among Italian Elites," *American Journal of Political Science*, Vol. 23, No. 3, August 1979, 463–494.

Putnam, Robert D. *Making Democracy Work*. Princeton: Princeton University Press, 1993.

Rayside, David M. "The Impact of the Linguistic Cleavage on the 'Governing' Parties of Belgium and Canada," *Canadian Journal of Political Science*. Vol. 11, No, 1, 1978, 61–95.

Rettskrivingsnemndi åt Noregs Mållag, Merknader til tilråding frå den departementale rettskrivingsnemnd av 1934. Oslo: Noregs Boklag, 1936.

Riker, William. "Implications from the Disequilibrium of Majority Rule for the Study of Institutions," *American Political Science Review*. Vol. 74, 1980.

Riker, William. *Liberalism Against Populism*. San Francisco, W. H. Freeman, 1982.

Riksmålsvernet, Rettskrivningen. Uttalelse av Riksmålsvernets og Riksmålsforbundets komiteer om tilrådningen fra den departementale rettskrivningsnevnd av 1934. Oslo: H. Aschehoug & Co., 1936.

Riksmålsvernet et al., Kritikk av "Framlegg til læreboknormal 1957. Fra Norsk språknemnd." Oslo: No publisher listed, 1958.

Rokkan, Stein, Derek Urwin, Frank H. Aarebrot, Pamela Maleba, and Terje Sande, *Centre-Periphery Structures in Europe*. Frankfurt: Campus Verlag, 1982.

Rosengarte. Frank. *Antonio Gramsci, Letters From Prison, Volume One*. New York: Columbia University Press, 1994.

Runblom, Harald. "Ethnic Minorities in Sweden, 1500–1980," *L'image de l'autre: Étrangers—Minoritaires—Marginaux*. Stuttgart: Congrés International des Sciences Historiques. Vol. 2, 1985, 499–531.

Rykkja, Åshild. *Det Norske Arbeiderparti og språkstriden, 1903–1937*. Unpublished M.A. Thesis, University of Oslo, Department of Scandinavian Studies, 1978.

Safran, William. "Language, Ideology, and State-Building: A Comparison of Policies in France, Israel, and the Soviet Union," *International Political Science Review*. Vol. 13, No. 4, 1992, 397–414.

Savard, Jean Guy, and Richard Vegneault, *Les Etats multilingues: Problems et Solutions*. Quebec: Presses de l'Universite Laval, 1974.

Schattschneider, E. E. *The Semi-Sovereign People*. Hinsdale, IL: The Dryden Press, 1960.

Schildkraut, Deborah J. "Official-English and the States: Influences on Declaring English the Official Language in the United States," *Political Research Quarterly*. Vol. 54, No. 2, June 2001, 445–457.

Simonsen, Dag Finn. "Sámigiella—almmolas giella. En sammenlikning mellom lovregler for bruk av samisk i Norge, Sverige og Finland," *Språk i Norden*. Oslo: Gyldendal, 1992, 101–109.

Smith, Anthony. "Culture, Community and Territory: The Politics of Ethnicity and Nationalism," *International Affairs*. Vol. 72, No. 3, 1996, 445–458.

Smith, Carsten. "The Sámi Rights Committee: An Exposition," in *Self-Determination and Indigenous Peoples*. Copenhagen: IWGIA, 1987, 15–56.

Social-Demokraten.
Solheim, Hilde Charlotte. "Må beherske nynorsk i statlige stillinger," Dagsavisen, August 25, 2000.
Solheim, Hilde Charlotte. "Nynorskfritak kan gi utdanningsforbud," Dagsavisen, August 25, 2000.
Statistisk Sentralbyrå, Historisk statistikk. Oslo: SSB, ongoing series.
Statistisk Sentralbyrå, Statistisk årsbok. Oslo: SSB, ongoing series.
Stengers, Jean. "Belgian National Sentiments," in Arend Lijphart, Ed. Conflict and Coexistence in Belgium. Berkeley: Institute of International Studies, 1981. 46–60.
Stortings Forhandlinger (1885), Indst. S. No. 111.
Stortings Forhandlinger (1906–07), Ot. prp. nr. 11.
Stortings Forhandlinger (1937), Innst. S. nr. 216.
Stortings Forhandlinger (1959), Instillingen fra Samekomiteen.
Stortings Forhandlinger (1959), Lov om folkeskolen.
Stortings Forhandlinger (1962–63), Stortingsmelding nr. 21.
Stortings Forhandlinger (1969), Lov om grunnskolen.
Stortings Forhandlinger (1989–90), Ot. prp. nr. 60., Samisk språk.
Stortings Forhandlinger (1986–87), Ot. prp. nr. 33.
Suleiman, Ezra. Elites in French Society. Princeton: Princeton University Press, 1978.
Sørensen, Ernst. "Foreldreaksjonene mot sproget i lærebøkene," Ordet, 1951, No. 2, 27–31.
Sørensen, Ernst. "Hvorfor får vi ikke lærebøker med moderate former?" Ordet, 1951, No. 4, 83–87.
Sørensen, Ernst. "Riksmålsbevegelsen i året som gikk," Ordet, 1964, No. 10, 359–364.
Tarver, Heidi. "Language and Politics in the 1980s: The Story of U.S. English," Politics & Society. Vol. 17, No. 2, 1989, 225–245.
Thuen, Trond. Quest for Equity: Norway and the Saami Challenge. St. John's, Newfoundland: ISER, Memorial University of New Foundland, 1995.
Torp, Arne, and Lars S. Vikør, Hovuddrag i norsk språkhistorie. Oslo: Ad Notam Gyldendal, 1993.
Vaagland, Per Ivar. Målrørsla og reformarbeidet i trettiåra. Oslo: Det Norske Samlaget, 1982.
Valen, Henry, and Stein Rokkan, "Norway: Conflict Structure and Mass Politics in a European Periphery," in Richard Rose, Ed. Electoral Behavior: A Comparative Handbook. New York: The Free Press, 1974, 315–370.
Valgprogrammer—Norwegian Parliamentary Archives, Oslo, Norway.
Vikør, Lars S. The New Norse Language Movement. Oslo: Novus Forlag, 1975.
Vikør, Lars S. "Rettskrivingsvedtaka i Språkrådet: ei oppsummering og ei vurdering," Mål og Makt, Vol. 9, No. 3, 1979.
Vikør, Lars S. "Den nasjonal revolusjon (1814–1905)" in Olaf Almenningen, Thore A. Roksvold, Helge Sandøy, and Lars S. Vikør, Ed. Språk og samfunn gjennom tusen år. Oslo: Universitetsforlaget, 1981.

Vikør, Lars S. "Jamstillingsvedtaket i 1885: Ein replikk," Norsk Lingvistisk Tidsskrift. Vol. 8, 1990, 68–80.

Vlerick, A. J. Baron. "Flanders Socio-Economic Emancipation Since the Industrial Revolution," Plural Societies, Vol. 17, No. 3, 1987, 9–16.

Walker, Jack L. "A Critique of the Elitist Theory of Democracy," American Political Science Review. Vol. 60, No. 2, June 1966, 285–295.

Weaver, Kent, and Bert Rockman, Eds. Do Institutions Matter? Washington, DC: The Brookings Institution, 1993.

Weinstein, Brian. The Civic Tongue: Political Consequences of Language Choices. New York: Longman, 1983.

Witte, Els. "Belgian Federalism: Towards Complexity and Asymmetry," West European Politics. Vol. 15, No. 4, 1992, 95–117.

Wittgenstein, Ludwig. Philosophical Investigations. New York: MacMillian Publishing, 1953.

Zolberg, Aristide. "The Making of Flemings and Walloons: 1830–1914," Journal of Interdisciplinary History. Vol. 5, No. 2, 1974, 179–235.

Zolberg, Aristide. "Transformation of Linguistic Ideologies:The Belgian Case," in Jean Guy Savard and Richard Vegneault, Les Etats multilingues: Problems et Solutions. Quebec: Presses de l'Universite Laval, 1974, 445–472.

Zolberg, Aristide. "Splitting the Difference: Federalization without Federalism in Belgium," in Milton J. Esman, Ed. Ethnic Conflict in the Western World. Ithaca: Cornell University Press, 1977.

Newspaper articles with no author listed:

"Elever bør slippe nynorsk," Bergens Tidende, August 6, 2000.

"Foran en hel revisjon av norsk sprogpolitikk?" Aftenposten. December 21, 1963.

Index